THOUGH MURDE

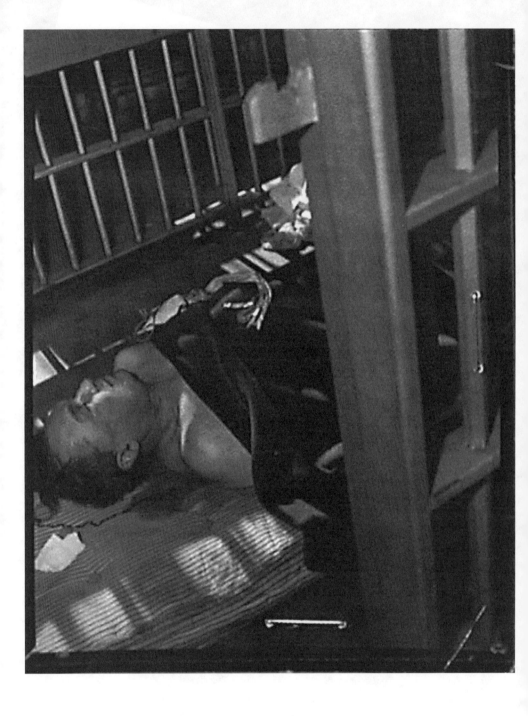

Though MURDER Has No TONGUE

THE LOST VICTIM OF CLEVELAND'S MAD BUTCHER

James Jessen Badal

WITH AN AFTERWORD AND APPENDIX BY CATHLEEN A. CERNY, M.D.

BLACK SQUIRREL BOOKS   KENT, OHIO

BLACK SQUIRREL BOOKS

The Black Squirrel Books imprint includes new nonfiction for the general reader as well as re-prints of valuable studies of Ohio and its people, including historical writings, literary studies, biographies, and literature.

ISBN 978-1-60635-062-1

Manufactured in the United States of America

Frontispiece: August 24, 1939: one of two photographs taken of Frank Dolezal's corpse lying in a corridor in the county jail. The unknown photographer who snapped this picture obviously had a better eye for gloomy atmosphere than "crime scene" documentation. Courtesy of the Cuyahoga County Coroner's Office.

Library of Congress Cataloging-in-Publication Data are available at the Library of Congress.

British Library Cataloging-in-Publication are available.

14 13 12 11 10   5 4 3 2 1

For veteran Cleveland newspaper reporter
Doris O'Donnell Beaufait:
for her friendship, encouragement, and
unswerving devotion to the truth

For murder, though it have no tongue, will speak
With most miraculous organ.
—William Shakespeare, *Hamlet,*
act II, scene II, lines 521–22.

First principles, Clarice. Simplicity. Read Marcus Aurelius.
Of each particular thing ask: what is it in itself? What is its nature?
What does he do, this man you seek?
—Hannibal Lecter in *The Silence of the Lambs*
by Thomas Harris

CONTENTS

PREFACE

The birth pangs associated with this book were especially protracted and difficult. The Kent State University Press published my book *In the Wake of the Butcher: Cleveland's Torso Murders* in spring 2001: the product of ten grueling years of digging into the city's most notorious unsolved cold case; a string of murder-dismemberments from the 1930s—rivaling Jack the Ripper's rampage through Whitechapel in sheer gruesome brutality—a case that has enjoyed legendary status in the city for over seventy years. As the publication date neared, I wrestled with the nagging fear that some new piece of significant information—something that could alter the whole fabric of the book—would come to light before *Butcher* ever hit the bookstore shelves. And, indeed, such a scenario almost occurred. As I chiseled away at the final set of revisions and corrections, Marjorie Merylo Dentz (daughter of Peter Merylo, the lead detective on the case) came upon an old box containing several hundred pages of her father's papers that had lain undiscovered in the family garage for years. Thankfully, she unearthed that treasure trove while I was still tinkering and rewriting; the inclusion of all that material added fifty pages to the book.

In the years since *Butcher* took its bloody bow, I have continued to speak formally about the murders to various groups. Inevitably, on such occasions, the children and grandchildren of those touched by the murders come forward to share a precious piece of family lore—some tidbit handed down from one generation to the next with a seriousness and devotion approaching reverence. Many thank me for acknowledging the role, however minor it may have been, that a near relative played in Cleveland's most agonizingly prolonged murder spree; some have, quite frankly, taken issue with the portrait of a father, an uncle, or a grandfather that I had fashioned from the surviving case documents. Though invariably interesting and often colorful, none of this "new information" altered my thinking about the case or added substantially to what I had already written. As a member of the board of trustees of the Cleveland Police Historical Society, however, I enjoy relatively easy access to historical police case records, personnel and documents at the Cuyahoga County Coroner's Office, and the artifacts that surviving family members of recently deceased former officers donate to the police museum. As attics are cleared out, old file drawers emptied, and the contents of long-forgotten trunks examined, new pieces of the old Kingsbury Run murder puzzle turn up at the museum's door: personal manuscripts, memoirs, never-before-seen photographs, stray official documents, hastily scrawled notes, and the like. Bit by bit, in a constant trickle, they continue to appear. At the very least, some of this material substantially fleshed out aspects of the case; suddenly pencil drawings morphed into full-color oil paintings. At best, some of the newly discovered documents heralded revelations about the killings, the investigation into them, and the political background against which this all occurred—some of them rather startling.

My eighth-grade American history teacher first opened my eyes to the ghosts of Kingsbury Run; and they were my constant, occasionally obtrusive, companions all through those years devoted to researching and writing *In the Wake of the Butcher.* During the time I spent on *Twilight of Innocence: The Disappearance of Beverly Potts* (Kent State University Press, 2005), they hovered quietly and patiently in the background. But when my book on Cleveland's most famous missing child lay behind me, those specters from the brutal past moved silently closer. What more could they possibly want from me? Though the intriguing prospect of an expanded edition of *Butcher* began to loom, both the KSU Press and I resisted the idea; putting those consumers deeply interested in the case, who had already shelled out for *Butcher,* into the position of having to buy a second book—much of which would be merely a repeat of the first—seemed unfair. But would it be possible to write a second book about Kingsbury Run and its aftermath, a companion volume to *Butcher* that would deal more fully with certain aspects of the case, such as the political situation in Cleveland at the time, but could also stand on its own without being overly repetitious? For three years or so, the answer seemed to be "No!" But by 2005, some newly found material of major importance changed all that. *Though Murder Has No Tongue: The Lost Victim of Cleveland's Mad Butcher* now became a real possibility. But digging into any cold case, especially a very old one, poses difficulties—obstacles that range anywhere from mildly troublesome to virtually insurmountable. Imagine a bratty child of seven or eight on a luxury cruise ship with his parents! To keep junior occupied while they do others things, Mom and Dad have fixed him up with a puzzle from the ship's stock of games and other diversions. Unfortunately, the puzzle's difficulties place it far beyond the child's abilities; so after some frustrating and unsuccessful attempts to fit pieces together, he loses patience and chucks the whole thing overboard, box and all. Several weeks later, the pieces begin to wash up on the beach. Though many of them are more or less intact, others have been faded by the sun, badly warped by the water, or nibbled on by various forms of marine life. And, of course, many of the pieces have been swallowed up by the sea, never to make it to shore. The box with the picture of the completed puzzle on the cover has been so badly damaged by the elements that the beachcomber who gathers up all this debris can get only a general, overall impression of the image. It is, perhaps, a landscape, a portrait, a still life of a fruit bowl. Beyond that, it is hard to discern the nature of some of the details: too much has been lost; too much has been damaged. Far too often, a cold case is that faded, damaged image on that waterlogged box cover. The overall image is there, but some—perhaps, many—of the important details are simply missing. The newspaper articles, police reports, autopsy protocols, records of witness testimony, inquest and trial transcripts (assuming there was a trial), and other sorts of public documents often add up to an incomplete picture, occasionally a very incomplete picture. Isolated facts in the story of a major crime may be well documented and, therefore, beyond dispute. We know without a doubt that certain events took place, that certain things were said; but the tissue that connects these actions and utterances may sometimes be difficult to see clearly and the motivations behind them virtually impossible to discern. Some of these surviving puzzle pieces may be so compellingly lurid in their own right—even in isolation—that the urge to turn the whole puzzle into the contemporary equivalent of a yellow journalistic wallow becomes almost irresistible.

Essentially, these were the issues with which I had to contend while researching and writing *Though Murder Has No Tongue*. On the one hand, the events were luridly sensational and the political circumstances surrounding them potentially downright explosive; on the other hand, this was history—legitimate historical questions, woven into the fabric of Cleveland's most infamous series of murders—that needed to be addressed objectively and without bias. I did not undertake this project lightly. In *Butcher* I had managed to deal with some of the hot-potato issues associated with the Kingsbury Run killings and the investigation into them with a certain delicacy and finesse without backing away from them entirely—at least, so I thought; but these controversial and unpleasant realities would undoubtedly have to be faced far more squarely and openly in a new book. The inferences that could be potentially drawn from the surviving hard evidence, all the attendant anecdotes, and the legends associated with the case could add up to some very serious allegations. The buds of these allegations have been an integral part of the Kingsbury Run story for decades. But they have never fully flowered or been explored in depth except in my private conversations and brainstorming sessions with members of my research team. And when reasonably hard evidence is lacking, all sorts of wild and unsupportable notions rush in to fill the void. Rather than let these assumptions fester unchallenged and unexplored, perhaps it would be best—I reasoned—to gather up as many of the recoverable puzzle pieces as I could and see what the completed picture actually looked like, at least to the degree that this even remained possible. I have, therefore, done my best to accept the inevitable limitations of cold-case research and tried to avoid the traps; I have stressed the verifiable facts but have remained cautious and conservative in my interpretation of them. Not all the recovered puzzle pieces will fit. As John Douglas observes in *The Cases That Haunt Us*, every crime has its anomalies; an investigator may not like them, but he learns to live with them.

The veins of information that make up the full story of Kingsbury Run lie deeply buried: some of them simply lost; many hidden beneath layers of secrecy and private shame. Mining them successfully has turned out to be an arduous long-term, ongoing process. Like a massive nineteenth-century Russian novel, the unfolding story presented here embraces a huge, disparate cast of characters and stretches over decades; like Orson Welles's *Citizen Kane*, the narrative sometimes moves forward with a series of flashbacks during which different witnesses explore the same territory from their own vantage points. And, like Welles's groundbreaking screen classic, there is a *Rosebud* at its core—a mystery, seemingly just out of reach, demanding elucidation—a crucial piece to the puzzle that may explain everything. At its base, this is also the story of two men of widely differing backgrounds, who, as far as I know, never met. One was a common laborer, the other a respected professional. They shared nothing beyond their first names; but their lives and ultimate fates became tangled in and inextricably linked with the most infamous and gruesome murder case in Cleveland history.

ACKNOWLEDGMENTS

First, I would like thank the powers that be at Cuyahoga Community College for granting me time off from teaching to do some of the necessary research and the editorial staff of the Kent State University Press for their steady patience as I stubbornly and repeatedly dug in my heels, insisting there was more work that needed to be done before I could submit the manuscript.

I owe an enormous debt to documentary filmmaker Mark Wade Stone of Storytellers Media Group. Our collaboration began in 2003 with the TV documentary project *The Fourteenth Victim: Eliot Ness and the Torso Murders* (obviously based largely on *In the Wake of the Butcher*). The program reaped high ratings and good reviews when it aired on local PBS stations. When Mark began taping *Dusk and Shadow: The Mystery of Beverly Potts*, my research into the Beverly Potts disappearance was already well underway and my notions about that case were more or less set. This second documentary repeated the critical and ratings success of *Fourteenth Victim* and picked up an Emmy Award as well. Throughout the research and writing of *Though Murder Has No Tongue*, he remained a dedicated partner and a reliable sounding board. At the time of this writing, he is working on a documentary—tentatively titled *Broken Rosary: The Frank Dolezal Affair*—that will serve as a companion piece for this book.

I also owe a major debt of gratitude to Dr. Cathleen Cerny for her insightful afterword to this book.

I remain extremely grateful to the following for their assistance, cooperation, and support: Dr. Elizabeth K. Balraj, former coroner of Cuyahoga County; Marilyn Bardsley; Doris O'Donnell Beaufait; Winifred Merylo Beube; David Ciocca, PC network technician, Cuyahoga Community College, Eastern Campus; Marjorie Merylo Dentz; Dr. Dennis C. Dirkmaat, associate professor of anthropology, Mercyhurst Archaeological Institute, Mercyhurst College; Sgt. Dennis Donovan, Pennsylvania State Police, retired, and adjunct professor in the Department of Applied Forensic Sciences, Mercyhurst College; Carol Fitzgerald; Dr. Marcella F. Fierro, former chief medical examiner for the

Commonwealth of Virginia; Charlotte Ilc, coordinator of continuing medical education and research, St. Vincent's Charity Hospital; John Kemmerling, media technician I, Learning Resource Center, Cuyahoga Community College, Eastern Campus; John Neundorfer, supervisor VI, Learning Resource Center, Cuyahoga Community College, Eastern Campus; Robin Odell; John Panza; Donald Rumbelow; Mary Dolezal Satterlee; Mary Suva, Copy & Print Service Center, Cuyahoga Community College, Eastern Campus; Dr. Steven A. Symes, Department of Applied Forensic Sciences, Mercyhurst College; Jennifer Thomas; and Kenneth A. Zirm, attorney at law, Ulmer & Berne, Cleveland, Ohio.

Considering the sheer brutality and sensational nature of the Kingsbury Run murders, the crimes have attracted remarkably little attention outside of Cleveland. In the city on the shore of Lake Erie, however, they remain a powerful legend. Even today, no Clevelander can look at that blighted industrial landscape at the heart of the city without feeling a chill. For the descendents of those individuals who were swept up in that four-year nightmare of seventy years ago, that chill can still be especially haunting and oppressive. I owe a considerable debt to a number of individuals who, by their own request, must remain anonymous.

I also gratefully acknowledge the assistance provided by staff members from the following organizations and institutions: the Western Reserve Historical Society library, the *Cleveland Press* Archives at Cleveland State University, the Cleveland Police Historical Society Museum, the Cuyahoga County Archives, the Cuyahoga County Coroner's Office, the main branch of the Cleveland Public Library, and the Ohio Soldiers' and Sailors' Home in Sandusky. I also would like to express my gratitude to the students in the Forensic Sciences program at Mercyhurst College for their willingness to participate in this endeavor and fellow members on the board of trustees of the Cleveland Police Historical Society for their continuing interest, support, and encouragement.

Part 1
CHAOS

Chapter 1

THE MAELSTROM

August 24, 1939, was a typical late summer day in Cleveland, Ohio: hot, with temperatures well into the mid-eighties, with the kind of humidity that brought handkerchiefs to faces and sweat spots to shirt fronts, the sort of humidity that could wilt a man by late afternoon. For Captain Floyd O'Neil, member of the Cleveland Fire Department assigned to Rescue Squad No. 1 at Engine House No. 23, it was a relatively routine day—until early afternoon. At 1:52 P.M. the call came in: emergency at the county jail, fourth floor, cell no. 11! Six minutes later, O'Neil rushed into the imposingly grim building and the familiar dank humidity of the jail, with its characteristic institutional smell of bodies and disinfectant. On the fourth floor, the stark prison lighting cast a harsh, impersonal glow; the heat and humidity had become an oppressive wall. Later that day, Captain O'Neil would relate to Cleveland police what had happened that afternoon in a formal deposition: "When I arrived at the County Jail I was informed by Sheriff [Martin L.] O'Donnell that the Torso Murderer had hung himself."

† † †

Frank Dolezal had hanged himself! Was it even remotely possible that it was all over? Could the grisly series of brutalities that had lurched through Cleveland for five years and made the city an embarrassing target of national attention really be at an end? It had been going on since September 1934—a series of mind-numbing, gruesome decapitation-dismemberment murders that could have come straight from Shakespeare's *Titus Andronicus*. Referred to locally as either the torso murders or the Kingsbury Run murders—named after the desolate stretch of industrial land near the downtown where some of the first victims were found—the killings had both fascinated and frightened the city populace for almost half a decade. As the violent crime scenes in this sickening drama succeeded each other over the years, the intensity of local press coverage and the pressure placed on law enforcement institutions

A grim, desolate corridor in the Cuyahoga County Jail. *Cleveland Press* Archives, Cleveland State University.

to do something about them increased substantially, straining resources and tempers to the breaking point. It was truly a catalog of horrors, nearly without precedent in the history of American crime.

It had started in September 1934. The lower half of a rotting female corpse had washed up on the shores of Lake Erie east of the city. Determined searching on the part of authorities had uncovered only a couple more of the body's pieces. Dead for six months and in the water for about four, the woman frustrated all attempts at identification. The Lady of the Lake, as she was known to law enforcement personnel, would have faded into history had it not been for a similarly grisly discovery a year later in a different part of the city. In September 1935, two neighborhood boys happened upon the decapitated, emasculated remains of two men, dumped at the base of a sixty-foot elevation known as Jackass Hill close to East 55th. Four months later, the severed remains of a woman, minus her head, turned up: two different sets of body parts discovered about ten days apart in two different downtown locations. The Butcher's pace increased markedly during summer of 1936, just as Cleveland was playing host to the Republican National Convention and the city's movers and shakers were hoping to offset some of the Great Depression's more debilitating economic consequences by attracting visitors to the Great Lakes Exposition. Between June and September, the remains of three more male victims were found—variously mutilated but all decapitated. And so it was through the rest of 1936, 1937, and most of 1938: unwary Clevelanders making exceptionally gruesome discoveries—stumbling across the severed body parts of men and women, white and black, distributed all over the Cleveland area though usually in the blighted industrial landscapes in and around the Flats and Kingsbury Run. By August 1938, the official body count stood at twelve, thirteen if the Lady of the Lake from 1934 is added to the tally. Operating on the long-held assumption that men and women were invariably murdered by people they knew for such understandable reasons as revenge and greed, Cleveland police made almost superhuman attempts to identify the butchered victims. But their Herculean efforts added up to only two positive identifications: Edward Andrassy (found on September 23, 1935, and generally considered victim no. 1) and Florence Polillo (victim no. 3, the initial set of her remains having been discovered on January 26, 1936), both sporting police records and judged low-lifes by authorities. The others passed into oblivion unknown and, as far as anyone knew, unmourned.

As time went on and disarticulated body parts accumulated to a disturbing degree, public fear, especially in the near-downtown neighborhoods where the pieces of many of the murdered victims had turned up, spread with the deadly inexorability of a plague. The seeming inability of the police to make any real progress in the case generated as much apprehension as the gruesome crimes themselves, and Cleveland's three competing daily papers frantically fanned the hysteria whenever a new victim turned up.

Authorities were at a loss as to what to make of the crime scenes; even a modern-day forensic investigator thoroughly schooled in profiling would find the disparate details conflicting, troubling, and ultimately bewildering. The police seemed to be dealing with some sort of diabolical joker, a twisted artist who packaged and arranged the pieces of his victims as if they were flowers, as if he were decorating his own personal chamber of horrors. In September 1935, police found the heads of the first two officially recognized victims buried in the dirt, close to their emasculated corpses and near enough to the surface to ensure that even the most unobservant of investigators could not overlook them. The first of two different sets of remains belonging to victim no. 3, Florence Polillo—found in late January 1936—had been carefully wrapped in newspapers, packed neatly into two produce baskets, and covered with burlap.

The killer had then placed his two surprise packages in the snow behind Hart Manufacturing on East 20th, (jokingly?) close to a butcher shop. Victim no. 4's head had been carefully wrapped in his pants and deposited under a small tree or large bush, where two terrified African American youngsters discovered it in early June 1936. It was impossible to escape the notion that the killer was taunting both the police and the public, thumbing his nose and laughing at a city fascinated by his horrific activities even as it turned away and shuddered in revulsion. However, he was also an artist who seemed to suddenly lose interest in his own canvases, one who simply turned away after casually dumping body parts in the Cuyahoga River or Lake Erie, abandoning his handiwork to the vagaries of wind, wave, and current.

† † †

If politics is a blood sport, then Depression-era Cleveland was a gladiatorial arena. A life of public service was certainly not for the fainthearted, thin-skinned, or easily intimidated in the city along the Erie shore during the 1930s. Some would assert, not without cause, that the political life in Cleveland and the rest of Cuyahoga County was not for the honest and upstanding either. By the mid-1930s, the once-prosperous industrial center had virtually collapsed into the economic doldrums; the numbers of unemployed workers in the area sometimes skyrocketed to close to a quarter of a million. Hobo jungles and shantytowns sprawled through the Flats and crept into the desolate areas surrounding the railroad lines in Kingsbury Run. In a deeply partisan atmosphere, it was inevitable that local political positioning and posturing would turn the torso murders into a soccer ball. In the 1920s and early 1930s, the Cuyahoga County Democratic Party machine ranked among the strongest and most formidable political organizations in local history. W. Burr Gongwer, often regarded as one of the last old-time political bosses, assumed chairmanship of the county organization in 1924, controlling both the patronage system and the fortunes of the party faithful with a proverbial iron hand. Born near Mansfield, Ohio, Gongwer actually started his political career as a Republican but shifted party allegiance in the early years of the twentieth century, when he fell under the charismatic spell of Cleveland's Democratic mayor Tom Johnson. The Democrats consolidated control over local political affairs in 1931, when, following the death of Congressman Charles A. Monney, lawyer and former Cleveland Municipal Court judge Martin L. Sweeney won election to the 20th Congressional District and again in 1932, when the city electorate voted Raymond T. Miller into the mayor's office. (The activist Miller immediately adopted tough but necessary measures to cope with the disastrous economic consequences of the Great Depression; he cut city spending drastically and successfully urged utility companies to slash their rates.)

Sweeney was a political maverick in the best (or, perhaps, worst) sense of the term. A staunch opponent of Prohibition, he used his seat on the court as a bully pulpit for launching strident vocal attacks on a law that he regarded as idiotic and virtually unenforceable. Often dubbed "colorful," "feisty," and "a rebel," he held strong opinions on just about everything; and he had no qualms about sharing them or indulging in very public verbal sparring matches to defend them. He was an enthusiastic supporter of Father Charles Coughlin, the Canadian-born, ultra-conservative Roman Catholic priest who used his radio program to rail against everything that displeased him, including the Jews, international bankers, and Roosevelt's New Deal. Upon arriving in Washington in 1931, Sweeney startled and angered many of his congressional colleagues by complaining that they were behaving like a bunch of old women; in 1940, he got into a fistfight on the floor of the House with Representative Vincent of Kentucky. Love him or hate him, Martin Sweeney was always good copy for Cleveland's daily papers.

The Democrats were truly riding high, but all that changed at the 1932 Democratic National Convention when delegate Sweeney—pledged to support Al Smith's bid for the presidency—suddenly switched his allegiance to Franklin Roosevelt. (In 1936, Sweeney would abruptly turn against Roosevelt—a man he had once praised as a "second Messiah.") Since Gongwer prized party loyalty and obedience as the highest of all political virtues, Sweeney's renegade move predictably precipitated a deep split in the county's Democratic structure, with both men publicly jockeying for power and control. By 1939, even though every county office was under Democratic control, destructive wrangling and internal mud slinging had so tarnished the party image that the *Press* openly lamented, "The party of Cleveland's grand Mayor Tom L. Johnson" was "in the hands of so-called leaders" who were "filled with the lust for power and personal aggrandizement."

In 1935, Republicans exploited the division among the Democrats by plunging a wedge deep into the unhealed fracture. Perhaps in response to the unsettling fact that Cleveland ranked as the country's most dangerous city, voters elected Republican Harold Burton as mayor. He would win reelection to the high city office twice, go on to serve in the U.S. Senate, and ultimately win appointment to the Supreme Court. (In 1936, local Democrats regained some of their lost territory, partially through a Sweeney-engineered-and-led coalition of disaffected party members. Independent Democrat Martin L. O'Donnell, one of Sweeney's staunchest allies and personal friends, won the race for Cuyahoga County sheriff, and Dr. Samuel R. Gerber became the new county coroner. O'Donnell would die of a heart attack five years later, but Gerber would serve as coroner for the next fifty years.) Called a reformer by his supporters and sarcastically dubbed a do-gooder by his enemies, Burton moved quickly to clean up a metropolis blighted by gang activity, labor racketeering, corruption in the police department, illegal gambling, political patronage, a high rate of homicide, and an off-the-chart number of traffic fatalities. In December 1935, Burton offered the job of city safety director to the most famous lawman in the country, Eliot Ness—who, according to well-crafted legend, finally brought down Al Capone. Armed with what he clearly regarded as a political and public mandate to do whatever it took to get the job done, the former G-man immediately attacked the festering social ills that had been brought on, at least in part, by the economic devastation of the Great Depression; and in the process, he would anger some very powerful men and create—in the person of Martin L. Sweeney—a virulent and very noisy enemy. Nominally a Republican, but essentially apolitical, Ness may have seen himself as a white knight riding to the rescue of a city held hostage by any number of deeply entrenched social dragons; but at least some of the battles he waged could not be so easily resolved into simple black and white terms. Gambling, for example, was illegal; and Democratic sheriff Martin L. O'Donnell often took heat from various quarters—specifically William Edwards, head of the crime commission—for allegedly being soft on vice. But O'Donnell saw the issue as one of "home rule" or "states' rights." Gambling may have been illegal, but it was not the job of Cuyahoga County—or the city of Cleveland, for that matter—to police what went on in the suburbs. That responsibility rested with the individual municipalities. (O'Donnell also turned a partially blind eye to gambling because he knew that some good Irish boys were earning their college tuition by working in the illegal gaming parlors.) This local witch's brew of fierce political wrangling and posturing came to a ferocious boil in 1935 when circumstances added the torso murders to the unsavory mix.

Responding to intense pressure from all sides—press, public, and the political establishment—Cuyahoga County coroner A. J. Pearce (immediate predecessor of the county's most famous coroner, Samuel Gerber) orchestrated what the newspapers dubbed the torso clinic in September 1936. Mindful that law enforcement had hit an impasse and, perhaps, painfully aware that city police, due to a simple lack of understanding of exactly what they were dealing with (the term "serial killer" wasn't coined until the 1970s), did not possess the investigative tools necessary for dealing with a possibly psychotic perpetrator who murdered total strangers for reasons known only to himself, Pearce invited to a meeting all the police officers who had worked the case so far, anatomists from the Western Reserve Medical School, and mental health professionals from area psychiatric institutions. His idea was to bring together knowledgeable individuals from these various professional fields to share and analyze all the information that had so far been collected. This was revolutionary for the time; in the 1930s the police did not routinely consult with psychiatrists while trying to solve a crime. Though no one in the journalism fraternity fully appreciated the coroner's foresight, the meeting was a brilliant, forward-looking move on Pearce's part. It stands as, perhaps, one of the first examples of what we might regard as modern FBI profiling. There was no preexisting game plan or path for the assembled participants to follow; they were truly feeling their way and formulating the rules as they went along.

The portrait that finally emerged from this collective endeavor was remarkably detailed. No one was sure whether or not drugs were involved with incapacitating the victims, so they decided the killer had to be a large and powerful man—strong enough to overpower his prey (or suave enough to lull them into a false sense of momentary security); large enough to carry the remains—in some cases, a corpse intact except for the head—over substantial distances of occasionally rugged terrain at night. He probably owned or at least enjoyed access to a car, hardly a common situation during the Great Depression. Coroner Pearce noted the obvious skill behind the decapitations and dismemberments, and the doctors from the medical school concurred: no hacking or sawing, few (if any) signs of hesitation. Whoever was committing these grisly crimes possessed considerable knowledge of human anatomy. A butcher or a hunter, perhaps? More likely an intern or a medical student? The killer was obviously no stranger to Kingsbury Run. He knew the geography of the desolate landscape and the adjacent industrial areas as well as he knew the geography of a dead body. He could move purposefully through the darkness with uncanny assurance, without attracting any attention. He either lived nearby or had grown up in the area. He must live alone and, perhaps, work odd hours, since he appeared to come and go as he pleased without notice. The lack of blood at or near most of the discovery sites clearly pointed to a hidden laboratory of some sort—a place where the murderer could dismember his victims in relative security, dispose of the blood, and clean up the corpses before he got rid of them. A derelict, abandoned building, perhaps? There would certainly be no lack of such structures in a rustbelt metropolis reeling under near economic collapse. Perhaps an undertaking establishment? Most frighteningly, he probably appeared normal and went through his daily activities without attracting any attention. The city's newspapers may revel in notions of werewolves, ghouls, and vampire killers, but the ease with which the Butcher accomplished his work and disposed of the remains argued against anyone so luridly obvious.

† † †

The dog days of July 1939 settled over an emotionally battered and exhausted city. There had been no horrific killings and dismemberments since August of the preceding year, but any mention in the Cleveland press of an unearthed bone, abandoned clothing, or a missing person sent the public's collective hearts surging into their throats with Pavlovian predictability. The most massive, intense, and publicized police investigation in city history had snared hundreds of potential suspects, shined an embarrassingly revealing light on the deplorable living conditions in and around the downtown area, presented local citizens with an astonishing array of deviants and mentally ill residents subsisting in their midst, exposed the seeming inadequacy of local law enforcement, and tarnished the image of Cleveland's safety director, Eliot Ness.

The legendary lawman may have been able to clean up the police department, muzzle labor racketeering, and cripple the gambling industry; but the Kingsbury Run murders seemed to have stymied him. The term "serial killer" did not appear in the index of the Federal Agent's Handbook; and the brutal cycle of killings simply remained a phenomenon outside his experience, indeed, outside the experience of any contemporary lawman. Law enforcement training in those days didn't cover tracking down and rounding up psychopaths who murdered and dismembered perfect strangers for their own murky, twisted personal reasons. Initially, Ness seems to have wisely adopted a hands-off policy toward the murders and allowed his police department to bear the brunt of both the investigation and press scrutiny. In summer of 1936, however—given the city's full calendar, Mayor Harold Burton advised his safety director that he had to get more directly involved. After the eleventh and twelfth canonical victims turned up in a city dump in August 1938, Ness led a well-publicized raid of the shantytown sprawl in the Flats and Kingsbury Run, rounding up its impoverished, desperate residents and reducing their hovels to ashes. He saw and defended his action as a valid response to an unprecedented situation; he was clearing out the hunting grounds where the unknown Butcher apparently tracked his prey. The local press, however, tended to characterize his actions as cruel and draconian. And the crumbling inner city still lived in a constant state of barely suppressed panic; the gnawing fears had spread to the outlying suburbs, as well. Cleveland was a city under siege, groaning under the weight of a frightening enemy no one could see. The public wanted answers; officialdom and law enforcement craved redemption; the city needed closure. It seemed that the answer to all those prayers came in early July 1939 when agents acting under orders from Cuyahoga County sheriff Martin L. O'Donnell arrested a fifty-two-year-old Slavic immigrant named Frank Dolezal for the most savage and heinous murders in Cleveland history.

Notes

Captain Floyd O'Neil's account of his arrival at the county jail on the afternoon of August 24, 1939, is drawn from his sworn deposition taken by the city's Criminal Investigation Bureau and dated that same day at 6:45 P.M.

The summary of the local political scene comes from several different articles in *The Encyclopedia of Cleveland History* (edited by David D. Van Tassel and John J. Grabowski [Bloomington: Indiana Univ. Press, 1987]) and my conversations with Doris O'Donnell Beaufait, formerly a reporter with both the *Cleveland News* and the *Plain Dealer*. (She is also the niece of then county sheriff Martin L. O'Donnell.)

The account of Coroner A. J. Pearce's torso clinic of September 1936 is drawn from the reports in Cleveland's three daily newspapers.

Chapter 2

THE BRICKLAYER, THE COP, AND THE PRIVATE EYE

It's impossible to say exactly when Frank Dolezal took those first tentative steps on the path that would inevitably lead to his destruction; but by summer 1939, he was a deeply troubled man. Our understandable desire to see the world of law enforcement and crime in simple terms of black and white, of villains and heroes, can sometimes lead us to view those who potentially suffer injustice at the hands of the establishment as totally innocent of any wrongdoing; but the fifty-two-year-old bricklayer was hardly an angel. There is no way to know when his serious drinking problems began; but by July 1939, Frank Dolezal battled full-blown alcoholism and a Jekyll-Hyde personality. When he was sober, he could be gentle, even sweet; his nephews and nieces, children of his brother Charles, treasured fond memories of a kind uncle who, on those rare occasions when he visited, invariably brought them candy and readily treated all the neighborhood youngsters to ice cream. Similarly, his neighbors recalled a gregarious man who enjoyed company—someone who would happily spring for steaks when he had the money and treat his friends to a cookout. But when he had had too much to drink, Dolezal wrestled with a legion of frightening personal demons. Crying jags would consume him, only to be replaced by deep black depressions, intense—almost paranoid—fears, and occasional violent rages. Whisperings about the exact nature of his sexuality also hung over him, and there were vague reports alleging he had been seen loitering around the Terminal Tower on Public Square trying to lure young men to his apartment. A common laborer who never married, by 1939, Dolezal supported himself by practicing his bricklaying trade on a variety of WPA projects. Except for some rumored casual on-again, off-again living arrangements with both men and women, he seems to have spent most of his life alone in a series of small, dilapidated apartments in the crumbling neighborhoods on Cleveland's near west and east sides. At five feet, eight inches, he was a relatively short, though stocky, man. He was hardly the sort of individual people would notice; he was just another nondescript working stiff trying to put together a meager living in the middle years of the Great Depression. He was, however, also plagued by what was then commonly referred to as a wandering eye, a condition that gave him a vacant, blank, distracted stare—as if he were never quite focusing on the objects and people in front of him. He had glasses to correct the problem but seems to have rarely worn them.

Frank Dolezal was born on May 4, 1887, in what was then simply referred to as Bohemia, to Vaclav and Mary, née Spinka, Dolezal, one of ten children. In 1910 at the age of twenty-three, he immigrated to the United States, apparently making the long sea journey alone. (Over time, Cleveland would absorb three major waves of Czech immigrants, the largest occurring between 1870 and the onset of World War I.) Whatever may have prompted, or forced, him to leave his homeland remains a mystery. Grinding poverty, high taxes, and lack of work drove many of his countrymen to the United States during this period; and as, perhaps, one of the older males in a large family, he may have seen it as his duty to lessen the financial burdens on his beleaguered parents by seeking his fortune on the other side of the Atlantic. In the early years of the twentieth century, Cleveland was a thriving and growing industrial center with a reputation as an ethnic melting pot that rivaled New York's. These circumstances alone would have been sufficient to attract a young Czech man on his own for the first time in his life. Frank Dolezal, however, was following an older sister, Anna, who had already come to America, in 1903 or 1904, and made her home in Cleveland. (An obscure piece of Dolezal family legend maintains a second sister, Antonia, or, perhaps, Antonie Dolezal Lesky, had also made the journey to the United States, though when she came and where she may ultimately have settled are unknown. There is no record of her in Cuyahoga County, which raises the possibility that "Anna" and "Antonie/Antonia" may have been the same person.) In 1913, on the eve of the Great War, one of Frank's younger brothers, Charles, became the third or fourth Dolezal sibling to cross the Atlantic. (Charles's given name was actually Karel. "Frank," therefore, may have been a similarly Anglicized version of something else, possibly Franz.)

Apparently, the two brothers lived quietly together for the next seven years, though exactly where is difficult to determine. None of the several Charles and Frank Dolezals listed in the Cleveland city directories between 1913 and 1919 would seem to fit the bill. It was not until 1920 that directory compilers took note of the brothers, both bricklayers, living at 3217 West 56th. In 1920, Charles married Louise Vorell, and from that point on, Frank was essentially on his own. In the years immediately following Charles's marriage, the first signs of a curious introverted silence—something akin to

The Frank Dolezal that Cleveland never knew. This photograph documents the 1920 marriage of his brother Charles to Louise Vorell. From left: Frank Dolezal, Louise Dolezal, Charles Dolezal, unidentified child, Lillian Vorell, Frank Vorell, and unidentified female. Courtesy of Mary Dolezal Satterlee.

estrangement—developed between the two brothers. They saw each other rarely and remained steadfastly oblivious to the mundane details of each other's lives. This same emotional distance and unwillingness, even inability, to communicate openly would characterize Dolezal family relationships in succeeding generations. Little or nothing of the family past was ever discussed openly; everything Mary Dolezal Satterlee (Charles's granddaughter and Frank's great-niece) learned about her family history came to her in vague whispers or through her own determined digging.

Whether one marks the beginning of the Kingsbury Run murders some-time in 1934 (when the Lady of the Lake turned up on the shore of Lake Erie) or September 1935 (the deaths of Edward Andrassy and his never identified companion), by late summer 1936, the string of gruesome atrocities had pro-pelled Cleveland into an embarrassing national spotlight. Cleveland's movers and shakers dreaded the constant stream of negative publicity the city was attracting internationally. The Great Lakes Exposition was also scheduled to open that summer—potentially attracting thousands of visitors—and the

Republicans were holding their 1936 national convention here, as well. All this activity could add up to a major economic shot in the arm for an old industrial city still reeling from the disastrous effects of the Great Depression. The torso killings were stretching law enforcement to beyond the breaking point and testing its institutions as they had never been tested before. Every sector of public safety—even the fire department—was mobilized to fight the elusive menace who perpetrated such grisly horrors in the middle of one of the nation's larger cities. Something had to be done, and quickly. In early September 1936, Mayor Harold Burton placed his safety director, the legendary crime fighter Eliot Ness, at the head of the investigation and ordered his chief of police, George Matowitz, to assign his best detective to work the case full time. Every city resident who had been marked as an odd character or a sexual deviant came systematically under intense official scrutiny. And that virtually unending tally of weird and strange Clevelanders would come to include the bricklayer with the severe drinking problem and uncertain sexual orientation who lived alone in a shabby apartment building in a dying neighborhood on Cleveland's near east side.

Detective Peter Merylo could have come straight from Central Casting; he was everyone's image of the ideal Depression-era cop—tough, smart, dedicated, scrupulously honest, a crack shot with his pistol, and obsessively thorough (he boasted the police department's most impressive arrest record). On the one hand, he was a team player who respected the lines of authority (even when he didn't particularly care for the individuals in authority) and did his job without complaint or fanfare; on the other hand, there was just enough of the maverick, the lone gunman, in his personality and professional conduct to endear him to an American public that worshipped individuality, personal initiative, and the Hollywood cowboy. Generally, he worked within the rules, but he remained more than willing to bend procedural guidelines when necessary to get the job done. Clevelanders saw only the dedicated professional, the tough cop who could sometimes be the proverbial bull in the china shop. But there lurked a gentle, even tender side to his personality that few outside his immediate family ever saw. He once considered joining the priesthood and harbored an abiding love for the sound of a violin. Crimes against the helpless, especially children, sparked his personal rage and drove him to give his all to the job. Ironically, his background was remarkably similar to that of Frank Dolezal, the man who would ultimately become his quarry. Born in 1895 in the Ukraine, Merylo immigrated to the

Detective Peter Merylo. The veteran cop could boast of the Cleveland Police Department's finest arrest record. He was placed on the torso murders full-time in 1936 by Chief of Police George Matowitz. *Cleveland Press* Archives, Cleveland State University.

United States sometime around 1915, joined the army—though he saw no active service—and gravitated to police work in 1919. By the mid-1930s, he had been a detective in the Cleveland Police Department for several years and had built a reputation for handling difficult and dangerous assignments.

Following orders from Mayor Harold Burton, Chief of Police George Matowitz assigned Merylo to work the torso killings full time in the early days of September 1936—just as transients who lived in the city's sprawling shantytowns spotted the first grisly piece of the Butcher's sixth victim floating in a fetid waterway at the heart of Kingsbury Run. Along with his partner, veteran detective Martin Zalewski, Merylo began reviewing the voluminous pile of police reports that had been accumulating since the torso killings began. Even for a cop of Merylo's vast experience and intelligence, absorbing and classifying all the diverse pieces of information gathered and recorded by the men who had worked the case from the beginning was a daunting task. A couple of days after Chief Matowitz gave his lead investigator his marching orders, Safety Director Ness incurred Merylo's displeasure—if not his wrath—by summoning him to his office and demanding to know how much progress he had made on the case. Merylo fixed Ness with an incredulous stare and most likely bit his tongue; he was still sifting through all the files, he replied, though he had come to the conclusion that the killings were sex crimes. The meeting was a clash of opposites: on the one hand, the tough, older, streetwise cop who personally ranked his colleagues by their gritty determination, willingness to give their all to the job, as well as their demonstrated competence and accomplishment; on the other hand, the younger, dapper, ex-G-man (already a legend) who courted the press, hobnobbed with the society set, and could usually call on enough political savvy to deal effectively with the ruling elites of the city. It was not an auspicious beginning; the professional relationship between Merylo and Ness would follow a strained and difficult path for the duration of the investigation.

In late November 1936, just two months after having been assigned to the Kingsbury Run murders, Merylo and Zalewski pulled Frank Dolezal into the central station for questioning. The bricklayer had come to their attention through an unidentified "pervert" they had rounded up and interrogated thanks to a tip. The suspect admitted frequenting a dive at the corner of East 20th and Central, a sleazy neighborhood watering hole where both Edward Andrassy and Flo Polillo—the only two victims to be positively identified—often drank. He also fingered Frank Dolezal as an establishment regular, branded him a pervert, and said he had spent a lot of time in the bricklayer's run-down apartment at 1908 Central Avenue. For the two veteran cops, the possible link between the mysterious Dolezal and the only two victims to whom a name could actually be attached was enough. It was a simpler time for law enforcement officials; the procedural guidelines dealing with the arrest and questioning of potential suspects were considerably more lax in the 1930s than they are today. Merylo and Zalewski simply barged into Dolezal's apartment and surprised their uncomprehending quarry sitting at his kitchen table. With only a slight nod to any sort of legal ceremony, the pair identified themselves as detectives, searched his apartment for weapons (they found nothing), arrested him (apparently without charges), and hauled him in for interrogation. Unfortunately, neither of the two different sets of memoirs Merylo left behind provides much evidence as to their line of questioning and also fails to give any indication as to how they handled Dolezal (the good, old-fashioned third degree? or something more gentle and humane?) or how long they held him. Dolezal, however, maintained that he did not know Edward Andrassy at all and insisted he knew Flo Polillo only "slightly." "We went over his background," Merylo wrote; "we talked to his friends and neighbors. We investigated his job record; we found out where he had worked before he went to work for the WPA; we talked to the 21-year-old pervert who lived with him as his 'lover,' and we talked to prostitutes who had visited his apartment." Merylo also checked with police officers who had known Dolezal for years; and, though they maintained he was a pervert, they reported his relatively clean record, declaring him an honest man. Though the two detectives subsequently cut Dolezal loose, they continued to keep him under some sort of surveillance. "We kept pretty close tab on Frank during those days," Merylo declared in his memoirs. "We knew where we could find him—whenever we wanted." In August 1938, Merylo pulled Dolezal in for questioning a second time. Unfortunately, the details surrounding this second interrogation are extremely sketchy; there is virtually nothing in Merylo's memoirs or his surviving official reports that provides any of the details—the reasons behind this reexamination, how or in what circumstances they snared him, or what form their line of questioning took. This reinterrogation of Frank Dolezal, however, seems to have occurred in the days following the discovery of victims nos. 11 and 12 on August 15 and Eliot Ness's high-profile shantytown raid three days later.

Just why Merylo and Zalewski kept Frank Dolezal under continued surveillance for close to two years after their first recorded encounter with him is hard to say. Merylo does not provide any explanation in either set of memoirs or any of his extant police reports for their ongoing interest in him. On the one hand, it would seem that the pair still harbored suspicions about the bricklayer in spite of the lack of any solid evidence against him. On the other hand, after Dolezal's arrest by the sheriff and his forces in July 1939, Merylo insisted to his superiors and anyone else in officialdom that approached him that he was convinced of the bricklayer's innocence. "I advised the Prosecutor that I had this man in custody on two different occasions, that if I had a case against him I would never have turned him loose." If Merylo was so convinced of Dolezal's innocence, why the continued surveillance? The most likely explanation is that, as a more-or-less admitted homosexual, Dolezal would have contact with other "perverts" and those contacts might ultimately lead to the killer. Law enforcement during the 1930s seems to have been operating on the assumption that perverts—like ducks and geese—gathered in flocks.

Lawrence J. (Pat) Lyons had worked for years as a special investigator—sometimes for various official agencies, sometimes on his own. He had put in a stint for the Cleveland Chamber of Commerce and had worked for former mayor

Ray T. Miller during his term as Cuyahoga County prosecutor. Sometime before April 1938, when the Butcher's body count stood officially at nine, Pat Lyons became deeply interested in the torso case. "As a criminal investigator it was natural that I was interested," he wrote in his memoirs. "I decided to assemble all of the known facts and make a comprehensive study of them. I enlisted the aid of my brother, GV, and together we gathered facts from every reliable source." Consequently, Lyons and his brother trolled through the newspaper accounts, gained access to morgue records, and studied— what he simply refers to, somewhat cryptically, as—"written statements of the county coroner." In a high-profile case such as this, the possibility of turf warfare among the competing law enforcement agencies always looms large—especially in a city like Cleveland where the police department was controlled by Republican safety director Eliot Ness and the Cuyahoga County sheriff's office was ruled by Democrat Martin L. O'Donnell. By early 1938, Sam Gerber (also a Democrat) had occupied the coroner's office for a little over a year, having beaten out his predecessor—A. J. Pearce—in the November 1936 elections. The new coroner guarded his territory with the vengeful ferocity of a dragon sitting on a pile of gold in the bowels of a cave. Yet the Lyons brothers apparently explored the string of murders without attracting any unwanted official attention or animosity—at least, not at first.

Among his papers related to the investigation, Lyons left a formal, relatively detailed summary of his methods and procedures that he titled simply "A Discussion of the So-Called Torso Cases." This precise account of his methodology reveals him to have been considerably more than an amateur private sleuth amusing himself by poking around in a sensational series of grotesque killings. He clearly approached the task with the methodical thoroughness of a seasoned professional; and if, in hindsight, some of his assumptions prove questionable, the carefully reasoned logic behind them is unassailable. The Lyons brothers decided to explore the run-down areas around Kingsbury Run searching for telltale signs of the Butcher's base of operations. "We were of the opinion," Lyons wrote, "that a person could not dismember this many bodies and not leave some traces, regardless of the care he exercised in cleaning up." Thus the brothers went from door to door with a prepared list of questions, passing themselves off as workers making a survey of population trends and taking a real estate inventory. (Lyons does not give a precise date for the initiation of this house-to-house search, but in his memoirs he states he and his brother were already "underway" when the first piece of victim no. 10 appeared on the shores of the Cuyahoga River in early April 1938.) If something about the resident or his abode set off any alarm bells in their minds, they marked that individual down for a return visit. "As I would hold the attention of the resident under pretense, GV would go [to] the bathroom, shut the door and give the entire room the preliminary chemical test for blood." By August 1938, Pat and G. V. Lyons had revisited a total of twenty-three dwellings, but G.V. found blood in only one—which, unfortunately, turned out not to be human. Eliot Ness launched a similar search for the Butcher's lair through the same geographical area employing identical tactics in late August 1938. Six three-man teams—two detectives and a fire warden (who could check dwellings without a warrant)—moved methodically through the dilapidated neighborhoods surrounding Kingsbury Run. Astoundingly, neither the Ness forces nor the Lyons brothers seemed aware of each other's activities at the time. Because the element of surprise was so crucial to his entire operation, for obvious reasons Ness kept the whole business away from the press as long as he could, but it is still difficult to believe that two separate well-organized, carefully planned search efforts could proceed over the same ground at roughly the same time and remain oblivious of each other.

By early January 1939, the Lyons brothers had hit an impasse. They found it impossible to proceed without some kind of outside financial assistance, so Pat began shopping his ideas around to various city agencies in search of monetary backing and, perhaps, some sort of official sanction. He tried the Cleveland Chamber of Commerce, which apparently expressed interest but declined to back him with any funds. Here matters get a little murky; regrettably, Lyons's account of his actions and with whom he may have talked at this point is not entirely clear. In his memoirs, Lyons reports that he next "talked to the City Safety Department without success." He does not specify with whom he talked: Eliot Ness himself, or, perhaps, an assistant? He then writes, "I next went to the County Coroner." But again, he does not specify whether he dealt with Sam Gerber directly or with someone else. Lyons, however, ultimately found himself presenting his plans for apprehending the killer to Sheriff Martin O'Donnell: "The sheriff referred me to the Police Department. This was accomplished on January 9, 1939. I started on a part time job in the civil branch as a Real Estate Appraiser." (Again, the exact nature of this sequence of events remains unclear. What exactly did he mean by "The sheriff referred me to the Police Department?" Subsequent events make it obvious that the police—especially Peter Merylo—were totally unaware of his activities.)

Sometime in the first half of 1939, an informant pointed Lyons and his brother—now working with deputies Jack J. Gillespie and Paul McDevitt of the sheriff's department—toward a suspicious character named "Frank." Thus, like Merylo and Zaleweski before him, Pat Lyons picked up a trail that ultimately led to Frank Dolezal.

That path began while Lyons was trying to establish the movements of Edward Andrassy—traditionally identified as the Butcher's first victim—in the days before his murder and decapitation. Andrassy had been sticking to his room and appeared reluctant to leave his parents' Fulton Avenue home. When his sister pressed him for an explanation of his behavior, he confided to her (in Pat Lyons's words): "He finally admitted that he had stabbed a man by the name of Frank over near East 20th Street[,] and he was afraid he had killed him." Further, Andrassy's sister told Lyons that her brother knew "a fellow with a cast in his left eye" who "might be able to tell us something of Ed's activities that the family didn't know." (Was "cast" a reference to Frank Dolezal's wandering eye? In Lyons's memoirs, the reference would seem to be to two different people; is it possible, however, that the "Frank" Andrassy had stabbed and the man "with a cast in his left eye" were a single individual?) Yet another lead pointed toward a "pervert," also named Frank, who had the strange habit of borrowing butcher knives from his neighbors and who had occupied a Cedar Road apartment from 1935 to roughly early September 1938, when he abruptly moved out—suspiciously, just as Eliot Ness's forces were working their way through the same neighborhood. (A third "Frank," or, are these all the same person? And is this individual Frank Dolezal?)

When Lyons and his brother gained access to the apartment once occupied by the mysterious Frank number three, G.V.'s on-the-spot examination—as well as subsequent tests run on samples collected from various surfaces—indicated the presence of human blood. One of the confiscated knives once apparently used by their suspect also showed the presence of blood. Thus it came to pass that in the early summer of 1939, Pat Lyons and his associates finally set their sights firmly on Frank Dolezal. Tracking him down in his current address on East 22nd proved no problem. As the days rolled by, Lyons watched and waited patiently. Finally, one day Frank Dolezal, with the fruits of his paycheck clutched in his hand, went on a shopping expedition. The account of his behavior that Pat Lyons left in his memoirs shows a pathetic, lonely, and troubled man.

> He purchased a sailor-type hat, two white shirts, a pair of white pants, white shoes, and white socks. By the time he returned to his room with these purchases he had stopped into many places for drinks. He returned to his room and spent about two hours changing clothes. When he again came upon the street, I was hardly able to recognize him. It was about 1 P.M. He staggered a little, but he appeared very pleased with himself. He took a streetcar to Bolivar Road and East 9th Street and stood before a store window admiring himself for about

ten minutes. He would change the angle of his hat and turn sideways to get a side view.

Over the next few days Lyons watched patiently as Dolezal wandered aimlessly around to his favorite drinking spots in the downtown area, apparently trying to pick up male companionship. In just one evening, Lyons counted eighteen unsuccessful attempts at apparent seduction. (Dolezal did have a job, but Lyons does not record him going to work.) While the Lyons team kept him under surveillance, they dug into his background—just as Merylo and Zaleweski had three years before. Among the potentially damning discoveries they made was that Dolezal apparently knew all the murder victims who had either been positively or tentatively identified: Edward Andrassy, Flo Polillo, and Rose Wallace. In the early days of July 1939, the long, winding paths of the bricklayer, the cop, and the private eye finally came together in a violent clash that would leave one man dead and the lives of the other two irrevocably altered, spawn a host of damning charges and countercharges, and carve streams of bitterness that would persist into the twenty-first century.

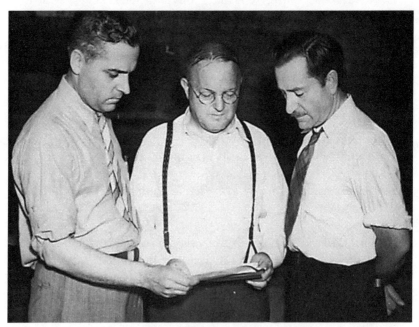

The trio responsible for Frank Dolezal's arrest. From left: Sheriff's Deputies Paul McDevitt and John J. (Jack) Gillespie; Special Sheriff's Deputy Pat Lyons. *Cleveland Press* Archives, Cleveland State University.

The desolate reality of day-to-day life in Cleveland's inner city during the Great Depression. A crowd gathers outside Frank Dolezal's apartment. Courtesy of the Cuyahoga County Coroner's Office.

At 6:00 P.M. on July 5, 1939, Pat Lyons, along with sheriff's deputies John Gillespie and Paul McDevitt, arrested Frank Dolezal, presumably on the order of and in the name of Sheriff Martin L. O'Donnell. The only account of this climactic moment in the unfolding drama that survives is in Pat Lyons's memoirs: "At 6 P.M. on July 5, 1939, Jack, Paul and I drove to his rooming house. As we stopped in front of his place, Frank was just coming around the corner of his house. We didn't get out of our car but opened the door and called to him. He came out to the car, got in, and we drove to the County Jail. All of this time Frank didn't say a word. He didn't ask who we were or where we were taking him." The behavior Lyons describes seems utterly incomprehensible. Why would Dolezal, or anyone else for that matter, docilely and without question enter a car occupied by three strangers and remain silent while the trio drove him off to an undisclosed location? Could the curtain really have descended that softly on the first act of the unfolding tragedy?

Exactly what prompted Sheriff O'Donnell into action at that precise moment is unclear. The only point upon which the accounts from Pat Lyons and Peter Merylo agree is that the Cleveland Police Department—specifically Merylo— somehow got wind of the Lyons team's activities, and Merylo does record in a police report dated April 2, 1940, that he learned that Pat Lyons was preparing to arrest Frank Dolezal the day before it occurred. At first blush, the fact that serious disagreements remain over who did or said what leading up to Frank Dolezal's arrest seventy years ago may seem of little consequence; but the torso butcheries had been the most sensational ongoing story in Cleveland history—a veritable feast for the city's three competing daily newspapers. After five years of intense coverage, the arrest of a suspect—the only arrest made in the case—was more than just big news; it meant, potentially, that it was all over, that the city could rest easy at last. But during the weeks following Frank Dolezal's arrest, the media circus would roll on with the inevitable force of a juggernaut. There would be a ransacking of Frank Dolezal's past and current lifestyle, acrimonious charges of mistreatment leveled at the sheriff's staff, resulting in ACLU involvement, a high-profile lie detector test, two alleged suicide attempts, three separate confessions, wrangling and squabbling in the courts over the legality of the system's conduct toward the suspect before charges were even leveled against him, a suspicious death, and a rancorous public inquest. When, on March 27, 1940, Frank Dolezal's brother Charles sued Sheriff O'Donnell and members of his staff for their treatment of their prisoner in two separate petitions, the conduct of everyone involved in the bricklayer's arrest and death came under intense legal scrutiny.

Pat Lyons's account of the events leading up to the arrest in his memoirs is regrettably brief and sketchy. He alleges that one of his team's prime informants witnessed a robbery, totally unrelated to the torso killings, during which the victim received a viciously severe beating. "And thinking we should know of this, he called the local office of the F.B.I. and asked for Jack [Gillespie], Paul [McDevitt] or Pat [Lyons], the investigators on the Torso Case. Naturally, they didn't know us and told him we must be from the Police Department. To make a long story short, the license plate number of Paul's car was obtained and Paul was identified as a deputy sheriff." With the proverbial cat out of the bag, at a subsequent meeting with Sheriff O'Donnell, the team decided to bring Dolezal in for questioning—perhaps before the police department, specifically Peter Merylo, could interfere.

Merylo's papers, however, contain two separate accounts of his version of events. In his memoirs he writes, "On June 12, 1939 [almost a full month before Dolezal's arrest], a license number was furnished us by a woman who was residing and conducting a place on Central Avenue, only a stone's throw from the locality where Florence Polillo's body was found, that a man was in her place of business who was very much intoxicated, telling her that he was working on the torso murder[s] and he was the investigator from the Chicago *Herald*.... We advised this woman that in the event this investigator ever showed up, to give us a telephone call, as we thought that he may be a good suspect." Apparently, almost a month went by before "this woman" furnished Merylo and Zalewski with the license plate number; on July 4—one day before Pat Lyons arrested Frank Dolezal—Merylo was checking out the individual (unidentified in his memoirs) to whom the license plate number belonged. Merylo's memoir is as vague as Pat Lyons's; his recapitulation of events does not provide any specifics. Neither the woman nor the intoxicated investigator is identified; her place of business remains unnamed; the type of business she owned (or, perhaps, only ran) is not even specified. All of that changes, however, in an official police report, dated April 2, 1940, that Eliot Ness specifically requested from Merylo. At the top of the three-page, single-spaced document (totaling approximately sixteen hundred words), Merylo has typed, "Report requested by Eliot Ness, Director of Public Safety." It is no coincidence that Ness asked for this report six days after Frank Dolezal's brother Charles filed his two lawsuits against Sheriff O'Donnell and five others, including Pat Lyons. Charles Dolezal was asking for $125,000 in damages, an astronomical sum by the standards of the early 1940s. Though Cuyahoga County itself was not specifically liable financially since the sheriff and his deputies were covered either by the Massachusetts Bonding and Insurance Company or the National Surety Corporation of New York, local reputations and the integrity of Cleveland's legal system were at stake. The safety director was crossing his *T*s and dotting his *I*s with a vengeance.

If Merylo demurely pulled his punches in his memoirs, the gloves were off in the report of April 2, 1940. All the participants in the unfolding drama, left unidentified in his memoirs, are named in his report; and the events that occurred are spelled out with much greater specificity. "On June 12, 1939, one Helen Merrills, at that time living at 1963 Central Ave. called our office and informed Detective Peters that she wanted the Detectives working on [the] Torso Murders." Mrs. Merrills was the proprietress of the Forest Café, a run-down neighborhood joint that served lunches and operated with a license for beer and wine. When Merylo and Zalewski arrived at her establishment, Mrs. Merrills had a tale to tell. "She then stated," Merylo writes, "that a man came to her place several days previously with a small brief case under his arm, and who was in an intoxicated condition, and he introduced himself to her as being Sergeant Pat Lyons of the *Chicago Herald*, and that he was working on the torso murders." Then, according to Mrs. Merrills, Lyons opened his briefcase and displayed a series of photos and newspaper clippings relevant to the murder-dismemberments and bought "everybody a drink who were [sic] in the place; who consisted mainly of prostitutes and 'pimps' from that vicinity, most of them colored." "Mrs. Merrills further stated that she had seen a gold badge on Pat Lyons, and that she was 'convinced' that he was a police officer, and that on a different occasion he came there with another man in [a] Ford automobile, and at that time Mrs. Merrills promised us she would procure the license number of this auto and call our office: which she did at a later date." At this point, the two differing accounts come together in agreement: Pat Lyons concedes that Paul McDevitt was identified as a deputy sheriff by the police through the number on his license plate, and Merylo concurs, noting a "license number as being BU954, same being listed to Paul McDevitt." Before the summer was out, Frank Dolezal would lie dead on the fourth floor of the county jail.

† † †

Pat Lyons's children and grandchildren vigorously dispute Peter Merylo's account of his actions in the Ness report of April 2, 1940, arguing that the obnoxious, raucous behavior the detective described is totally out of keeping with the father and grandfather they remember (especially the man who penned the charming lyrics to a song called "Mary Not Contrary") and further pointing out that Merylo harbored deep animosity against Pat Lyons for intruding in "his" investigation and being successful where he had failed. And there is some evidence to suggest that this could be, to a certain degree, the case. Merylo clearly saw the sheriff and his team as interlopers, and it was no secret that he could react with pit-bull ferocity when guarding what he perceived as his territory. (Pat Lyons gives due credit to Merylo in his memoirs for his talents as an investigator and his impressive arrest record; nothing in Peter Merylo's papers reciprocates that respect.) A newspaper article from early 1940 brands Lyons as the veteran cop's "arch-rival and favorite abomination." A second, undated clipping describes a meeting between the two men, apparently in early 1940, during which Merylo reportedly lectured his rival on the inadequacy of his investigative methods. "You've got the wrong technique. Don't believe everything drunks tell you. Furthermore, I hope you know that you bungled up everything when you arrested Frank Dolezal." Yet Merylo assured the press, "I bear the man no ill will. None whatsoever." The political storm swirling around Pat Lyons's arrest, trial, and conviction on drunk driving charges in January 1940 further clouds and complicates an accurate assessment of Merylo's attitude toward him. Though the exact circumstances leading to the arrest remain in dispute, Municipal Court judge Frank C. Phillips tossed out the original conviction when Lyons's attorney, Charles W. Sellers, produced sworn affidavits alleging that the two arresting officers had perjured themselves. Sheriff O'Donnell injected a heavy dose of local politics into the resulting legal wrangling when he wrote Lyons on June 22, 1940: "I considered your arrest and the flimsy circumstances which surrounded the charge as being the spleen of an envious police department [Peter Merylo?], whom you had bested in solving the Dolezal case. Further, when they [word illegible] before Detective Merylo, who questioned you on the Dolezal case rather than the traffic case, is positive proof that you were the victim of their jealousy." A point well taken? Perhaps—but Martin O'Donnell accusing others of acting out of political motivation is a prime example of the proverbial pot calling the kettle black. Also, in 1940 Sheriff O'Donnell was heavily invested in the notion of Frank Dolezal's guilt, since the lawsuits Charles Dolezal brought were still being litigated and the integrity of the sheriff and his office clearly hung in the balance. And why did the sheriff wait almost six full months after Lyons's January arrest before writing this token of support to his former special deputy?

Pat Lyons's account of the events that precipitated Frank Dolezal's arrest is sketchy enough to suggest that he is, indeed, hiding or at least glossing over something; and the behavior Merylo describes and attributes to Lyons in his report to Ness—if true—would easily explain Lyons's seeming evasiveness. One must also consider the nature and ultimate purpose of the two manuscript accounts Merylo left behind. Though they were never published, both sets of his personal memoirs were intended for public consumption; therefore, his relative and somewhat uncharacteristic reticence to name names and provide specifics could be read as reflecting his desire to protect the reputations of those involved. The report of April 2, 1940, however, was an entirely differ-ent matter. It was an official police document specifically requested by his superior, Eliot Ness; and as such, it would probably never have been seen by anyone aside from the Ness circle and Chief of Police Matowitz. Every little detail had to be nailed down and fully explained. The chances that anyone else would ever see it were virtually nil. The notion that a detective of Peter Merylo's reputation and stature would lie knowingly in an official report to his superior—even though he did not particularly like Ness—is untenable, especially when the details of that report could have been so easily checked. But Merylo was repeating what others, specifically Helen Merrills, reported to him; and it is possible that the good proprietress of the Forest Café was simply misinterpreting some of what she was seeing.

On the one hand, the suggestion that Lyons was drunk when he came into her place of business appears a couple of times in the Merylo report, and some of the behavior Mrs. Merrills described could only be attributed to intoxication. The charge of intoxication was obviously also central to Lyons's drunk driving arrest in 1940. And there were at least two other arrests for intoxication in his past—one in 1918 and another in 1933. Coincidentally, the later incident also involved charges of perjury on the part of the arresting officers. On the other hand, it is difficult to believe that anyone with a drinking problem could have conducted the sort of calculated investigation Lyons and his team had, while also keeping it out of the papers and away from the attention of the police department for so long. In his memoirs, Lyons states that he was careful never to say he was a policeman; he always went simply by his first name, as did the sheriff's deputies working with him. (In his report to Ness, however, Merylo does write that Helen Merrills saw a gold badge.) He adopted this strategy essentially for two reasons: outright fabrications and falsehoods can come back to haunt a careless investigator; and the people from whom he was trying to extract information lived in the destitute, run-down neighborhoods on the fringes of society and—given the nature of their lives, experiences, and color—were not about to trust the police. Thus, Lyons walked a thin line—presenting himself as an authority figure of some sort who was also a "regular guy" who could be counted on to spring for a round of drinks. It is possible to read at least some of the boisterous behavior that Mrs. Merrills reported to Merylo as a heavy-handed attempt on Lyons's part to ingratiate himself to the poor, black regulars that hung out at the Forest Café.

The Pat Lyons who survives in old newspaper stories and official documents, both public and private, is an imperfect reflection of the father and grandfather his family remembers. It was an important lesson, one I had already learned and of which I would be reminded several times during the course of my research. From all of this diverse and incomplete evidence, two seemingly different portraits of Pat Lyons emerge: on the one hand, a careless would-be detective who couldn't hold his liquor; on the other, a shrewd investigator trolling for significant information in the murky, dangerous swamps of tenement life in Depression-era Cleveland.

NOTES

Frank Dolezal's great-niece Mary Dolezal Satterlee provided the details relevant to Frank Dolezal's family background and his early days in Cleveland—as well of those of his brother Charles. Other details were culled from public documents, such as the city directories and government census reports.

When he died in 1958, Detective Peter Merylo left behind two extensive, unpublished manuscripts detailing his work on the Kingsbury Run murders. The longer of the two comes in at 155 typed legal-sized pages, and the dry formality of its prose strongly suggests that Merylo was the document's sole author. Though the second manuscript, 107 typed legal-sized pages, bears the name Frank Otwell—a *Cleveland News* reporter as well as Merylo's personal friend—on its first page, Merylo's hand is still evident; and Otwell's participation in this version may have been an attempt to lighten the rigidly official tone of the veteran cop's style, thus producing a far more reader-friendly account. Both of these manuscripts are part of the vast collection of documents related to the case in the possession of Peter Merylo's daughter Marjorie Merylo Dentz. Though most of these papers are copies of Merylo's official police reports, the assemblage also includes tip letters from a variety of sources, many of them unsigned, and other pieces of official and personal correspondence. Totaling well over two thousand pages of diverse material, the Merylo papers constitute the largest single collection of documents pertaining to the Kingsbury Run murders.

Pat Lyons's daughter, Carol Fitzgerald, graciously provided me with copies of all her father's papers dealing with his role in the torso investigation. Though nowhere near as voluminous as the Merylo collection, the random notes, lists of people to be interviewed, various letters, and Lyons's formal manuscript, "A Discussion of the So-called Torso Cases," provide significant insight into the thinking behind his working methods and flesh out a considerable number of the significant details leading up to Frank Dolezal's arrest in July 1939. The song "Mary Not Contrary," for which Lyons supplied lyrics, was composed by A. Leopold Richard and published by Legters Music Company of Chicago.

An extensive account of Pat Lyons's 1933 arrest for intoxication and being a "suspicious person" can be found in the clipping files of the *Cleveland Press* housed in the library of Cleveland State University. The document is not a published story clipped from the pages of the *Press;* rather it is a typed, three-page manuscript for a story that apparently was never printed.

Chapter 3

HISTORY THROUGH A GLASS DARKLY

Frank Dolezal was arrested on Wednesday, July 5, 1939; on August 24 he would lie dead on the jailhouse floor. Until the beginning of the twenty-first century, the only record available to the public of what happened in the county jail on those hot summer days and during the rancorous aftermath would be the bits and pieces recorded in Cleveland's three daily newspapers—fragments of history hurriedly gathered to meet a deadline, with little, if any, in-depth investigation—offered to a public hungry for details. A predictable wave of local excitement and relief washed over the city after Sheriff Martin L. O'Donnell's public announcement on July 6 that the torso killer had finally been apprehended. The city was now safe from the elusive killer who had prowled through its neighborhoods and haunted its blighted interiors since late 1934. Clevelanders could now breathe their collective sigh of relief and celebrate the crack investigators under the sheriff's command who had finally tracked down the Butcher—a man O'Donnell luridly described to the *Cleveland News* as "gorilla-like"—and put him behind bars.

THURSDAY, JULY 6, 1939

"Find Human Blood in Torso Hunt," blared the headline in the *Press* that afternoon. Thus murder-weary Clevelanders first learned that the cycle of mutilation and blood-letting might finally be over. Sheriff Martin O'Donnell announced that a chemical analysis performed by G. V. Lyons—brother of Pat Lyons—of stains found on the walls and under the bathroom baseboard at the 1908 Central Avenue apartment where Dolezal had lived in August 1938 proved they were human blood. He then continued to outline what the *Plain Dealer* termed the "strong circumstantial case" that he and his office had built against Frank Dolezal so far. Allegedly, Dolezal's initial explanation for the telltale blood in his Central Avenue apartment was that he had bought a pig at the central market and had butchered it in his bathroom. When informed that the central market did not sell pigs, he immediately insisted it was a chicken he had bought and killed. Though he had at first denied he had been acquainted with any of the torso victims, Dolezal ultimately confessed he had known Flo Polillo (victim no. 3) and had been drinking with her in his apartment the night before the first set of her remains turned up behind Hart Manufacturing, less than a block away, on January 26, 1936, thus potentially making him the last person to have seen her alive. Allegedly, Dolezal had borrowed "a large knife" from a neighbor and later returned it stained with human blood. He had suspiciously moved from his apartment to a Scranton Road address (to get cheaper rent, he insisted) on the near west side following the discovery of victims no. 11 and no. 12 in August 1938—just as Eliot Ness was sending teams of police and firemen to search the dilapidated dwellings in the run-down east side neighborhoods close to downtown—and had just as suspiciously moved back to the east side to 2491 East 22nd Street a few months before his arrest. In spite of his constant denials that he knew any of the Butcher's victims other than Flo Polillo, unidentified witnesses, most likely Dolezal's neighbors, had assured the sheriff's men that they had seen him with a man who strongly resembled the first officially recognized victim, Edward Andrassy, and another man, clearly a sailor. (Because of his distinctive tattoos, authorities had always surmised that the unidentified victim no. 4—discovered on June 5, 1936—may have been a navy man or, at the very least, a sailor.) He reportedly also had a "passionate craving for knives." A thorough search of Dolezal's apartment had turned up a notebook filled with names and addresses, as well as a photo album from which pages had obviously been torn. According to the sheriff, Dolezal would not or could not offer any explanation for these missing pages. Finally, he had worked as a "sticker" and then a "stamper" in a slaughterhouse for three months twenty years before, apparently around 1918, thus potentially providing him with the necessary experience to disarticulate a human corpse with surgical precision. A very circumstantial case, indeed! But it all added up to an incriminating picture, and it was certainly a promising beginning. Dolezal, however, had so far confessed to nothing beyond the alleged facts that he had known Flo Polillo and had been drinking with her the night of January 25, the day before some of the pieces of her corpse turned up in the snow behind Hart Manufacturing on East 20th.

Apparently, some unidentified members of the press corps decided it might be a good idea to check with Peter Merylo and ask what he thought of all this. After all, the torso murders had been the exclusive property of the Cleveland Police Department since the beginning, whether one officially marked that beginning at September 1934 or September 1935. Merylo had worked the case virtually full time since September 1936 under the guidance of Safety Director

Eliot Ness. And the police had repeatedly come up empty; the most massive investigation in city history had seemingly crashed against an impregnable wall of mystery. Yet the county sheriff's office, with the aid of Pat Lyons, had blown the case open in a bit less than a year. Though the *Press* reported on July 6 that Merylo was "angered by the sheriff's intrusion into his specialty," the wily detective played his cards carefully and close to the vest—at least, for the time being. He pointed out to the *Plain Dealer* that Dolezal's alleged assertion that he had been drinking with Flo Polillo the night of January 25 could not possibly be true, since then-coroner Pearce had determined she had been dead two to three days before January 26, when her partial remains were found. At this point, Merylo's shot across the bow did little damage to the sheriff's case, but the veteran cop was silently and deliberately arming his torpedoes.

FRIDAY, JULY 7

That evening, Sheriff O'Donnell announced with great fanfare that he had obtained a confession—at least a confession of sorts. "Dolezal said he killed Mrs. Polillo and I believe him," Pat Lyons told the *Plain Dealer*. "Suspect Says He Struck Woman with Fist When She Threatened Him with Butcher Knife in Quarrel," proclaimed the *Press*. Deputy Harry S. Brown, Chief Deputy Clarence M. Tylicki, and Chief Jailer Michael F. Kilbane had subjected Dolezal to a continuous and brutally intense interrogation—no less than forty hours, according to the *Cleveland News*—since his arrest two days before, and the suspect had finally broken. "We were in my room drinking Friday night. . . . She was all dressed up and wanted to go out. She wanted some money. She grabbed for $10 I had in my pocket. I argued with her because she tried to take some money from me before. . . . She came at me with a butcher knife. . . . Yes, I hit her [Flo Polillo] with my fist," the *Plain Dealer* reported the next day. "She fell into the bathroom and hit her head against the bathtub. I thought she was dead. I put her in the bathtub. Then I took the knife—the small one, not the large one—and cut off her head. Then I cut off her legs. Then her arms." (The *Press* also "quoted" Dolezal's narrative; and although the story is the same, the wording is rather different, thus raising a significant issue: how accurate were these reporters when it came to quoting a source? Just how rigorous—or casual—were press standards when it came to the use of quotation marks? The problem is further compounded in this case by the suspect's reportedly very poor command of the English language; by all accounts from friends and family, he spoke broken English at best. Just whose words were those that the eager press establishment was quoting?) Dolezal placed this deadly confrontation at 2 A.M. on January 25, the day before the initial set of her remains was discovered. Following his confession, the sheriff and his men whisked their prisoner off to the lakeshore at East 49th just so he could point to the exact spot where he allegedly tossed Flo Polillo's head into the frigid waters; then they headed back to Hart Manufacturing so he could similarly indicate where he had deposited the produce baskets containing the initial set of Polillo's body parts. That evening, Cleveland's press corps got their first look at the alleged Mad Butcher of Kingsbury Run—the monstrous fiend who had terrorized the inner city for four years, given Cleveland a black eye in the national press, and stumped Ness and his legion of detectives and other law enforcement personnel. The most massive investigation in Cleveland history had resulted in the arrest of a short, stocky man in a sweat-stained shirt who gazed blankly into space as the assembled photographers snapped his picture.

The main problem with the Dolezal confession was that the rest of his story simply did not match the documented and widely publicized details of the Polillo murder. After carefully packing some of her remains in produce baskets and depositing his handiwork in the snow behind the manufacturing company, Dolezal supposedly told his captors that he transported the remaining pieces of her corpse to the foot of East 49th, where he unceremoniously tossed them into Lake Erie. But it had been widely reported that the second set of Polillo's body parts had been located at 1419 Orange on February 7; and, working cautiously behind the scenes so as avoid attracting the attention of either Sheriff O'Donnell or Chief of Police George Matowitz, Merylo pointed out to the press that Dolezal could not have disposed of Flo Polillo's remains in Lake Erie on the night of January 26, 1936, in the manner alleged because the biting winter cold had frozen lake waters well beyond the breakwall. All reporters had to do was check with the U.S. Weather Bureau to verify the claim. The press also reported that Dolezal had claimed he burned Flo Polillo's clothing, save for her coat and shoes; those, he is alleged to have insisted, he left behind the Hart Manufacturing Company building on East 20th with the first set of her remains. If that were the case, why weren't they found? They don't appear in either of the two official photographs of the scene, nor are they mentioned in any of the surviving police reports. Merylo wryly reflected on the situation in his memoirs: "This was my first experience where a man is making a confession to a murder or any other serious crime and does not know the details of the crime which he is alleged to have committed." Thus, at the very moment the juggernaut began rolling inexorably forward and gathering speed, the wheels started to fall off. "There are some discrepancies between what Dolezal says he did and what are known facts in the Polillo case," the sheriff acknowledged to the *Plain Dealer.* "We want to get a confession that will hold up in court before we place any charges against him." According to the *Press*, the sheriff was far more specific. "But I still want him to confess that he actually murdered Mrs. Polillo." Though serious allegations of mistreatment at the hands of the sheriff and his deputies would materialize later, at this point there was no way for the reading public to tell what had happened to Frank Dolezal behind the jailhouse walls in the two days since his arrest. But some of the wording in the *Press* made it clear that he must have been subjected to a horrendous ordeal: "questioned all night" (July 6); "the suspect . . . has been grilled for two days," "suspect is weakening under the long hours of grilling" (July 7); "the questioning continued thus, in relays" (July 8). According to the *Cleveland News* on July 6, Dolezal endured "more than twenty hours of intermittent grilling"; and the *Plain Dealer* casually informed its readers that the prisoner had not been allowed to sleep from the time he was arrested on July 5 until 9:00 P.M. on July 7. It was a different time, and law enforcement

Western Reserve University chemist Dr. Enrique Ecker (kneeling) looks for blood-stains on the bathtub in Frank Dolezal's apartment. Also present are Sheriff Martin L. O'Donnell (second from left) and Head Jailer Michael Kilbane (fourth from left). *Cleveland Press* Archives, Cleveland State University.

operated under a much looser set of rules than it does in the early twenty-first century. The rights of possible defendants didn't count for much, and obtaining a confession by any possible means was often the norm.

Dolezal added a nail to his own coffin when he finally "admitted" that he socialized and drank with Edward Andrassy and Rose Wallace (the tentative identification assigned to victim no. 8). Though the *Plain Dealer* reported that the case against Dolezal had obviously been strengthened by his admission, the fissures in the dam continued to spread. Edward Andrassy's father, Joseph, insisted to the *Press*, "I never saw that fellow [Frank Dolezal] in my life." (The official assumption was that the two were at least acquainted.) Also, without providing any explanation, the *Plain Dealer* cautiously indicated, "There appear to be some question [*sic*] as to whether Dolezal is the 'mad butcher of Kingsbury Run' and is responsible for all twelve of the torsos discovered in Cleveland between September, 1935, and last August." In the meantime, Sheriff O'Donnell occupied himself by arranging for his prisoner to take a lie detector test at the police department in East Cleveland (the only municipality to own one), lining up chemist Dr. Enrique E. Ecker of Western Reserve University to validate G. V. Lyons's analysis of the supposed bloodstains in Dolezal's bathroom, and checking hospital records to see if the scar on Dolezal's arm could be linked to the knife fight Edward Andrassy told his sister about in the days before his death.

SATURDAY, JULY 8

Frank Dolezal amended his story: as the *Press* so quaintly put it, "Dolezal Amplifies Confession." It seems he was mistaken when he initially told his interrogators that he had dumped Flo Polillo's head into Lake Erie along with other parts of her body. Upon further reflection, he remembered that he had actually burned her head under an East 34th bridge after pouring gasoline over it. The press dutifully reported these changes in the basic story, but the stark contrast between the two versions of the head's fate passed by without editorial comment—at least for the time being. The sheriff and some of his deputies immediately and, apparently, in relative secrecy—the few photographs that document the excursion show only Dolezal, the sheriff, and his men—whisked their prisoner over to East 34th so he could point out the exact spot where this minor conflagration had taken place. A half-hour search turned up only a few bones, later identified by Coroner Gerber as having come from a dog, cat, or sheep.

Dolezal's adamant refusal to admit he had been responsible for any of the torso killings other than Flo Polillo's murder raised the issue of whether those victims may have been dispatched and disarticulated by someone else, that Frank Dolezal's guilt only extended to the death of victim no. 3, Flo Polillo. Could there be two perpetrators? Consequently, Coroner Sam Gerber announced that he would restudy all the autopsy protocols and related evidence since the killings began. Gerber was something of a Johnny-come-lately to the Kingsbury Run murders. He had been elected to the coroner's office in 1936. The first six victims—seven if one includes the Lady of the Lake killed in 1934—had been murdered on A. J. Pearce's watch; and, thanks to his activist, hands-on approach, Gerber's predecessor had already placed his own indelible stamp on all the evidence in the coroner's office related to those murdered during his tenure. The groundbreaking torso clinic had also been Pearce's brainchild, not Gerber's. By publicly announcing his intention to reexamine all the killings—not just those that had occurred since his election—Gerber was, in a sense, taking ownership of the entire murderous cycle. Whether he realized it or not, his first public statements tended to damage the sheriff's case against Frank Dolezal. "Our records show some slight differences in the manner in which Mrs. Polillo's body was dismembered and the manner in which others were," he told the *Plain Dealer*, "but I still feel that the murderer of Mrs. Polillo is responsible for all the crimes. While it is possible that two men committed the crimes, it is unlikely that one would pick up where the other left off or that the manner of dismembering would be so similar. It is more probable that, as the murder series continued, the torso murderer changed his style." Dolezal's refusal to admit he killed the other victims now became an obstacle for the sheriff. O'Donnell's first step was to shore up Dolezal's confession to Flo Polillo's murder and then try to link him to the others, but the notion that he was only responsible for the death of Polillo had been established and would stubbornly persist.

Always mindful of how useful city newspapers could be in publicizing—even supporting—his crime-battling initiatives, Eliot Ness courted the press with the practiced finesse of a Hollywood press agent. Perhaps taking a page from the safety director's playbook, Sheriff O'Donnell now began trying to exploit and manipulate the press to the advantage of both his office and its case against Frank Dolezal. Unfortunately, he lacked the safety director's suave style, and his approach to reporters was considerably more heavy-handed. To O'Donnell's credit, he staged some of the scenes in the unfolding Dolezal drama for maximum public effect, allowing reporters and photographers full access to his activities; but when newspapermen turned too nosy or belligerent in his estimation, or when he could not control the situation, he turned defensive, often displaying a petulance that simply convinced the press corps that he was hiding something, that here was something deliberately left unsaid worth digging for. One of O'Donnell's more successful operations, however, was a very visible, highly publicized return visit to the scene of the supposed crime, Frank Dolezal's former residence at 1908 Central Avenue, for a thorough reexamination of its bathroom. His men tore out the bathtub and examined the stains and filth underneath and along the bathroom walls. Western Reserve University chemist Enrique E. Ecker scrapped samples of the various stains for further analysis. The coroner's office promised to search through the collected evidence of the Polillo murder to see if there was anything with her blood on it that could be compared to the samples gathered at the Central Avenue apartment; there were even some rather pointed comments about exhuming her body if necessary.

At the time of his arrest on July 5, Dolezal had been sharing his apartment for a month with Harold Kiersner, a twenty-three-old ex-con who had served two years in Leavenworth for liquor-law violations. On July 8, Kiersner wrote an article for the *Press* recounting his experiences with his recently arrested roommate. (Though Kiersner's name appears at the top of the piece, it is extremely doubtful he actually wrote it. Attributing the article to him was probably an editorial ploy to increase circulation; an article actually written by someone who had lived with the accused would obviously be seen as a major scoop.) "I slept with him the night before he was arrested for the torso murders," the article declares. "I don't know whether he killed that woman. Sometimes I don't think he did. He liked a pretty face, but he never did go for women." Kiersner painted a disturbing portrait of a troubled man who drank at least twenty bottles of beer a day, angered easily when intoxicated, and was overwhelmed by frequent crying jags. Almost as an afterthought, Kiersner noted, "He speaks English very poorly." Again, the issue of Dolezal's command of the language becomes crucial. It's far more than a matter of whether newspapers were quoting him accurately or rewriting his utterances in Standard English. Did he fully understand the nature of his interrogators' questions? Also, his signature later appears on some extremely significant, not to say incriminating, documents; did he actually understand what he was signing?

In the midst of all this excitement, veteran *Cleveland News* reporter Howard Beaufait pulled off a major scoop. He seemed to enjoy access to some levers of power beyond the reach of his colleagues: in the early hours of the morning, he was allowed to spend fifteen minutes with Frank Dolezal. Rather than merely outline the sheriff's case against him as his colleagues from rival papers had done, Beaufait gave his readers a graphic portrait of a pathetic, terrified, and deeply confused man. "I saw a man on the verge of hysteria," he wrote.

Cuyahoga County sheriff Martin L. O'Donnell. He was a friend and close political ally of Congressman Martin L. Sweeney. He had formerly been mayor of Garfield Heights, a Cleveland suburb. *Cleveland Press* Archives, Cleveland State University.

"He sat in his small, hot cell at County Jail, wringing a dirty handkerchief in his coarse, thick hands. . . . As he sat in his cell, his watery blue eyes heavy from a sleepless night, Dolezal drank glass after glass of water. . . . He was drenched in perspiration. It came through his soiled blue work shirt in dark spots. . . . His eyes are filled with fear, and he moves his head from side to side in quick, nervous jerks." In a clear echo of the vain behavior Pat Lyons described on the day of Dolezal's arrest, Beaufait commented, "He seemed rather ashamed of his ragged appearance. He said he wanted a shave and a haircut and a clean shirt. He was wearing dark, unpressed trousers and white kid shoes with fancy, pointed toes. These were soiled. He looked at them frequently and tried to tuck them out of sight under his bunk. Now he looks at all men as if they were his enemies. Each stranger who enters his cell brings a threat to his safety." "It is a curious fact that rarely does a murderer look like one," Beaufait mused in closing. "This is particularly true of Frank Dolezal. If he hadn't said so, you would find it rather preposterous to believe that he could turn his humble home into a slaughter house."

SUNDAY, JULY 9

"Woman Says She Jumped Seeing Knife" proclaimed the lead of a page one *Plain Dealer* story. A twenty-two-year-old—later identified as a black prostitute named Lillian Jones—insisted that she had been in Frank Dolezal's East 22nd apartment a week before his arrest and had been forced to jump out of the window when he came at her with a knife. "I was in Dolezal's room when he came at me with a knife. I jumped out of a second-story window to get away from him. The heel of one of my shoes was broken when I landed." Though the morning daily wondered how the woman could hurl herself out of a second-story window and fall to the ground without breaking anything else, Sheriff

O'Donnell seized on the sensational tale as further evidence that Dolezal was connected to the killings. The story "strengthens my suspicions that Dolezal was connected with other torso murders," he insisted to the *Plain Dealer.*

MONDAY, JULY 10

It would be a very busy day, marked by stunning revelations and troubling questions. Sheriff O'Donnell began the morning by showing reporters a letter he had received from Mrs. Nettie Taylor of Wheaton, Illinois. The woman, who identified herself as Frank Dolezal's sister-in-law, alleged that his sister Mrs. Anna Nigrin had apparently been murdered in July 1931 on the Geauga County farm near Chardon, Ohio, that she shared with her husband. When her son, Joseph, came to Cleveland from Chicago seven years later to clear up details related to his mother's estate, he stayed with his uncle Frank—never to be seen again! (There is some confusion here. The *Cleveland News* reported that the letter had actually come from Sheriff E. R. Burkholder of Wheaton, Illinois.) The implications of all this remained unstated; clearly, though, O'Donnell saw Nettie Taylor's suggestions of a mysterious death and an unexplained disappearance in the family as further proof that Frank Dolezal was a vicious murderer. But, cautioned the *Press,* "Neither the sheriff's office in Chardon nor the county prosecutor could find any record of the death of a Mrs. Nigrin." Alarm bells of some sort should have sounded at this point, but they apparently didn't. (See the epilogue for a full discussion of the Taylor letter and the fates of Anna and Joseph Nigrin.)

The real bombshell of the morning, however, was the sheriff's announcement that Frank Dolezal had made two unsuccessful suicide attempts overnight. At around 12:30 A.M., he tried to hang himself with his shirt from a hook in the wall of his cell, only to be foiled when Chief Jailer Michael Kilbane discovered him and pulled him down, ripping the shirt in the process. Reportedly, Dolezal tried again at about 4:30 A.M., this time fashioning a noose from his shoelaces. Apparently, however, they weren't sufficiently strong to bear his weight; Deputies Nick Miller and John Mulroy found him lying, stunned, on the cell floor. Again, though no public statements were made, the unspoken subtext was clear: withering under an unrelenting series of nonstop interrogations, a guilty, desperate man had decided to end it all rather than face the rigors of the justice system. (Among the coroner's papers, there is a signed deposition dated July 10 in which Dolezal admits his attempts at suicide, but the document remains troubling for several reasons. Had he been coerced into signing it? Given his questionable command of English, did he even understand what he was signing? Was it standard procedure to take such a deposition under the circumstances? If so, it would logically follow that there would be some sort of official form. The existing document, however, is not an official form; it is simply a typed statement with the heading "Criminal Courts Building" appearing at the top.)

But the story that Dolezal would be given a lie detector test in the late afternoon under the stewardship of the East Cleveland Police Department became the most newsworthy event of the day. The east side municipality owned an early version of the Keeler polygraph—named for Leonard Keeler of Northwestern University, the man who had perfected the machine and was widely regarded as the best in the business at administering the tests and interpreting the results. At around 3:00 P.M., sheriff's deputies escorted a dazed Frank Dolezal out of the county jail to an official car for the drive out to the municipality on the city's east side. Until this ceremoniously staged appearance, reporters hadn't had many opportunities to get a look at the sheriff's prisoner; staring vacantly ahead and stumbling slightly, Dolezal allowed himself to be steered toward the waiting automobile while flashes exploded around him as

Frank Dolezal being escorted to a car that will take him to East Cleveland for a lie detector test. This photograph was taken hours after his two suicide attempts. His pain is palpable. *Cleveland Press* Archives, Cleveland State University.

Frank Dolezal pathetically tries to hide from newspaper reporters and photographers. *Cleveland Press* Archives, Cleveland State University.

press photographers jockeyed for position. Suddenly, alarmed murmurs began to spread through the crowd of onlookers. Where had the clearly visible black eye come from, and why was he holding his side in obvious discomfort and pain? Dolezal had injured himself, explained the sheriff, when he had fallen on his face during his second suicide attempt. But the *Press* was dubious. "This seemed unlikely in view of the instinctive and automatic reflex action which makes anyone falling forward throw his arms out before him to protect his face." And when reporters realized that Dolezal's shirt—the same sweat-stained garment he had been wearing since his arrest—was intact, they began to wonder openly why there was no sign of the rip that had supposedly occurred during the first attempt at taking his life. Even as it relayed the sheriff's tale of his two suicide attempts, the *Press* looked at the report with a jaundiced and skeptical eye. "Not completely convincing," it declared.

Once in East Cleveland, the sheriff and his men were greeted by that city's police chief, L. G. Corlett. Dolezal was escorted to a basement soundproof room, where Paul F. Beck, a recent graduate of the Western Reserve University

Law School, would administer the test. The formal questioning started around 3:30 P.M. and continued uninterrupted until shortly after 6:00, at which point everyone took a supper break. The grueling interrogation began again at 8:15 and ran until Dolezal was returned to the Cuyahoga County jail at 10:30—a staggering five-and-a-half-hour ordeal. At first, Dolezal retracted his murder confession and insisted he had not killed Flo Polillo. When the machine indicated he was lying, he reverted to his initial claim that he had killed her when she came at him with a knife and had dismembered her corpse in his bathtub. Whenever the words "murder" or "blood" came up during the examination, Dolezal's "pulse and respiration jumped," the *Press* reported the next day. According to Beck, the final results of this interrogation were clear. Frank Dolezal was, indeed, guilty of Flo Polillo's murder.

At the end of what had to be an extraordinarily exhausting day for the prisoner, Dolezal finally got some medical attention for the pain in his side. After duly examining him, the male nurse on duty couldn't find anything specific wrong with him, but he proceeded to tape his side anyway.

TUESDAY, JULY 11

The day began with Frank Dolezal finally receiving his first visitor—his sister-in-law's brother Patrolman Frank Vorell of the Cleveland Police Department. (Whether Sheriff O'Donnell allowed Vorell to see his prisoner because he was a relative or because he was a policeman is not clear. Though Cleveland's dailies took scant notice of the patrolman's appearance, Vorell would later provide damning testimony relevant to the sheriff office's treatment of Dolezal.) In a move calculated to head off any insanity defense on Dolezal's part, the sheriff had two psychiatrists, K. S. Kent and S. C. Lindsay, examine him for about an hour and a half. "Dolezal Ruled Not Insane after Psychiatrists' Test," proclaimed the lead in the *Press*. O'Donnell now offered yet a third confession, a new version of what Dolezal had allegedly done with Flo Polillo's still missing head. It seems he had not thrown it into Lake Erie at the foot of East 49th as he had initially claimed, nor had he poured gasoline over it and burned it at East 34th; rather he had taken it to the WPA Lake Shore Drive project (on which he said he had been working) and discreetly buried it where he knew a steam shovel would further cover it with endless loads of dirt. O'Donnell lamented that trying to find it under those circumstances would be a typical needle-in-a-haystack proposition, so he regretfully called off the hunt.

Cleveland's press corps and legal fraternity became increasingly alarmed over the conduct of the sheriff and his office toward their prisoner and began to air their concerns openly. "Is Frank Dolezal the torso murderer? Or is he a harmless psychopath who has been forced into admitting a crime he did not commit?" asked *Press* reporter William Miller. "Lawyers agree Dolezal's rights have been infringed on," the paper declared. "He has been held six nights and five days without charge. Courts have held that 72 hours is the reasonable length of time a man may be held without charges." The civil liberties committee of the Cleveland Bar Association fired off a formal letter to Sheriff O'Donnell asking him to appear at their noon meeting at the Hotel Allerton on July 12 and explain, according to the *Plain Dealer*, "why the usual procedure of preferring charges against confessed criminals had not been followed in this case." In an unsigned, page one editorial, titled "The Sheriff and the Law," the *Cleveland News* openly questioned the legality of O'Donnell's conduct.

> This editorial has to deal with the strange case of Frank Dolezal, the extra-legal tactics of Sheriff O'Donnell, and civil liberties. Without attempting to determine the guilt or innocence of Frank Dolezal, *The News* does not believe the cause of justice is being served in a high degree by the apparent political campaign which has claimed headlines of newspapers throughout the nation. Sheriff O'Donnell has had one week in which to make up his mind as to the guilt or innocence of Prisoner Frank Dolezal. So far he has shown no indication of this intent. He has detained a prisoner without risking a formal charge against the prisoner. He has presented no evidence to the County Prosecutor's office. He has made no contacts with the Cleveland police department with a view to turning the prisoner over to this department. [As nearly as I can determine, this is the first and only time this jurisdictional issue was ever raised by the press or anyone else.] Frank Dolezal happens to be a derelict without money or influence. He has lived in a half-world of clouded and rather shady surroundings. But the Constitution of this land states that he may not be deprived of his liberty without due process. Sheriff O'Donnell knows as well as any one what due process means. Dolezal has been in the custody of Sheriff O'Donnell one week without any charge filed against him. It is time for some tangible legal action.

The legal chickens were, indeed, coming home to roost! Sheriff's detective Harry S. Brown, however, obligingly fell on his sword for his boss, insisting that O'Donnell had, indeed, wanted to press formal charges against Dolezal but that he, Brown, had counseled against the move until they had what they deemed a more solid case. In spite of the *News*'s very public and deliberate slap in the face, it would seem that the sheriff finally had reason to celebrate; after nearly a week of on-again, off-again interrogation and endless statements to the press, the case against Frank Dolezal had finally come together: his guilt had been confirmed through lie detector examination; the possibility of an insanity defense had been headed off; and O'Donnell finally had a confession he felt was legitimate. Exactly what that confession said, however, remained something of a mystery. "The confession will be for the grand jury's consumption and will not be made public," the sheriff told the *Plain Dealer*. The next step would be an arraignment on a charge of murder. At 3:30 that afternoon, Dolezal appeared in court before Justice of the Peace Myron J. Penty and was formally charged with first degree murder in the death of Flo Polillo. The onetime bricklayer entered no plea and was held without bail; his case was handed over to the Grand Jury, which would reconvene on July 24. The *Plain Dealer* indignantly reported that while the formal proceedings were moving forward, state senator William J. Zoul stood outside Penty's door flagging down passersby and inviting them "to come inside—the torso killer's in there."

But questions about the case against Frank Dolezal stubbornly persisted. After the sheriff had arrested him, Peter Merylo complained to his superior, Police Chief George Matowitz, that the bricklayer was innocent, that he had

Frank Dolezal, in a clean shirt, being escorted to his arraignment hearing. The bruising around his eye is still obvious. Pat Lyons and Sheriff O'Donnell are to the left. *Cleveland Press* Archives, Cleveland State University.

Frank Dolezal's deeply worried brother Charles (third from left) and his wife, Louise (second from right), at the arraignment hearing. *Cleveland Press* Archives, Cleveland State University.

investigated him thoroughly and questioned him on two separate occasions. He never would have released him, he insisted, if he had any lingering suspicions about him. Counseled by Matowitz that political realities dictated the sheriff must be allowed to build his case without interference, Merylo initially stayed in the background and, for the most part, reluctantly held his tongue. But the entire affair had further lowered the veteran detective's already abysmal assessment of the sheriff and his office, and he began to grumble openly. If no one in the press took his protestations too seriously at this point—in spite of their own doubts about some aspects of the Dolezal drama—it was probably because circumstances had cast Merylo in the unenviable role of sore loser. The sheriff and his men had invaded his territory and succeeded where he had failed. Anything Merylo said at this juncture ran the risk of being branded as simply sour grapes on his part. In his unpublished memoirs, however, Merylo pointed out that Dolezal's third explanation regarding Polillo's head was as ludicrously absurd as the previous two. Dolezal's WPA time card not only showed that he had been working at East Technical High School at the time of the Polillo murder but clearly proved he had never even been assigned to the Lake Shore Drive project. "This same record was open to inspection to the Sheriff or any member of his staff," he snorted contemptuously, "but no such attempt was made to examine those records." And, once having admitted to the murder-dismemberment of Flo Polillo, why would Dolezal lie, apparently twice, about what he had done with her head? At that point, what difference did it make? (In fairness, however, I must point out that the sheriff and his office considered the possibility that Dolezal remained reluctant to reveal the location of Flo Polillo's head because it would have led to the discovery of other heads, thus implicating him in the other murders, in spite of his adamant refusal to admit that he had anything to do with them.)

Suddenly, the local legal tangle became a Gordian knot of national proportions: enter the American Civil Liberties Union! The involvement of the ACLU's national office in the Dolezal affair attests to the nationwide press coverage the entire torso case was receiving and shines an embarrassing light on the laxity of Sheriff O'Donnell's office in safeguarding its prisoner's rights under the law. A July 8 article in the *Nashua (New Hampshire) Telegraph*—originally carried by the Associated Press—reported that Frank Dolezal had been held without charges for days by Cleveland authorities. The revelation prompted Mrs. Sidney Knight (presumably a Nashua native) to fire off a letter of alarm and protest to the ACLU's national office. "If true," Mrs. Knight wrote, "it would appear that Cleveland has reverted to barbarism and has disregarded the hard-won rights of us all—that they have ignored the principle that 'A man is innocent until he is proved guilty,' they have violated the right of habeas corpus, and they have usurped the powers of judge and jury." Strong words, indeed, and no doubt fighting words to the ACLU. The office in Cleveland was duly alerted that a gross miscarriage of justice festered on its doorstep, but, coincidentally, the local chapter already had the sheriff and his office lined up in its crosshairs. At around 2:00 in the afternoon of July 11, a six-man legal team—including former Common Pleas judge David R. Hertz, former assistant U.S. district attorney Martin A. McCormack, and acting chairman of the local ACLU chapter Russell W. Chase—went to the county jail to meet with the sheriff and demand an explanation for his office's conduct toward their prisoner. O'Donnell, however, pleaded that he was tied up in meetings, so the members of the ACLU committee were left to stew in their indignation and twiddle their collective thumbs for the rest of the afternoon. "After a considerable wait," reported Chase angrily to the national office in a letter dated July 17, "it became clear that the Sheriff refused to meet with our committee." The disgruntled team left around 5:00 or so, leaving only David Hertz to battle with the sheriff's office.

The good judge found himself cooling his heels and sharing his frustration with attorney Fred P. Soukup, who had apparently been hired, somewhat belatedly, by Charles Dolezal to represent his brother. Unfortunately, there is no record of how or exactly when Soukup became involved in the case, but he had been as unsuccessful as Judge Hertz and the ACLU committee in gaining access to his beleaguered client and the sheriff. Though O'Donnell finally granted Soukup permission to meet with Dolezal for the first time, he insisted Hertz would have to stay put unless he was a member of the defense team. "I am not interested in this case beyond whether this man was mistreated in the jail," the judge told the *Plain Dealer*. When Soukup left the county jail later that evening, after finally meeting with his client for thirty-five minutes, he informed the press that Frank Dolezal "did not act like a normal person" and had retracted his third confession. "He denies the killing [of Flo Polillo]," Soukup told the *Plain Dealer*. "He denies he is the torso murderer. He says he was in a daze when he made the confession. I know a lot about how the confession was obtained, but I'm not prepared to say anything yet." In a move that spoke volumes about what Soukup knew, or at least suspected, about "how the confession was obtained," the lawyer arranged—with the sheriff's consent—for an independent physician, L. J. Sternicki, to examine his client at 10:00 that night.

The extraordinarily hectic and dramatic day ended with Frank Dolezal receiving his second visitor: Monsignor Oldrich Zlamal of Our Lady of Lourdes Catholic Church on East 53rd. Dolezal's religious affiliation had not been of any particular interest to the men of Cleveland's press corps as they pieced together their portrait of the alleged sexual deviant and torso killer, but whatever Dolezal's beliefs may have been, he was finally granted some sort of spiritual comfort in the sixth day of his incarceration. Reportedly, Dolezal admitted to Zlamal that he had, indeed, attempted suicide twice in the early morning hours of Monday, July 10, citing sheer desperation and feelings of abandonment by his family and friends as his rationale. (Up to this point Charles Dolezal had apparently made no attempt to visit his beleaguered brother since his arrest.) Obviously, the admission was not a formal penitent-to-priest confession recognized by the church; if it had been, Zlamal could never have revealed its contents to the press. But that a man raised a strict Catholic would even think of taking his own life testifies to the incredible level of distress Dolezal must have been enduring. And the problem of the visible injuries noted by onlookers on the afternoon of July 10 remained: Were they caused, as the sheriff insisted, by his botched suicide attempts or by something far more sinister?

WEDNESDAY, JULY 12

East Cleveland police chief L. G. Corlett dropped his own bombshell on top of this ever-developing legal imbroglio. "Says Dolezal Told of Beating," screamed the *Press*. At one point, the sheriff left the room in which Paul F. Beck was conducting the lie detector test; Dolezal quickly turned to Corlett and desperately insisted that he had been beaten by men in the sheriff's office. According to Corlett, Dolezal had bitterly complained that his ribs hurt. "They made me. They kept at me until I got crazy. They beat me up." Though Corlett was inclined to dismiss what he regarded as wild allegations, a bell had been rung, and there was no way to un-ring it. Two days before, the entire city had watched as sheriff's men led a dazed Frank Dolezal to a waiting car for his trip to East Cleveland; everyone had noticed the fresh black eye and the obvious signs of pain as the prisoner gripped his side. Add to this both Soukup's having called in an independent medical man to examine his client and his own ominously chilling words to the press the night before: "I know a lot about how the confession was obtained." But Soukup refused to disclose the conclusions about Dolezal's physical condition that Sternicki had arrived at following his examination the previous evening, nor would he clarify or expand on what he implied he knew about the sheriff's methods in extracting the string of confessions from his client. "He [Dolezal] has to stay in jail and if he has been beaten it won't do him any good to say so," Soukup told the *Press*. "I won't say whether he has or whether he hasn't."

THURSDAY, JULY 13

The test results were in! Ecker had submitted his findings relevant to the stains and other material found in the bathroom of Dolezal's former apartment at 1908 Central to O'Donnell but adamantly refused to make them public. "That is up to the sheriff," he told the *Press*. But O'Donnell was silent. "O'Donnell Keeps Torso Test Secret," shouted the headline of the paper's page one story. "Sheriff Martin L. O'Donnell today was keeping secret the results of chemical tests on stains found in the alleged 'murder den' of Frank Dolezal, accused torso killer." In spite of silence the evening before, attorney Fred Soukup leaked some of the details of Sternicki's examination of Dolezal to the press: injuries to the ribs, a black eye, and a number of bruises to the body. "There is no doubt in my mind the man has been pushed around," he declared unequivocally.

The moment Frank Dolezal was arrested on July 5, Sheriff O'Donnell had gone on the offensive, courting and teasing the press with the details of his office's ongoing interrogation of their prisoner and its efforts to build a solid case, but events had turned against him. Increasingly, the sheriff found himself and his office retreating and taking up defensive positions. The ACLU committee that had tried unsuccessfully to see O'Donnell on Tuesday afternoon issued a statement claiming in no uncertain terms that he had clearly violated the law when he initially refused Fred Soukup permission to see his client, thus—according to committee member Edgar S. Byers—opening himself up to a possible fine of between twenty-five and one hundred dollars, thirty days in jail, or both. Further, Byers asserted, the arraignment before Judge Penty on July 11 had not only been meaningless but downright illegal as well, since Dolezal had not had an attorney present and Penty had failed to inform him of his right to have one. (In a grim stroke of irony, at the very moment Dolezal was being arraigned Soukup was actually waiting for the sheriff to grant permission to see him.) Like many a politician under fire, Sheriff O'Donnell responded to the legal onslaught by adopting a code of silence and charging the media with mounting a viciously biased campaign against him. "I am convinced that the newspapers intend to misconstrue everything I say," he angrily declared to the *Press*. "I will have nothing more to say on the case until the Grand Jury takes action [on July 24]." He further declared that he would present the case himself, with no help from the Cleveland Police Department or the prosecutor's office.

The case against Frank Dolezal was in deep trouble; at the very least it was falling apart at the seams. Virtually the only remaining reasonably solid planks upon which the sheriff could conceivably build his case were the suspect's three confessions—of which two had been discredited and the third retracted—and the still undisclosed test results submitted by Ecker. And that plank would collapse the next day.

Friday, July 14

"Scientist's Test Fogs Torso Case," proclaimed the *Plain Dealer* that morning. "W.R.U. Pathologist Reports Stains Are Not Blood." "Chemists Disagree on Torso 'Blood' Stains," shouted the *Press* later in the afternoon. Ecker dismissed as nothing more than "plain dirt" the stains that chemist G. V. Lyons had pronounced human blood at the time of Frank Dolezal's arrest on July 5. Oddly, Lyons chose not to respond publicly to this curt rebuttal of his professional opinion. He may have been waiting for a more serious forum than the city press for a scientific exchange with Ecker—something like a formal trial; but his silence at this juncture further damaged the sheriff's already faltering case. In recent years, questions have been raised over whether Ecker and Lyons may have collected their samples from different places, but the question is moot. Given the age of the building and the nature of its occupants, it does not strain credulity to assume there could have been some blood present, though it would be impossible to determine whose. Moreover, the whole blood debate again raises the issue of exactly how many of the victims, if any,

Frank Dolezal actually dispatched and dismembered. According to his trio of confessions, he had killed Flo Polillo before he disarticulated her corpse. If she were already dead, the blood flow would have been minimal. But some of the victims—Edward Andrassy, for example—were still alive when the killer removed their heads; in fact, the coroner determined that the cause of death in some cases actually was decapitation. If the heart were still beating when the Butcher's knife sliced through the neck, there would have been a veritable geyser of spurting blood. Traces of it would be everywhere, no matter how diligently Dolezal tried to clean up the mess: on the walls, in the grouting of the floor, in the cracks of the tub surface, and around the drain.

The *Press* now turned against the sheriff and openly criticized his behavior, branding him "Lone Hand O'Donnell" and questioning his conduct during the entire Dolezal affair. "The conduct of Sheriff Martin L. O'Donnell in the torso case grows more amazing day by day," the paper declared. "Is the sheriff interested in furthering the ends of justice or is he interested in making a grandstand play for personal glory and acclaim? . . . His conduct of the case arouses the suspicion that however sincere he and his deputies were in making the arrest, the desire to put one over on the Cleveland police has played a strong part in his subsequent behavior." To add to the sheriff's growing list of woes, later in the day, attorney Fred Soukup and former judge David Hertz—now officially a member of the Frank Dolezal defense team—went before Common Pleas judge Frank S. Day asking him to void the July 11 arraignment, since Dolezal had not been represented by an attorney. If Day granted their writ, O'Donnell would have to appear in court as a defendant—certainly a new role for the sheriff of Cuyahoga County.

SATURDAY, JULY 15

And so it was. "To deny this man the right to counsel is to abrogate all civil liberties and the bill of rights which is the law in every state of this union," Day thundered, with all the weight of his high office behind him. According to the *Plain Dealer*, the judge decreed that his colleague Myron Penty had seriously erred in presiding over an arraignment in which the accused stood before the law without legal counsel. Then, turning his outrage on the sheriff, Day declared O'Donnell had "adopted a procedure [of] which this court does not approve." As a county official, O'Donnell stood before Day represented by Acting County Prosecutor John J. Mahon. Apparently, the sheriff endured this dressing-down in grim-faced, stony silence and left the courthouse without making any comments to the press. Penty accepted his colleague's censure and scheduled a second arraignment for Frank Dolezal at 9:30 on the following Friday, July 21. David Hertz exploded: "A hearing as late as next Friday would make a laughing stock of this procedure." After a rancorous legal skirmish—during which Penty unsuccessfully asked to be removed from the case—the re-arraignment was moved up to Monday morning, July 17.

MONDAY, JULY 17

Detective Harry S. Brown, one of the more important witnesses and apparently the only member of the sheriff's team called to testify, was nowhere to be found. Reportedly, he was fishing near Sandusky. There is no proof that anything conspiratorial should be read into his failure to appear, but it remains ironic that Brown's absence necessitated rescheduling the arraignment to Wednesday—two days earlier than the original date Penty had specified, but also two days later than the date David Hertz had forced on him in Judge Day's court.

WEDNESDAY, JULY 19

Detective Brown was still numbered among the missing, but Frank Dolezal's second arraignment proceeded without him. By all accounts, events moved smoothly in Judge Penty's court. The parade of witnesses, including Coroner Gerber and members of the police department, passed in review without incident. As he had done in the past, Gerber cast some doubt on Dolezal's guilt in the murder of Flo Polillo by testifying that only an individual who commanded extensive knowledge of human anatomy could have performed such a skillful dismemberment. For David Hertz—now dubbed "chief of defense counsel" by the *Plain Dealer*—it was a day of both frustration and satisfaction. On the one hand, that no one from Sheriff O'Donnell's office offered testimony prevented him from probing such contentious issues as his client's multiple confessions and the allegation that he had been beaten; but, on the other hand, Penty dropped the first degree murder charge down to manslaughter, insisting, according to the *Plain Dealer*, that "the testimony failed to show Mrs. Polillo's slaying was purposeful or premeditated." Frank Dolezal was duly bound over to the Grand Jury, and bond was set at fifteen thousand dollars, an astronomical sum by the financial standards of the late 1930s. Hertz later tried to get the amount lowered to five thousand dollars, so he could take his client to a psychiatrist, but Common Pleas judge Hurd blocked the move, declaring, "A bond of fifteen thousand dollars for a man accused of cutting up a woman is low." Hertz had obviously undergone a major personal odyssey of conscience in the week since he stood outside the county jail. On that Tuesday evening, he had described himself simply as a representative of the ACLU, concerned only with the question of Frank Dolezal's rights under the law; now he was actively participating in his defense with attorney Fred Soukup before Judge Penty.

The prosecutor's office was faced with what appeared to be an almost insurmountable obstacle—at best, Herculean, at worst, absolutely impossible. The Grand Jury would reconvene on Monday, July 24 for a week; and Acting Prosecutor John J. Mahon was reluctant to take the remaining shreds and tatters of the Dolezal affair before that legal body without some sort of review. He, therefore, announced to the press he would personally be going over the police records of the torso killings in—what the *Plain Dealer* described as—a search "for clews not generally known by persons outside the police department which would tend to give credence to Dolezal's reported confession." It was the sort of reassuring but ultimately meaningless pronouncement public officials often make when they find themselves caught in a bind. The hunt for the Mad Butcher of Kingsbury Run ranked as the most massive and intense police investigation in Cleveland history; the combined departmental records coupled with the papers from the coroner's office would total literally thousands upon thousands of pages. (Peter Merylo's surviving reports alone add up to a stack of paper over a foot high.) The notion that anyone in the prosecutor's office not already deeply immersed in the details of the case could sift through this veritable Everest of documentation in time for a presentation before the Grand Jury five days later is ludicrous. It would take legions of clerks and other legal personnel months to process all the existing information, and Mahon finally conceded that his office would have to wait until the Grand Jury reconvened in September to outline its case and seek an indictment.

Mahon clearly knew he was in trouble. "It was about this time that I was called into the county prosecutor's office and asked what I knew about Frank Dolezal," Merylo writes in the memoirs he coauthored with *Cleveland News* reporter Frank Otwell. "I told the prosecutor [apparently John Mahon, although Merylo does not specifically name him at this point], and I suspect he knew it already, that I had Frank Dolezal in on two occasions and that if I had thought there was enough to make a case on him, I would not have turned him loose." When Mahon cautioned the detective that he would probably be called to testify before the Grand Jury, Merylo fired back, "I can't tell the grand jury much more than I have already told you about the suspect." Then he stormed out of the office thundering indignantly that when he arrested anyone, he didn't need to subpoena the sheriff to help him make the case.

In the two weeks following his arrest, Frank Dolezal was the city's biggest story. All three Cleveland dailies followed and reported on every new development in the emerging case against him; Sheriff O'Donnell and his deputies initially became instant celebrities courted, quoted, and photographed by a press establishment eager for details. Everything about Dolezal became grist for the voracious newspaper mill. Reporters dug into his background, explored his work history, ransacked his personal life, and canvassed his acquaintances in an ongoing campaign to keep the story of him and his alleged connections to the Kingsbury Run murder-dismemberments on the front pages of city papers. They mulled over his apparent jovial sociability when he was sober and leered at his rages and crying jags when the demons of alcohol possessed him; they examined his reported craving for knives and traced in detail all the lurid tales of his odd behavior willingly supplied by his neighbors. Newspapers ran photographs of the dilapidated East 20th–Central Avenue neighborhood to show the suspicious proximity of some of the relevant sites in the Kingsbury Run murder cycle: Frank Dolezal's old apartment on Central, the bar at the corner of East 20th and Central where he and Flo Polillo both drank, the spot behind Hart Manufacturing where the initial set of her remains had been found so neatly and tidily packed into those half-bushel produce baskets. And, of course, city dailies ran photos of Frank Dolezal himself, making his blank, unfocused gaze instantly recognizable.

Few, if any, noticed during those first heady days of excitement in early July that there was a problem; the portrait of the killer that had emerged from the careful deliberations of former coroner A. J. Pearce's torso clinic seemed to have been largely forgotten. Few, if any, among law enforcement, members of the press, or the public seemed to notice that Dolezal came nowhere near fitting the profile that had been so carefully crafted almost three years earlier. True, the press had grumbled about problems and inconsistencies in the official version of the Dolezal saga in the days following his arrest; but those doubts had been prompted by the immediate circumstances, not any lingering memories or respect for the torso clinic's profile. There had been unanimous agreement among the clinic participants that the Butcher had to be large and powerful. Though a stocky, strong working man, Frank Dolezal was smaller than some of the victims; how did he overpower them—especially Edward Andrassy, who, besides being a taller man, was rumored to have carried an ice pick? Dolezal had been a bricklayer for most of his working life; where did he learn to cut up a corpse with the surgical precision noted by the medical men at the torso clinic? Would three months of employment in a slaughterhouse give him the necessary skill? Though he lived in a succession of shabby apartments in run-down buildings in the central city's crumbling core, he would seem to lack the necessary familiarity with Kingsbury Run. There was nothing that specifically tied him to the desolate industrial landscape or the adjacent shantytowns. Dolezal certainly had no car, nor is there any indication anywhere he even knew how to drive; how did he transport the remains? Certainly not on a public conveyance. It is ludicrous to imagine him sitting on a bus with his sack of body parts beside him. Complicating the transportation issue considerably more is the fact that some of the male bodies were intact except for their heads. Edward Andrassy and his never-identified companion had been discovered at the base of Jackass Hill near East 49th on the south side of Kingsbury Run. Frank Dolezal's apartments and drinking haunts were all on the north side, closer to East 20th. Given the distance between these two spots and assuming—as the sheriff and his allies did—that Dolezal carried out the murders where he lived, it is impossible to imagine him lugging two heavy male corpses (minus heads and sex organs) across the Run without someone having noticed something out of the ordinary. And where was his laboratory—the isolated spot where he supposedly carried out his murderous activities and subsequent dismemberments free from any worries of detection? The only locations that came close to fitting the bill were the bathtubs in the various apartments in which he had resided. Even if he possessed the necessary anatomical expertise, could he have accomplished such exacting work while trying to maneuver the dead weight of a bulky human corpse in the narrow confines of an old tub?

There was also an additional, significant aspect of the Butcher's methodology that everyone in the late 1930s, including the hand-picked experts who had participated in the torso clinic, missed. The manner in which the Butcher had left the remains of some of his victims clearly indicated a severely warped sense of humor—the artist-joker proudly displaying his handiwork for all to see while at the same time thumbing his nose at the authorities. The heads of Edward Andrassy and victim no. 2 had been buried so as to ensure that the police could find them; some of Flo Polillo's remains had been carefully wrapped, packed, and covered with burlap bags; the head of victim no. 4 had been neatly rolled up in his pants and placed at the foot of a small tree. All such staging suggests someone with a high degree of intelligence deliberately taunting and mocking the police even as he horrified the public. "Look at what I can do!" "Catch me if you can." Such twisted but sophisticated antics hardly seemed to fit the personality of someone so simple as Frank Dolezal.

Had the torso clinic profile that had been so carefully fashioned and so proudly trumpeted by the press really been so readily forgotten? It would seem so. Granted, this crucial conference had occurred almost three years before Dolezal's arrest, and it hardly strains credulity to suggest that public and official relief was great enough to banish any nagging doubts or lingering suspicions about his guilt stemming from the conclusions drawn at that meeting. Perhaps politics had reared its ugly head. Coroner Sam Gerber would have certainly been acutely aware of both the conference and its findings, but he was a staunch Democrat, and the clinic had been the brainchild of his predecessor, A. J. Pearce. Political squabbling and brawling had been a nasty sideshow attraction of the entire investigation. There is no evidence to suggest that Gerber deliberately turned his back on clinic findings for political or even personal considerations; but even though he was only three years into his fifty-year tenure as Cuyahoga County coroner, he had already earned a reputation for zealously guarding his turf against encroachment from other official agencies and for publicly and vociferously defending the sanctity of his medical judgments—behavior that would be devastatingly apparent fifteen years later, during the high-profile investigation into the murder of Marilyn Sheppard. Yet some of Gerber's reported public utterances did reinforce the torso clinic's profile. On Saturday, July 8, the *Plain Dealer* told its readers, "Coroner Samuel R. Gerber asserted the expertness with which the cutting away of the organs had been done made it seem more than ever convincing that the slayer was a person trained in surgery and anatomy."

No one seems to have taken issue with Paul Beck's determination of guilt via polygraph examination in 1939. Even seventy years later, those who believe Dolezal innocent of the charges leveled against him have not challenged the results of the Keeler polygraph examination directly. And it is not necessary to impugn either Beck's integrity or experience with the machine to question the accuracy of the examination or his interpretation of it. Dolezal had, by his own admission to Monsignor Zlamal, tried to commit suicide twice before the interrogation; and, if he is to be believed, someone in the sheriff's office had beaten him severely. In either or both cases, he would have been in pain, tired, frightened, and, no doubt, extremely agitated—precisely the wrong state of mind and body for an accurate assessment of his veracity via the polygraph! Victor Kovacic, former head of the Cleveland Police Department's Scientific Investigation Unit, stressed that the subject of a polygraph examination must be well rested and as calm as possible to ensure accurate results.

It had been an extraordinary time for Cleveland: two weeks in July boiling over with intense, high-level legal wrangling; damning charges and countercharges;

vicious name-calling and character assassination; and a dramatic, ongoing story that seemed propelled from one sensational event to the next by some furious, demonic drive of its own. It all added up to a major newspaper feeding frenzy; and terrified Clevelanders, hungry for the raw meat being served, instantly devoured every scrap of information provided by the three obliging city dailies. As the ferocity of the media storm abated toward the middle of the month, some significant questions were left dangling—not only unanswered but seemingly unnoticed as well. Why had so many of the major players in both the torso saga and city politics remained curiously, even inexplicably, silent? Granted, the only surviving sources of utterances from public figures would be the city newspapers; but—given the sensational nature of this high-profile, ongoing story and the level of competition among Cleveland's major papers—one would think the armies of reporters might beat the bushes with a vengeance for every possible scrap of information, especially pungent quotes from the city's power elite. Yet, surprisingly little commentary from the involved politicians and law enforcement personnel survives. Merylo had been muzzled by his boss, Chief Matowitz; and the angry detective, convinced of Dolezal's innocence, had stood outwardly silent on the sidelines while at the same time secretly feeding information to the press to torpedo the sheriff's case. Matowitz himself had had nothing to say to the press, even though it was the men under his direct command who had struggled unsuccessfully for five years to crack the terrible series of murder-dismemberments. Ness seems to have limited himself to a single public comment. "The sheriff is to be commended for his investigation," he told the *Plain Dealer* on July 8. "The leads he has uncovered will, of course, be followed up to see what possible connection the Polillo case may have with any others. My department and I stand ready to make available to the sheriff any information or facilities that he might feel could be of assistance." Surely as neutral, politically safe, and empty a public statement as any crafted by a modern-day spin doctor! Mayor Harold Burton did not make any public comments, at least none that have survived. Coroner Gerber did make pronouncements relevant to the anatomical findings of his office; but he was strangely silent about Dolezal during the period he was in the sheriff's custody—although he would have much to say about him and his "guilt" in the years to come. Democratic congressman Martin L. Sweeney watched the entire brouhaha in utterly uncharacteristic silence. In the past, he had never passed on an opportunity to bash the Republican administration with its failure to save the city from the torso killer. Also, O'Donnell had been elected sheriff of Cuyahoga County in 1936 as part of an independent Sweeney-led coalition of local maverick Democrats; thus, the congressman's reticence to speak on the record about Dolezal's alleged guilt or to publicly defend his close political ally and personal friend when he was being besieged by events and battered by the press would seem absolutely inexplicable.

Dolezal had been indicted for the murder of only Flo Polillo, and even that single charge had been reduced to manslaughter. All of O'Donnell's repeated efforts to link him to the other torso killings had failed. During those rancorous two weeks in July, circumstances had created the notion that Flo Polillo may not have been a part of the murder-dismemberment series; and in spite of Gerber's insistence to the contrary—his repeated assurances that all the torso victims had been dispatched by a single perpetrator, that notion persisted. "I have never said or claimed the late Frank Dolezal committed all the so-called Torso crimes," wrote Pat Lyons in his memoirs. "By his suicide, he deprived himself [of] his day in court. Likewise, he denied the state its right to prove its charge." Obviously, if Frank Dolezal was not responsible for all those other grisly deaths, someone else was. The Mad Butcher of Kingsbury Run was still out there somewhere hidden in the shadows of inner-city grime and decay. Peter Merylo certainly thought so; in the coming weeks, months, even years, he would press his own personal, solitary investigation forward. After his second arraignment on July 19, Frank Dolezal faded from the front pages of city newspapers and then dropped out of them entirely. His case would never go before the Grand Jury when it convened in September, nor would Frank Dolezal ever see the inside of another Cleveland courtroom. But the two-week storm was not over; by the end of August, Cleveland would learn it had merely passed through the eye of the hurricane.

THURSDAY, AUGUST 24, 1939

Frank Dolezal was dead.

NOTES

To fill in some of the gaps in the newspaper reports of Frank Dolezal's first weeks in the sheriff's custody, I have included some information gleaned from the formal transcript of the coroner's inquest held on August 26. Similarly, I have fleshed out the account of ACLU involvement with documents originally obtained from the organization's national archives and provided to me by Frank Dolezal's great-niece Mary Dolezal Satterlee.

The small collection of ACLU documents relevant to Frank Dolezal comes from the organization's archives, volume 2136.

See notes at the end of chapter 2 for a full discussion of Peter Merylo's and Pat Lyons's papers.

Chapter 4

VIOLENT DEATH ON A HOT AFTERNOON

Hitler was on the march. By the end of August 1939, the erupting crisis that would lead directly to Germany's invasion of Poland on September 1 was in full swing. All over Europe heads of state postured, ambassadors negotiated, and armies mobilized. Thus, it should be no surprise that, with the very real and ominous threat of world war looming darkly on the horizon, the death of Frank Dolezal in the county jail on August 24 stirred minimal interest in the Cleveland press. Kingsbury Run and everything connected with it seemed to belong to a different age. Even a compellingly gruesome series of decapitation murder-dismemberments seemed relatively unimportant, indeed parochial, in the face of growing world tragedy. But Dolezal's fate prompted Cleveland's legal machinery into swift action, and—behind the news curtain of the gathering European storm—it rolled inexorably forward into a hornets' nest of bitter allegations, whose shock waves would reverberate throughout the city for years.

Initially, it all seemed rather cut and dried. Left alone for a few minutes, Dolezal had hanged himself from a coat hook in a jail cell. When deputies discovered him, they cut his body down and called for medical assistance. Efforts to revive him, however, failed; and when Coroner Gerber arrived on the scene a little later, he officially pronounced the death a suicide and declared—since he saw no evidence of criminal activity—that a formal autopsy would not be required. As far as Sheriff O'Donnell was concerned, the suicide was nothing less than a tacit admission of guilt on Dolezal's part; he simply did not want to face the Grand Jury and the subsequent rigors of the justice system. Reportedly despondent over his desperate situation, Dolezal had made two previous attempts on his life over a month before; this time, he had succeeded. But as the details of the "suicide" trickled in, the troubling questions mounted. Reportedly, he had hanged himself with a noose he had fashioned from muslin rags or cloths. Where had he gotten them? Ever since his two failed attempts on his life, Dolezal had been kept on suicide watch; his belt and shoelaces had even been taken away from him. An unidentified deputy volunteered that Dolezal had constantly badgered his captors for something to do, so they gave him the rags to clean his cell. Assuming this explanation is true, had no one taken notice of the fact that he was obviously stockpiling them? Apparently not! Why were additional rags found wound around Dolezal's waist underneath his pants? No explanation was forthcoming. If he was on suicide watch, why, and for how long, had he been left unguarded? Reportedly, Deputy Hugh Crawford had left him alone for no more than three minutes while he informed visitors in another part of the jail that the visiting period was over. But was a mere three minutes long enough for what Gerber officially termed "asphyxiation caused by strangulation" to occur? Gerber reasoned it was but conceded he thought it would have taken longer, perhaps fifteen minutes. How could this time discrepancy be explained? There was no immediate answer. Were there no signs that Dolezal had been depressed? Couldn't this suicide have been prevented if he had been more closely watched? Sheriff's deputies insisted he was far from being depressed, rather, in a good, indeed, jovial mood. They even alleged he played cards with them. Where was the coat hook from which he hanged himself? It was located about five feet, seven inches above the floor of the cell. Frank Dolezal, however, measured five feet, eight inches in height; how did he manage to hang himself from a hook so close to the floor? How was that even possible? By simply crouching down and letting his weight do the job, insisted the sheriff. But could that explanation be reconciled with the sheriff's statement that Dolezal's toes were barely touching the floor when he first saw his hanging body? (Gerber speculated he could have stepped off the toilet directly below the hook and swung free.)

A tin cup handle, clearly visible in one of the official death scene photographs, was found in his pocket. How did he get it, and what was it for? It could have been fashioned into a dangerous weapon, deputies hinted ominously, but no explanation of its provenance was offered. There were rumors that Dolezal had asked for and been given medicine of some kind just before his death. Exactly what was it, and who gave it to him? And, perhaps most troubling, where had the length of relatively thin rope clearly visible in the photographs of his corpse come from? Not only did this question slip by without comment, the telltale length of rope or twine was never mentioned again. "I had a hunch something like this would happen before he ever came to trial," raged attorney Fred Soukup to Chief Deputy Sheriff Clarence M. Tylicki, according to the *Plain Dealer* on August 26. "What kind of jail are you running here, anyway? I thought you were keeping a 24-hour watch on him." Sergeant James Hogan and Inspector

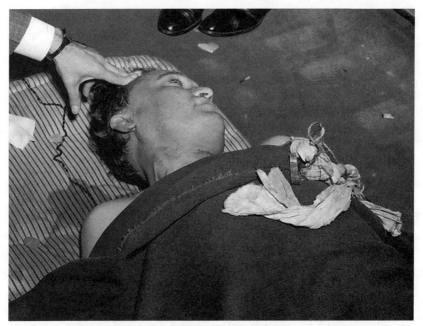

Frank Dolezal dead on the jailhouse floor. The cloth noose with which he allegedly hanged himself has been placed on his left shoulder. The black, stringlike object to the left of his head is his broken rosary. Its presence on the mattress raises questions. Why was it broken, and why was it not on his person? Since the Cuyahoga County Coroner's Office did not take its own photographs in the 1930s, it is somewhat unclear whether this shot should be attributed to the police or the press. Courtesy of the Cuyahoga County Coroner's Office.

Joseph M. Sweeney of the Cleveland Police Department, both with long torso case experience, showed up at the jail to look into the incident around 3:00, about an hour after it occurred. Whether they regarded Dolezal's death as suspicious at this point is not clear. Everyone involved, however, including the sheriff, was invited down to the department's main headquarters to make formal statements. Maybe it was just procedure; maybe—in contemporary parlance—the veteran cops were sticking it to the sheriff and his deputies.

It all proved too much for William E. Edwards, operating director of the Cleveland Crime Commission. Edwards had become involved in the Dolezal affair rather as former judge David Hertz had several weeks before: as an objective outside party concerned solely with making sure proper procedures were followed and Dolezal's rights under the law were protected. Hertz, however, had been so outraged at the manner in which the sheriff's office was handling their prisoner that he abandoned his initial neutrality and joined forces with Fred Soukup. Now Edwards seemed ready to follow a similar path. "In view of all the street corner rumors and other reports of brutal treatment of Dolezal," Edwards told the *Plain Dealer* on August 26, "I think it only fair to the sheriff and the public to make as thorough as possible an investigation to ascertain the truth or falsity of these reports." And as far as Edwards was concerned, that thorough investigation must include a formal autopsy, in spite of Gerber's initial pronouncement that it was not necessary. Such a "demand"—as the *Plain Dealer* termed it—surely rankled someone as touchy and protective of his turf as Coroner Gerber, but he held his tongue and bowed to Edwards's wishes on the condition that the Dolezal family formally granted permission for the procedure. Edwards immediately obtained the necessary affidavit from Charles Dolezal, who gave his consent, with the proviso that Edwards be allowed to designate a neutral and "recognized pathologist" to be present during the autopsy. It is hard to believe that such a legally sophisticated request could have come from someone whose command of English was elemental at best and who remained as naïve about the workings of the American justice system as Charles Dolezal; undoubtedly, either Fred Soukup or David Hertz had prompted him. The two-and-one-half-hour procedure was scheduled to take place approximately eighteen hours after Dolezal's death, on August 25 at 6:30 A.M. Harry Goldblatt, assistant professor of pathology at Western Reserve University (obviously the "recognized pathologist" Edwards chose per Charles Dolezal's request), joined Samuel Gerber and Reuben Straus, himself a veteran of several torso victim autopsies. In spite of the war hysteria howling in the press, the entire city of Cleveland turned its attention to the official procedure at the Cuyahoga County morgue. Arguably, this ranked as potentially one of the most important autopsies in city history. The reputations of some very prominent Clevelanders were on the line. Before the formal procedure began, someone on the coroner's staff took two photographs of the wound around Frank Dolezal's neck. (These were not shown nor even mentioned at the subsequent inquest. Even more perplexing is the photo taken of the empty cranial cavity after Dolezal's brain had been removed. No doubt Gerber, Straus, and Goldblatt would have examined Frank Dolezal's brain closely, looking for any suspicious abnormalities, but why photograph an empty skull?)

The autopsy results were shocking—so shocking, in fact, that the official report jockeyed for position with war fears on the front pages. Dolezal had six broken ribs: the third, fourth, eighth, and ninth on the left side; the first and seventh on the right. "The fractures are not of recent date," Gerber told the *Press*, "that is they were not suffered within the past two or three weeks.

There will be no definite verdict rendered until all sections [of the broken ribs] have been put through the laboratory and examined under the micro-scope." To help "determine whether the fractures are old or new ones," the coroner's office turned pieces of the broken ribs over to David Cowles, head of the Police Scientific Laboratory, and his assistant, Lloyd Trunk, for X-ray examination. But Soukup was convinced those breaks had to be new, and he didn't have to wait for any scientific verification of the obvious to say so publicly. "It is absurd to imagine that he could do the work he did [bricklay-ing] if he had received the fractured ribs before he went to jail," he scoffed to the *Plain Dealer* on August 25. O'Donnell stuck to his guns and insisted the injuries resulted from a fall during one of Dolezal's well-documented July 10 suicide attempts; but that seemed highly unlikely, as ribs are not easy to crack and Dolezal had suffered breaks on both sides of his body and in different places up and down his rib cage. It takes a very hard, direct blow to break a rib; a single fall to the floor of his jail cell, even if he also struck the bench on his way down, would not be sufficient to cause that much damage in so many different places. Without naming his source—though it was most likely Patrolman Frank Vorell, brother of Charles Dolezal's wife, Louise—Edwards told the *Press* on August 26 that he had evidence "that he [Dolezal] had been gagged, blindfolded and beaten until he became unconscious. . . . When he regained consciousness he was lying on the cement floor." In response to a reporter's inquiry as to who could have been responsible, Edwards wryly commented, "I suppose by inference we have to assume it was the sheriff's office." Battle lines were being drawn, and Edwards clearly seemed to be moving over into the Dolezal camp with Soukup and Hertz.

On August 25, Coroner Gerber bowed to intense pressure from Hertz and Edwards and called for a formal inquest. That evening twenty-two separate parties were served subpoenas ordering them to appear the next day—Saturday, August 26—to testify. The proceedings would commence at 10:30 A.M. at the Cuyahoga County Coroner's Office with Coroner Gerber presiding. The machinery of local justice had moved forward with remarkable speed—perhaps because the whole issue of Dolezal's death had become so contentious, complicated, and controversial, within hours of it being reported in the press. To allow such a poisonous morass of contradictions and ques-tions to fester publicly could raise major doubts about the competence, even the integrity, of city officialdom. The proceedings had four serious issues to address: the broken ribs, bruising on Dolezal's face and arm, and the atten-dant charges of brutality; the time line of events leading up to the discovery that he had apparently attempted suicide; how he had gotten a hold of the material with which he allegedly hanged himself; and the amount of time he had been left hanging before being cut down. The last of these questions was potentially the most vexing. The disparities surrounding this crucial bit of time had been covered by the press. Questions dealing with the nature of some of the other disagreements, however (who may have said what), were not specifically addressed publicly by city dailies.

Gerber issued his official verdict on Dolezal's death on September 5. Of all the cases over which he would preside in his long tenure as Cuyahoga County coroner, probably no other forced him into such a delicate, politically sensitive dance as this one did. In September 1939 Gerber was just ending his third year on the job; his position was touchy, to say the least. Though a Democrat, he was a Jew in a town where some of the most powerful politicians were Irish. Even allowing for the fact that Martin L. O'Donnell had endured a very public dressing-down in Judge Day's court on July 15 over his handling of the Dolezal case, the sheriff still wielded considerable power; and his oft-stated position that neither he nor his deputies had ever physically abused the prisoner could not be casually ignored. And yet, the Dolezal team of Hertz, Soukup, and Edwards—men with considerable clout of their own—were insisting their client had been repeatedly beaten; and Gerber could not afford to snub them, either. In an uneasy compromise between the allegations of the two opposing camps, he concluded that the suspect had, indeed, taken his own life as the sheriff and his deputies maintained. The broken ribs and other injuries, however, proved a vexing and politically sensitive problem, and the coroner juggled this hot potato as deftly as he could. After admitting that the broken ribs and other physical injuries had occurred while Dolezal was in the sheriff's custody, he immediately equivocated and speculated that they could have resulted from the alleged beatings, the previously noted suicide attempts, or even a combination of the two. The soldiers on both sides of the battlefield probably gritted their teeth but remained silent. A partial victory was better than none at all.

With Gerber's official determination that he had committed suicide, Frank Dolezal dropped from the pages of city dailies and faded from Cleveland's collective memory. His key role in Kingsbury Run lore and legend, however, had been firmly established. His family buried him quietly in an unmarked grave, but he did not rest easily. Uncertainty about his alleged guilt continued to fester. On the one hand, it was pointed out that the torso killings stopped after his death; but on the other, it was argued that they had already stopped in August 1938—almost a full year before his arrest. Shortly after his death, suspicion arose that his "suicide" was not as cut and dried as Coroner Gerber's official judgment suggested, that there were still nagging, uncomfortable questions. In time those questions would coalesce and grow into a dark urban legend that possibly, just possibly, Frank Dolezal had been murdered. And if that were, indeed, the case, who had done it, and why? His specter, with its blank, unfocused stare, would haunt his family for decades; and he would eventually splinter his coffin and rise from his grave, more than sixty-five years after his death.

NOTES

Most of the information in this chapter was gleaned from the coverage in Cleveland's three daily newspapers. The dates and names of the papers are provided in the text.

The official autopsy protocol reporting on Frank Dolezal's death bears the case number 49869 and is on file in the Cuyahoga County Coroner's Office.

Part 2
REVELATIONS

Chapter 5
AN INTERLUDE: MARY DOLEZAL

"**W**hy the hell should I tell you anything?" rasped the voice at the other end of the line, between bouts of heavy coughing. Momentarily flustered by the speaker's unanticipated vehemence, I rummaged for an appropriate response that would not add to her obvious distrust and anger. At the time, I was still doing the research for *In the Wake of the Butcher: Cleveland's Torso Murders;* all I wanted was a little information about Frank Dolezal—the only man ever arrested and charged in the brutal series of killings, the man who may or may not have committed suicide to avoid prosecution.

Whether guilty or innocent, a murder victim or a suicide, at that point I regarded the history of Frank Dolezal as only one of the later, longer, though very disquieting, chapters in the entire Kingsbury Run murders saga. But his story was a chapter I thought deserved closer scrutiny than it had received before. Certainly there must still be Dolezal descendants living in Cleveland, I reasoned—people who could give me their perspective on this dark, painful episode of family history.

My probes in the Cleveland telephone book ultimately led me to Los Angeles and Mary Dolezal, Frank's great-niece, the unofficial family historian who had learned the ugly story of her grandfather Charles's brother from her mother before she hit her teen years, in spite of the rest of the family's determination to keep silent about the entire affair. Working below the radar of older relatives, she unearthed as much information as she could find—inquiries that revealed to her virtually unacknowledged reservoirs of family anger, grief, and shame. Suddenly the reasons for her father's obsessive, aggressively defiant pride in the name "Dolezal" became clear: the name was something of which to be proud, not ashamed. She finally became convinced that her great-uncle was innocent of the crimes with which he had been charged and, far from having committed suicide, had been murdered while in the county sheriff's custody, by a person or persons unknown. Ultimately, however, there seemed some sort of curious, old-world attitude toward public humiliation at work among her older relatives, including her father—something that dictated that one bore one's shame, deserved or undeserved, in stoic silence. The tragic story of Frank Dolezal and everything connected with it became the proverbial elephant in the room—something that could not be ignored but, by tacit agreement, was never discussed or openly referred to. Senior members of the clan may have believed in Frank's innocence without question; however, they resented her determination to prove it publicly. Now, suffering with a terrible cold, she found herself potentially sparring over the phone with an unknown writer who seemed poised to pick at the scab covering her family's deepest wound for purely selfish reasons. I would later joke that those of us whose gyroscopes spin at odd angles have ways of recognizing each other, so, in spite of that phone call's shaky beginnings, Mary Dolezal and I ended our first conversation on amicable terms; and we have been the best of friends ever since. In December 2003, we endured biting winds and cold temperatures as we trudged through Cleveland's West Park Cemetery together looking for the exact spot of her great-uncle's grave. We gave up our search as darkness began to close in but found the cemetery gates locked when we tried to leave. Somehow we had managed to miss closing time, and I had to drive over the curb through cemetery grounds, sincerely hoping there would be no grave markers in the way, until I could get back to city streets. It was a hilarious excursion; it seems 'tis ever thus when Mary and I are together.

I am running a little late; and by the time I pull up in front of my house in the Tremont neighborhood on Cleveland's near southwest side, Mary is already there—perched comfortably on the top step outside my front door, waiting, languidly puffing a cigarette, her long hair sprawling across her shoulders. "Hey there!" she croons as I hop out of my hastily parked Grand Am. The smile on her face flickers characteristically between wry humor and genuine pleasure as she rises to her full five feet, ten inches. Her grace and height always come as a mild surprise, at least initially. The images of her short, burley, stocky great-uncle Frank have been deeply engraved in my mind for well over a decade; it is difficult for me to imagine a Dolezal looking any other way.

Over the next few days, we will hang out, chat over drinks, and catch up over a series of superb meals in Tremont's incomparable collection of first-rate restaurants. And, of course, we will carefully walk the ground we have traversed so many times before; we will talk about her great-uncle Frank—a palpable presence in her life even though he met his cruel fate decades before she was born. We will sift through her memory for any tiny bits of additional information—any stray, unguarded comment dropped by an older relative she may have neglected to mention before, any bit of family legend that could be remotely tied to her great-uncle. With fairy-tale regularity, the story of how she came to know this shadowy presence in her family always begins with its own "Once upon a time." Her mind wanders back to the late 1970s, when she was ten years old, to the time her mother, Joan—for no reason that Mary could discern—rummaged through a bureau drawer and retrieved a collection of *Plain Dealer* articles marking the fortieth anniversary of the Kingsbury Run murders. In a hushed voice, from her limited perspective, she laid out the history of the city's most gruesome series of killings and the role Mary's great-uncle had been forced to play in the terrible drama. "I had no idea that these killings had taken place," she muses softly. Her expression begins to alter almost imperceptibly; her eyes turn strangely vacant, as if something inside her were retreating into itself, curling into a ball for protection. Her voice drops to virtual inaudibility: "I did not know he [Frank Dolezal] existed up to that." Why was it, she wondered, that no one in her family ever spoke about this hitherto unknown and unidentified relative. "My grandmother [Frank Dolezal's sister-in-law Louise Vorell] in her life never spoke about it. She passed away in 1984, never saying a word. I became very curious about it, curious why my family would not speak of a relative—where I clearly knew all my other relatives at that point—and started digging into it, and really for the last twenty-five years have been extremely interested in it, and found out as much about Frank Dolezal as I possibly could." She does not remember specifically the first time she saw his picture. It may have been during her mother's introduction to the family's link with violent and terrible crime, but she remains unsure. But the haunted, unshaven face had been caught and chronicled many times over by Cleveland's press photographers in the summer months of 1939, and she has long been familiar with the vacant, unfocused, disturbing gaze that still stares from the pages of the city's old newspapers. During our first face-to-face meeting, in 1999, she handed me an old, lovingly framed family photograph from 1920, showing her grandfather Charles and her grandmother Louise formally posed with their wedding party. At the picture's extreme left stood a Frank Dolezal that 1939 Clevelanders never knew existed, neat and almost dapper in his quaint formal attire, polished shoes, and glasses. Marriage was a serious business in those days; there is no hint of joy on any of the faces—only a stiff severity.

She reflects on her teenage years and her first trip downtown to the Cleveland Police Historical Society Museum. The display devoted to Kingsbury Run was smaller and considerably less graphic than it is today, but it still conveyed the sheer horror of what had taken place fifty years before. For the first time, she saw the grisly visual record of the mayhem to which her mother had cautiously introduced her several years before. She stood silently before the old masks representing four of the Butcher's victims. Cast in the 1930s by the Scientific Investigation Unit, they bore the combined signs of age and neglect. Above them hung a single large picture frame containing a sickening series of old police photos: decapitated naked corpses, heads in various stages of decomposition, rotting body parts. She stared in mingled wonder and revulsion. Her eyes closed; a realization—a terrible recognition that could not yet be put into words or even molded into coherent thought—suddenly rose within her. *Someone related to me was accused of doing this!* The museum's then curator, Anne Kmieck, provided more details about the reign of terror that went on in the city for over four years and directed her to the accounts of the crimes chronicled by Cleveland's daily newspapers. Slowly, painfully, Mary began to understand the reasons behind the family reticence to speak openly of Frank Dolezal. "If the family name is shamed and accused of a crime, you would go back to the bunker, hunker down, and keep your face out of the public. And I think the biggest shame was that the Dolezal name became headline news. My aunts and uncles were anywhere from ten to twenty-two at the time, and they heard about it. They were ashamed; they were asked questions; they were jeered at. Several of my aunts were school-aged. Can you imagine going to school during that time?"

Suddenly, her eyes flash with determined resolution. "And I started from there, started to work my way back through a lot of the articles that Cleveland newspapers had at that time, and kind of putting my own scrapbook together." But the great wall of family silence had yet to be breeched. "I didn't ask my father any immediate questions. He felt it was something that still disgraced the family. It was shameful to the family. It was taboo to speak about." But the more she dug into the history of the crimes and her great-uncle's part in the investigation, older aunts and uncles began to relent; the formidable wall developed cracks. Bit by bit, small pieces of the story as family members remembered, understood, and experienced it began to materialize. "You go, girl," cheered one of her elderly aunts from the sidelines. It was not just some understandable blood-is-thicker-than-water family loyalty that left the Dolezals convinced of Frank's innocence and angered over his fate; it was their memories of the gentle uncle who always brought them candy when they were children. "The guy would never hurt a fly," grumbled Mary's father on those few occasions when he even mentioned his uncle. But family loyalty was not blind, nor was it even compromised by the proverbial rose-colored glasses. "I believe my grandparents thought he was an odd character," Mary declares. "That he did live alone. That he did go to bars every night. He worked hard, but he also drank hard. That is how he is remembered within the family."

August 21, 1999: Mary and I are at the library of Cleveland State University, sitting in the room devoted entirely to the *Cleveland Press* collection of photographs and clippings—a treasure trove of documentation that had somehow eluded her in the past. In those days, there were two different groups of old *Press* photographs chronicling the Kingsbury Run horror—one devoted exclusively to Frank Dolezal. She had never seen so many photos of her great-uncle in one place before. By fleeting turns, her eyes grow vacant, apprehensive, sad, even angry as she slowly works her way through the stack of yellowing, fading pictures: Frank Dolezal, dazed and frightened, with Sheriff Martin L. O'Donnell and his deputies; Frank Dolezal, looking tired and in pain, hand on his side, as law enforcement personnel escorted him in front of assembled press photographers—what old-time cops called a "perp walk"; Frank Dolezal stretched out on the backseat of an official automobile, pathetically trying to hide from the prying camera lenses by holding his hands over his face. "There's something about the 1930s and 1940s I identify with," Mary reflects in a barely audible whisper. "The style of the clothes, everything." She winces at some of the more graphic depictions of her great-uncle's humiliation and distress; at times, her entire expression turns strangely inward, as if she were trying desperately to recover memories that were not really hers to command. I learned more from Mary Dolezal than simple family history and the details marking the steps in her own personal odyssey of discovery; I learned what it meant to be a survivor. In monstrous crimes, especially murders, we generally think of "a survivor" as someone who had a direct tie to the victim or who had narrowly escaped being a victim him or herself. But, like her father and other relatives, Mary is also a survivor. She didn't ask for that black cloud that always hovers in her background, but she inherited it as surely as she did the color of her eyes and hair. And it is always there—a deep, haunting shadow that whispers, "I am here; I am a part of you." It's a lesson I would learn again many times over—from Peter Merylo's daughters, Marjorie and Winifred; from Pat Lyons's daughter, Carol; from the surviving relatives of those traumatized children who stumbled upon dismembered body parts or a rotting corpse more than a half century ago; and from the daughter and granddaughters of Edward Andrassy, traditionally

Uncovering a painful past. Mary Dolezal and the author look through the material related to her great-uncle in the *Cleveland Press* Archives at Cleveland State University. Photograph by Denise Blanda.

thought of as the Butcher's first victim. His daughter was only six when her father's grisly murder catapulted the aristocratic Hungarian name "Andrassy" into public notoriety, and her daughters knew their grandfather only through his reputation. And that reputation was nothing of which to be proud: run-ins with the police for drunken brawling, a spotty employment history, an arrest for carrying a concealed weapon, allegations of all sorts of low-level criminal activity, and dark rumors of sexual deviancy. "Everything is so negative," lamented granddaughter Tomi Johnson when I first spoke with her.

† † †

In spring 2001, the Kent State University Press and the Cleveland Police Historical Society cosponsored the official release of *In the Wake of the Butcher* with a reception, book-signing, and dinner at the Great Lakes Brewing Company in Ohio City on Cleveland's near west side, the oldest continuously operating bar and restaurant in Cleveland and one of Eliot Ness's favorite local watering holes. The ever-cautious Ness reportedly sat at a booth in the rear, where he could keep an eagle eye on those who came and went. (To honor their famous former customer, the present owners, the Conways, have named one of their excellent brews "Eliot Ness.") Mary flew in from LA for the event. It was quite an occasion. Peter Merylo's daughter Marjorie Merylo Dentz was there, with two of her daughters and other members of the family, as were two of Edward Andrassy's granddaughters. It was the first time any of the descendents of the major players in Cleveland's most notorious murders had ever been in the same place, let alone had the opportunity to meet and speak with each other. "These are people I never thought I would meet," reflected Marjorie Dentz, almost in awe. Mary and I scanned the large party room and caught sight of the two Andrassy granddaughters speaking to one of the trustees of the Cleveland Police Historical Society. "I'd love to talk with them," she murmured, "but what do I say?" It was perhaps the first and only time during our acquaintance that I have ever known Mary to be hesitant or even remotely at a loss for words. I kneed her in the rump. "You go up to them and say, 'Hi! My great-uncle was accused of murdering your grandfather and cutting off his head.' How often does life hand you an opening like that?"

NOTE

Some of the quotations I attribute to Mary Dolezal were culled from a videotaped interview that Mark Stone conducted in 2003.

Chapter 6

BEHIND THE VEIL

In the late 1960s, Michelangelo Antonioni's film *Blowup* caught the fancies of both the art-house crowd and the average movie buff. One of the great Italian auteur's few popular successes, it told the story of a beat-generation photographer, played by David Hemmings, who seems to stumble across evidence of a murder through a close-up examination of a recent batch of his photos. The immensely popular television drama *CSI* picked up on the same premise during its 2003–04 season, and, ironically, it was a series of old photographs of Frank Dolezal's corpse, long tucked away and forgotten in the musty archives of the Cuyahoga County morgue that provided the first inklings that Coroner Sam Gerber's 1939 determination that Dolezal had committed suicide, that he had died of asphyxiation by hanging himself from a jailhouse clothes hook with a noose fashioned from cleaning rags, was suspect.

In late 1999 and early 2000, as I was completing the final revisions to the manuscript of *In the Wake of the Butcher: Cleveland's Torso Murders*, the morgue archivist unearthed the original photographs taken of Frank Dolezal's corpse in the county jail at the time of his death and in the morgue just prior to and during the formal autopsy—huge documents of stunning clarity, easily eleven by fourteen inches or larger. Since the coroner's office did not start taking its own photographs until the 1950s, there is a real question as to who took these—especially the ones documenting the autopsy. City newspapers printed a few of the pictures taken at the jail, but there is no indication in any of the coverage at the time that photographers from Cleveland's dailies were ever present. The Scientific Investigation Bureau (the 1930s precursor to the modern Ballistics Bureau or CSI Unit) may have been responsible for some of the photos—perhaps all of them, including those taken in the morgue. (Was it standard procedure at the time for police to share their photographs with city papers or vice versa?) In the 1930s, it certainly was not common practice in the coroner's office to document a case with photos of such size, and my initial surmise was that they had served simply as visual aids at the August 26–29 inquest into Frank Dolezal's death. And, indeed, that may have been their original purpose; but when the full transcript of those official proceedings materialized in winter 2004, it became clear that the vast majority of those photos had played no role in the inquest. Except for one or two, they were never shown, nor did any of the testimony deal with them, even remotely. Two of the photographs taken just before the formal autopsy procedure clearly showed the mark on Frank Dolezal's neck supposedly left by the homemade noose. Among the first to get a look at these new finds were my good friends and research partners Rebecca McFarland (the Cleveland expert on Eliot Ness) and Andrew Schug. Both reported that the narrow wound seemed inconsistent with the instrument of his alleged suicide—a bulky-looking length of toweling that a stone-faced Coroner Gerber displayed to a *Press* photographer on August 24, 1939. At the last minute, I incorporated their views and reservations in the manuscript before turning it over to the Kent State University Press. And there the matter rested, at least for the time being.

In the final months of 2002, I teamed up with Mark Wade Stone of Story-tellers Media Group to produce a TV documentary, *The Fourteenth Victim: Eliot Ness and the Torso Murders*, based in part on my recently published book. Our collaboration eventually took us to the Cuyahoga County morgue for an intense reexamination of Frank Dolezal's death. We studied the pictures taken right after the alleged suicide as well as those taken before and during the subsequent autopsy—a treasure trove of documents that included the two photos that had aroused McFarland and Schug's suspicions three years before. To say they were disquieting, even upsetting, ranks as the proverbial understatement; the alarm bells that had sounded for McFarland and Schug in 1999 began to ring for us as well. Things just did not look right. A huge close-up of Frank Dolezal's head and the wound on his neck showed his open, vacant, dead eyes starring fixedly toward the ceiling. In a second photograph, a rubber-gloved hand descends from the upper right, obscuring a portion of the face, to pull his head slightly to the side to better reveal the telltale mark. For the first time since 1939, students of the Kingsbury Run murders could see what that wound looked like. The deep, narrow mark on Dolezal's neck just did not match up—at least to our untrained eyes—with photographs of the toweling or sheeting with which he was alleged to have taken his life.

All sorts of admittedly amateur notions about hanging and the nature of injuries to the neck intruded on our assessments of what we were seeing. The few photos I had ever seen documenting a lynching or a state execution by hanging showed a V-shaped mark that pulled upward behind the ears to the noose's coil at the back of the head. Also, if memory served, the wound left by the rope at the front of the neck was invariably positioned fairly high

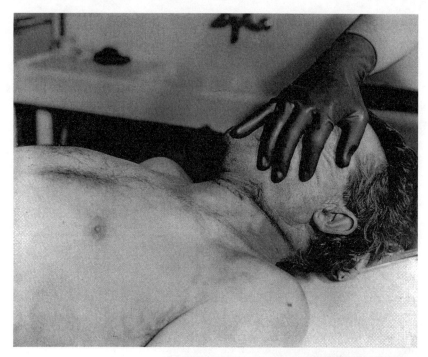

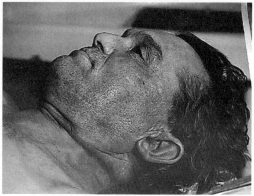

The two pre-autopsy photographs showing the deep, narrow wound on Frank Dolezal's neck. They were taken eighteen hours after his alleged suicide. If Dolezal had died from asphyxiation due to hanging from a cloth noose for a couple of minutes, the mark would have been faint and would have disappeared long before these pictures were taken. Courtesy of the Cuyahoga County Coroner's Office.

up, virtually right under the chin. Frank Dolezal's wound appeared to circle his neck about midway between the shoulders and head, with no sign of the characteristic *V*-shaped pattern. And those two revealing photographs were only the beginning.

When Mark and I made our initial visits in the winter of 2003–04, the archivist at the morgue had gathered every surviving photograph, document, and artifact related to the arrest and death of Frank Dolezal that lay hidden away in the coroner's old files. Some photos were duplicates of police or press shots familiar to anyone who has studied the Kingsbury Run murders; others, however, proved entirely new. (A substantial number showed Dolezal in the custody of the county sheriff's men, thus again raising the admittedly rather minor issue of who had taken them: the press, law enforcement personnel?) Some photos were difficult to identify, in spite of their huge size. One showed what looked like bone fragments. What were they? Dolezal's broken ribs? It was hard to be certain, because there was nothing else in the picture, no measurement scale that gave any indication of size. It was impossible to tell how large or how small these bones were.

One particularly shocking photograph—an eleven-by-fourteen-inch copy of a shot that had made it into the pages of the *Press* in August 1939—set off every alarm bell imaginable. The size and clarity of the original print revealed things that the cheap paper and the relatively poor photo reproduction techniques of the time had obscured. Frank Dolezal lay on the jail floor, his body partly covered by a sheet. His eyes were open and glazed; a hand resting on his head had turned his face toward the right of the picture. The noose with which he had allegedly hanged himself looked as if it had been hurriedly placed on his left shoulder, apparently for the sake of staging a powerfully compelling photograph—a circumstance that strongly suggests that a *Press* photographer had indeed taken the original picture. In the sheeting or toweling of the makeshift noose, however, curled a length of thin rope or twine. A second and much smaller photo of the death, taken at the same time but from a different angle, not only revealed the hitherto unnoticed piece of twine but showed that it seemed to be a part of an intricate series of lengths of rope or cord wrapped in sheeting. (See page 87. It is almost impossible to determine what this contrivance actually is, given the size of the original; the image degrades badly under magnification.) There was a single, fleeting, reference to the twine in one of the newspaper stories, but this curious rope failed to appear in any other photographic record of the scene, nor was it ever referred to or even mentioned in any of the surviving paperwork covering the case. Newspaper photographs—copies of which were among the morgue collection—showed a length of towels or rags hanging from the clothes hook in the death cell. If the rather fragmentary newspaper coverage of the inquest could be taken at face value, no one ever mentioned that twine during those official proceedings; all the testimony centered on "cleaning rags"—how Dolezal had gotten a hold of them, how he had secreted them. Yet that mysterious length of rope seemed more consistent with the wound on his neck than did the noose of rags. Why did only two photographs show it? What happened to this piece

A piece of the noose hanging from the cell hook. It has obviously been placed there to stage a compelling photograph. All the visible edges seem frayed, not freshly cut. Courtesy of the Cuyahoga County Coroner's Office.

of rope? Coroner Gerber had, somewhat reluctantly, convened the inquest on August 26, two days after Dolezal's death. For over six decades, the only surviving accounts of those proceedings available to the public remained the fragmentary coverage in Cleveland's newspapers—stories that offered only a dim reflection of what transpired during two solid days of occasionally explosive testimony.

† † †

In spring and early summer 2000, Marjorie Merylo Dentz, sent me copies of all her father's papers relating to the case—a staggering pile of documents over a foot high containing police reports spanning several years, tip letters, the manuscripts for two projected but unpublished books, close to one hundred photographs (many unseen by the public for over sixty years), and various other pieces of official documentation. As the lead detective on the Kingsbury Run murders, Merylo was present during the inquest, though he did not testify, and his papers fleshed out some significant details of the proceedings and recorded his negative assessment of some of the principal players involved. Those memoirs pointed to the hitherto unknown lawsuits buried in the archives of Cuyahoga County court proceedings: two causes of action undertaken by Frank Dolezal's brother Charles against the county, Sheriff Martin L. O'Donnell, and several others involved in his brother's arrest and death. Both sets of documents ended with the tantalizing statement, "Settled at defendants' cost." Exactly what that meant remained unclear. At the time, no one still alive in the Dolezal family seemed to know of the double-barreled legal assault initiated by Frank's brother. Did money change hands? If so, why didn't any of Charles's descendants know about it? Were the actions regarded at the time by local officials simply as nuisance suits to be settled as quickly as possible, or in all this legal sparring was there an implied recognition of Frank Dolezal's innocence? Or, perhaps more important, was the county acknowledging, however indirectly, that his death may not have been a simple suicide? Mark and I began to shop our concerns and doubts about his death around to various individuals in local officialdom whose training potentially made them far better judges of what we thought we were seeing in those revealing old photographs than we were. Everyone was polite, pleasant, and cooperative; but . . . was it a tinge of paranoia on our part, or were we being ever so elegantly stonewalled with a nod and a smile? And why? What was the point of being evasive? The crime—if that is what Dolezal's death actually had been—was nearly three quarters of a century in the past. Everyone we talked with conceded that, based on all the new recently unearthed evidence, Dolezal had been subjected to a brutal old-fashioned "third degree" interrogation by his captors—that he had been physically abused by a person or persons unknown and that his rights as a potential defendant, even by the far looser standards of the 1930s, had, indeed, been seriously violated. (An individual in the Cleveland Police crime lab—who, naturally enough under the circumstances, requested anonymity—even went so far as to speculate that Dolezal had been driven to take his own life by all the mistreatment meted out to him by his captors.) But no one seemed willing to question Coroner Gerber's suicide verdict; it was allowed to stand unchallenged.

Samuel Gerber was, of course, a Cleveland icon and legend; he had been Cuyahoga County coroner from 1936 to 1986. For many locals in and out of government, Gerber and the coroner's office were inseparable. His image,

A stone-faced coroner, Dr. Samuel Gerber, holding the alleged instrument of Frank Dolezal's suicide for the assembled newspaper photographers. Note that none of the edges look as if they had been freshly cut with a knife. *Cleveland Press* Archives, Cleveland State University.

however, had already been marred by at least one major black eye: his high-handed and arrogant behavior during the Sheppard murder case of 1954. And during the Butcher's reign of terror, one of the county pathologists,

Reuben Straus, had committed a major blunder during the autopsy of victim no. II, a female, and Coroner Gerber had blithely signed off on his wildly inaccurate results in the official autopsy protocol. Straus had judged the death a probable homicide, though he could not be certain about the exact cause. The disarticulated remains of the victim ultimately wound up in the medical school of Western Reserve University, where anatomy professor T. Windgate Todd examined them closely. This was not a legitimate torso victim, the anatomist later fumed to David Cowles, head of the Cleveland Police Department's Scientific Investigation Bureau and member of Safety Director Ness's inner circle. Not only had the unidentified woman been dead before disarticulation, she had already been embalmed. Whoever had placed her remains in the trash dump at the corner of East 9th and Lake Shore Drive had taken the time to cut up a body that had been previously prepared at an undertaking establishment. This tale of apparent sloppiness run amok in the coroner's office was never leaked to the press or even made public until 1983, when David Cowles talked about it in a taped interview with police lieutenant Tom Brown and Florence Schwein, the first director-curator of the Cleveland Police Historical Society Museum; but certainly such a serious blunder in such a high-profile case could not be kept entirely secret at the time. There had to be some who knew, whether in the county coroner's office or the Western Reserve Medical School, but no one seemed willing to say anything publicly. Was there still some sort of local good-ole-boy network left over from the Great Depression intact in the city in the twenty-first century, or was official Cleveland still simply unwilling to compromise Gerber's shining reputation further by conceding that in 1939 he had committed a couple of major mistakes in judgment in regard to one of the city's most notorious cases? There were no obvious answers to those troubling questions; and for the moment, at least, we were stymied.

Then in winter 2004, the archivist at the morgue located the original record of the inquest testimony, all 220 elegantly bound pages of it. Included with the impressively hefty tome was a sheaf of other extraordinary papers—the depositions taken by Cleveland police, late in the afternoon of Frank Dolezal's death, from everyone present and otherwise involved in his alleged suicide and its immediate aftermath. This was a find of enormous significance; the material added up to a huge missing piece in the puzzle that no one had seen since 1939. With our enthusiasm rekindled, Mark and I obsessively pored over copies of the original documents for weeks—reading and rereading, noting questions in the margins, underlining key bits of testimony, and comparing the various statements offered by different witnesses. It was a daunting task; the combined total of all the typed material easily topped 250 pages. Suddenly, the alarm bells that had sounded in 1999 when Rebecca McFarland and Andrew Schug first saw those autopsy photos became a jarring cacophony. The tension present in that room was immediately obvious, and gradually some of the discrepancies in the testimony only vaguely hinted at by the original 1939 newspaper coverage began to take shape. There seemed to be something sinister flowing just beneath the surface. But what?

Gerber had convened the inquest into Frank Dolezal's death on Saturday, August 26, 1939, at 10:30 A.M.—the day after the formal autopsy and two days following the bricklayer's death. The most obvious explanation for his initial reticence is that he saw no need for the formal procedure; his investigation of the scene at the county jail, coupled with statements from Sheriff O'Donnell and his deputies, had convinced him that Dolezal had, indeed, taken his own life with a noose he had secretly fashioned from "cloths" jail personnel had given him to clean his cell. Unfortunately, the reporters in attendance at the formal proceedings probably viewed inquest testimony in the same light as trial testimony—long, dry, and often rather dull. What interested them most were obviously the conclusions. They perked up and took more than casual interest, however, whenever something out of the ordinary occurred, such as when Sheriff O'Donnell almost got into a fistfight with William Edwards, crime commissioner, or when he lost his temper and challenged Gerber during the testimony of Patrolman Frank Vorell. But, for the most part, the gentlemen of the press establishment remained totally oblivious to the intricacies of the delicate dance going on before them. Thus, the public only got a vague, generalized notion of what was going on behind those closed doors.

Reading and absorbing the full inquest transcript was a monumental task. Though the troubling undercurrents rumbling beneath the placid surface of official question and answer were readily apparent even on a first read-through, gaining a full understanding of what was actually being said or inferred would require me—as well as the other members of the research team, principally Mark Stone—to comb through the testimony many times over, all the while taking voluminous notes and endlessly hashing out our impressions over gallons of coffee and uncountable boxes of doughnuts. Mark and I traded frantically dashed-off e-mails and shared our intense and rapidly developing excitement over the phone. This was real! This was *Cold Case* plus all the *CSI* and *Law & Order* shows rolled together and catapulted from the TV screen into real life; from all appearances, we seemed on the brink of making tantalizing, potentially explosive, entirely new discoveries in the accepted record of one of Cleveland's most notorious and gruesome murder cases. Gradually, the inconsistencies, the irregularities (at least by contemporary standards), the personal agendas, and the sometimes awkward procedural maneuvering came into focus. It just did not add up; and everyone who has studied the document has come away deeply troubled and with serious misgivings.

Most of the testimony dealt with such issues as the physical injuries Dolezal had apparently sustained (the bruising and broken ribs), his two suicide attempts, his state of mind, and the exact time line of events leading up to his death and the immediate aftermath: Who did what, where were they when they did it, and when did they do it? The first witness to testify on that Saturday morning was A. V. Fried, the Cuyahoga County jail physician—a position he had held for seven years at that point—and the first person on the scene to declare Dolezal officially dead. In his fifties at the time, Fried had once had his sights set on the coroner's office but had lost out to Gerber. Whether his then current position at the county jail was a consolation prize is impossible to say. Since he was the first to take the stand and there was no other testimony on the record to which his could be compared, it would not become clear until later in the day that Fried had dropped a troubling little bombshell regarding the official time of death. According to all the sworn depositions taken on August 24, Dolezal's death had occurred around 2:00 in the afternoon. Fried had been called immediately at his Broadway office and had arrived at the jail, according to his inquest testimony, about eight minutes later. At this point, Dolezal had supposedly been dead for less than a half an hour, yet Fried insisted the corpse was cold.

Fried: . . . and he was cold. The entire body was cold.

Gerber: Now, had he been given any resuscitation before you examined him, to your knowledge? Schaeffer resuscitation? Any method of resuscitation, to your knowledge?

Fried: I don't know anything about it.

Gerber: How long do you think Frank Dolezal was dead, when you examined him?

Fried: Well he must have been dead about half an hour.

Gerber: And you examined him at what time?

Fried: Well this is about 2:25 I guess or 2:28, around there. Exactly, I would—

Gerber: Two-twenty in the afternoon?

Fried: Sometimes [sic] in there.

Gerber: Two-twenty to 2:25, is that it?

Fried: I guess it was about that, wasn't it? I didn't pay too much attention to the time.

Gerber: Did you determine the condition of rigor mortis of the body at that time?

Fried: Beg your pardon?

Gerber: Did you determine the condition of rigor mortis in the body at that time?

Fried: Life?

Gerber: Rigor—rigor mortis?

Fried: Oh, absolutely.

Gerber: Was there any rigor mortis present?

Fried: He was dead as a doornail, and that is all.

It is a curious exchange. Gerber keeps hammering at Fried (who seems somewhat belligerent, even combative) because neither could the body simply be entirely "cold" nor could rigor mortis have set in after only a half an hour. The unstated implication of Gerber's badgering is clear: *Are you absolutely sure about the time? Are you absolutely sure the body was cold and rigor had set in?* If Fried is accurate about the state of the corpse, death must have occurred far earlier than 2:00 in the afternoon. And to whom was Fried's "wasn't it?" directed? Would it be reading too much into this part of the exchange to suggest that Fried's question makes him sound like an actor checking with the prompter to make sure he had delivered his lines correctly?

Gerber obviously attached crucial importance to the broken ribs and other injuries that Dolezal had sustained, according to the sheriff's office, during his two botched suicide attempts on Monday, July 10—and which the autopsy on August 25 had so graphically confirmed. Both Frank Dolezal's brother Charles and Charles's brother-in-law Patrolman Frank Vorell testified that the prisoner had not suffered any prior injuries nor had he been in the hospital, thus firmly establishing that the bruising on the face and arms (clearly visible in newspaper photographs taken on and after July 10) and the broken ribs (confirmed by the autopsy) had occurred while Frank Dolezal was in the sheriff's custody, sometime between early July and late August. Were these injuries caused by beatings? Absolutely not, insisted Sheriff O'Donnell. "He was questioned in the regular way by myself and Mr. Brown, and no force, no threats or no promises or anything made whatever. . . . I never raised my voice or threatened, and never heard Mr. Brown threaten or raise his voice in any way, shape or form all the time we talked to him." In fact, asserted the sheriff, "and if anything, treated him better than the average prisoner we had there, and he knew that and he appreciated it a whole lot[!?]. . . . treated him better than any prisoner who was ever in the jail in my time arrested for a like offense."

Called to testify immediately after his boss, sheriff's detective Harry S. Brown concurred. "Now, more than once there has been a lot said about lickings and beatings and all that sort of thing. I was there all the time up to the time this man got hurt [presumably, a reference to Dolezal's two suicide attempts], and some time a little after he got hurt. I know positively that there was no beating of any kind."

Witnesses more or less in the Dolezal camp, however—those outside the sheriff's office—had far different stories to tell. David Hertz recalled: "He said that at one time he was bound, blindfolded and gagged, and that he was kept in that condition . . . that he was bound, his hands bound and his legs bound, and blindfolded and gagged, and considerably punched throughout a period of time." George Palda (an attorney brought in by David Hertz because he was of the same nationality as Dolezal and could talk to him in his native language) said: "A cloth was suddenly thrown over his head, over his eyes and over his mouth, and he was jerked back onto the cement floor and while there on the cement floor he was kicked and punched."

Patrolman Frank Vorell remembered: "I spoke to him at the County Jail, and I asked him how he come with the injuries. And he said that he was beaten up. And I says 'Who done the beating?' He says 'I don't know,' he says. 'Well,' I says, 'didn't you see him?' He says, 'No,' he says, 'I was blindfolded and gagged when I came to.' And I says, 'Where were you at, at the time?' He says 'I was laying on the cement, in the jail.'"

Fred P. Soukup, the attorney obtained by the family to represent Frank Dolezal recalled:

> He told me practically the same story that you have already heard . . . and he said they commenced to punch him as they were taking him down to the County Jail in the car from his residence . . . and then he said that there were crews of men, seven or eight deputies kept shouting at him in turn day after day and night after night that he did it, he committed this crime, it was no use, that he should confess. . . . [H]e complained to me that people in the jail were taunting him, calling him vile names. . . . He had an obsession that someone was going to do something to him all the time.

The glaring contradictions among the accounts as to Frank Dolezal's state of mind during the period leading up to the early afternoon of August 24 were equally wild and jarring. Sheriff's detective Harry S. Brown, Deputy Sheriff Hugh Crawford, and elevator operator Clarence Smart maintained that he never complained to them about anything; and O'Donnell actually claimed he was so "satisfied" and "happy" that he played cards with the deputies. Brown insisted Dolezal was not depressed and was, in fact, "very, very, very, very friendly." Some of this testimony borders on absurdity. Did anyone present at the inquest really think for one moment that Dolezal would have complained openly about beatings or pain to the very people he alleged were mistreating him? In fact, he had grown so wary of everyone he saw in the jail that he initially refused to confide in either Fred Soukup or George Palda. "He was so confused," snorted Frank Vorell, "he didn't know a doctor from a deputy sheriff."

Interestingly, Gerber ran into some rather stubborn resistance when he tried to illicit some comment about Dolezal's state of mind from L. J. Sternicki, the physician brought in by David Hertz to examine the prisoner in the evening of July 11 and again on July 20.

Gerber: What was his mental condition?

Sternicki: Well, I don't know whether I should—I wasn't called in there to testify as to his mental condition. I would just as soon not say anything about the mental condition.

Gerber: Well, as a physician in the practice of medicine for a considerable length of time, you have a definite idea as to a man's mental attitude, so you have every reason in the world to tell me and the general public what type or what attitude your patient had at that time.

Sternicki: I was called in, though, to examine him physically, and I would prefer not to discuss his mental condition, or psychiatric—

Gerber: I am not asking you to discuss his mental condition, from a psychopathic standpoint. Just as an ordinary observation, was Frank Dolezal dazed, or was he depressed or something like that? I would like to know your observations on that point.

In spite of Gerber's hammering, Sternicki refused to budge beyond recounting that during the examination Dolezal had said he was not in any pain. (It's hardly surprising that Dolezal would say this, considering Sheriff O'Donnell was in the same room.) The coroner returned to the issue of Dolezal's mental state later in Sternicki's testimony, but the doctor still flatly refused to comment. Obviously, any trained medical professional with a sense of propriety would be reluctant to comment officially on anything beyond his areas of expertise, but Sternicki's adamant refusal to respond to Gerber's request for a simple "ordinary observation" remains both interesting and troubling.

When it came to the broad, general outline of the events that had led to the alleged suicide and what had transpired in the immediate aftermath, Sheriff O'Donnell, his deputies, and other jail personnel were mostly on the same page; and what emerged from their collective testimony was essentially

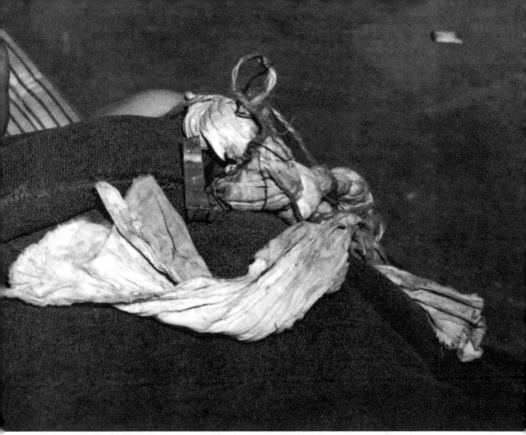

A close-up of the alleged noose clearly showing the length of twine and what looks like thin black cord wound in with the cloth. The twine and the cord appear in only one other photograph. It was this photograph that first alerted my research team and me that something might be amiss with Dr. Gerber's suicide verdict. The metal object at the left of the noose is the cup handle found in Frank Dolezal's pocket. Courtesy of the Cuyahoga County Coroner's Office.

a more detailed version of the account that had appeared in the press. Dolezal had been given his lunch in block B, cell 4 around 12:00. At 1:48 P.M., Deputy Sheriff Hugh Crawford found him hanging from the clothes hook in cell 11. (Crawford—who had been assigned to make his rounds of the fourth floor every ten minutes—testified that he had last seen the prisoner about three minutes before, at 1:45, and he seemed fine.) Immediately, he called out to stockroom worker Catherine Krial. "'Kate,' I says, 'call the jailor [Assistant Chief Jailor Archie Burns]. Dolezal is hanging.'" He tried to hold Dolezal up with one arm while, at the same time, attempting to loosen the knot of the noose around his neck. Hearing someone in the corridor, he yelled, "Number 11 cell." Burns and elevator operator Clarence Smart arrived on the scene; and while Burns ordered Krial to call the rescue squad, Smart tried to help Crawford hold Dolezal up and untie the noose's obviously very stubborn knot. Burns then encountered Sheriff O'Donnell at the elevator. "Just as I stepped in the elevator, Mr. Burns was in there, and he said, 'Come on right away to the fourth floor.' I said, 'What's the matter?' He said, 'Mr. Dolezal has tried to hang himself.'" Finding the knot impossible to loosen, someone called out, "Got a knife?" O'Donnell then passed his knife to Burns, who cut Dolezal down. According to Burns, they placed Dolezal on his bunk and "worked on him" until Del Young (the day nurse on call at the jail) arrived on the scene and gave him a hypodermic, apparently of adrenaline. The rescue squad showed up about 1:58—at which point Dolezal was removed from the cell and placed in the outside corridor on the floor. Fried, the jail physician, arrived around 2:15 and, after examining the prisoner, declared Frank Dolezal dead. The entire episode took less than a half an hour. (Curiously, neither Del Young nor Captain Floyd O'Neil of the rescue squad were called to testify at the inquest. And, though the police did obtain a deposition from O'Neil—which was accepted into evidence, Young was apparently not asked to give one.)

Some of the issues that had seemed so critical at the time of Dolezal's death took considerably less time to hash out during the inquest. The explanation of how Dolezal had gotten the rags with which he was alleged to have hanged himself was essentially identical to the newspaper accounts; the prisoner wanted something to do, so the deputies gave him the cloths to clean his cell. The medicine he had been given turned out to be aspirin. For the record, Gerber mentioned that Dolezal was entirely alone during his period of captivity. The fourth floor of the jail housed two cell blocks, A and B; though kept in cell 4, Dolezal had all of block B to himself. When Gerber questioned O'Donnell about this enforced isolation, the sheriff responded that he thought it advisable to separate him from other prisoners because of "the nature of the crime" and certain details about "the history of his past life"—a veiled reference to Dolezal's alleged homosexuality. Having established that Dolezal was kept by himself, Gerber moved on to other issues; but the unspoken implication of the brief exchange with the sheriff was clear: no one was around to see the manner in which the prisoner was being treated.

There was an interesting subplot playing out on the jail's fourth floor while this major drama was unfolding, and the contradictory accounts of it are decidedly perplexing. Oscar Delany; his wife, Agnes; and Earl Burtt arrived at the jail between 1:45 and 1:50 to visit Burtt's son Willard in block A, also on the fourth floor. In his deposition, taken in the afternoon of August 24, Deputy Crawford blandly and matter-of-factly describes the incident. "I went to notify some visitors [around 2:05] who were on the floor visiting other inmates that their time was up, and I accompanied them to the elevator and while walking by Cell Block B. I saw Frank Dolezal in his cell, he was walking up and down in the prisoners corridor."

Oscar Delany's account, given during the inquest, was considerably more dramatic: "Then the next thing I knew, why the Deputy came and said, 'You will have to go,' and he just naturally chased us out, and I was a little bit slow about moving and he grabbed me by the sleeve, he says, 'Come on Bud, come on,' and I could see there was something wrong with him because he was as white as a sheet, and he was awfully nervous and excited. Excited as the dickens, and I could see there was something wrong." The major contradiction in the two accounts is obvious. Crawford says Dolezal was alive when he escorted the Delanys and Earl Burtt to the elevator; Oscar Delany would seem to suggest that he was already dead.

There were other curious moments during the testimony of the sheriff and his men that set off alarm bells of varying decibels. When Gerber asked Hugh Crawford exactly what time he found Dolezal hanging, the deputy responded: "Well, I would say about three—1:48 P.M." Just what did Crawford start to say before he caught himself? While describing the way he and Smart cut Dolezal down, Crawford seemed to go out of his way to say the body was warm. "His body was still warm and he had a good color. Even when I had hold of his two arms, his wrists, raised him up and down, I could feel the warmth of his body and his arms." Why this emphasis on the warmth of Dolezal's body? Was this a deliberate attempt to counter Fried's insistence that the body was cold when he saw it less than a half an hour after it had been supposedly cut down? When the coroner asked Harry Brown to describe "as briefly and as concisely as possible and, at the same time, thoroughly" the chronology of events between July 5, when Frank Dolezal was arrested, and August 24, Brown began his response with, "Yes, sir, I would be glad to." Not only is this a rather curious opening, much of what Brown has to say unfolds with the smooth logic of a prepared dramatic monologue. Brown rarely stumbles; and his testimony is remarkably free from the hemming and hawing, the incomplete sentences, and the abrupt shifts of direction in midsentence that appear so frequently in the testimony of others. Had he been coached? Had his testimony been scripted?

The procedural rules governing a formal inquest may have been less strict in the 1930s than they are in the early twenty-first century. How else to explain Sheriff O'Donnell's presence throughout? Today, witnesses in an inquest are not permitted to hear the sworn testimony of other witnesses; and as the eighth person called to give evidence, O'Donnell should have not been in the room to hear what other witnesses had to say. Yet newspaper photographs of the sessions and his own occasional outbursts clearly establish his presence. Perhaps, as one of the most powerful political figures in the county, he simply inserted himself, no matter what the official guidelines may have been. Quarrelsome and edgy, even during his own testimony, O'Donnell obviously had an agenda and occasionally tried to exert some sort of control over the proceedings even though Gerber was officially in charge. No doubt it galled him in the extreme to hear sworn testimony that directly contradicted the accounts he and his deputies provided, but proper decorum demanded that he sit there in stony silence. He erupted, however, during Vorell's testimony when he suspected Gerber was asking questions passed to him by someone else in the room. "I would like to know whether or not you are asking questions that have been passed up from the outside," he fumed. "I want to know our rights, here." When Assistant County Prosecutor Saul S. Danaceau—apparently in attendance to advise Gerber on any legal issues that arose—assured him that Gerber had the right to accept questions from anyone he chose, O'Donnell raged, "I don't think he has, according to law, he is to conduct his examination. I want to register an objection. I know my rights, I know the rights in this inquest, too." Though the exact circumstances remain difficult to discern, because of a very curious and unexplained gap in the transcript, a similar incident occurred after the testimony of Charles Dolezal. But whatever the precipitating incident was, it involved the sheriff and almost led to a physical altercation.

Edwards: Now, if the Coroner please, I merely stated that the witness [Charles Dolezal] cannot speak the English language very well. Now if this is going to be turned into a personality scrap, in here, I will get up and take my coat off and go to bat.

Gerber: No you won't Mr. Edwards. This is going to be carried on in a normal way.

Edwards: Please, Mr. Coroner, I am sitting here, and this man [Sheriff O'Donnell] getting up and telling me I can't ask a question. I didn't ask a question. I told you that the witness could not speak the English language.

O'Donnell: I object to this.

Gerber: We won't go into any controversy. Let's not have any controversy.

O'Donnell's be-on-your-guard stance continued during his own testimony. When the issue concerning the amount of time Dolezal had been left alone arose—in other words, how long did he hang, how long would it take for him to asphyxiate—he turned especially combative: "I guess you [Gerber] came and you saw what took place, and in the course of the conversation different things were said, and one of them I remember you said, Coroner, 'A man that would commit suicide that way, it would be possible for him to be dead in two minutes,' and there were other things that were said, and if I remember right, you said, 'It is a clear case of suicide,' and that is as far as I can remember outside of what you saw and everybody else saw."

One can almost see O'Donnell wagging his finger at Gerber like an overbearing schoolteacher lecturing an errant student who had forgotten his lesson. Perhaps the most telling moment, however, occurred during a brief exchange over cutting Dolezal's body down.

Gerber: And they [Crawford and Smart] were attempting to get him [Dolezal] down?
O'Donnell: That is right.
Gerber: And you gave them your knife?
O'Donnell: My knife.
Gerber: To cut him down, to cut *the rope* [my italics].
O'Donnell: Cut the line.

The official version of Frank Dolezal's death, of course, was that he had hanged himself with a homemade noose fashioned from material alternately described as cloths, toweling, or sheeting. The pressing issue at the inquest was how he had gotten hold of this material in the first place. Though two of the photographs taken on the scene clearly showed a length of rope, this is the first and only time the word "rope" was used during the inquest. Was Gerber's "slip" inadvertent or deliberate? Either way, the term and the sheriff's refutation of it were now part of the official record. The most startling revelations in the inquest, however, were yet to come.

† † †

Formal proceedings reconvened on Tuesday, August 29, at 10:30, and that brief morning session ended with an interesting and, given the circumstances, somewhat mystifying statement by Danaceau: "I want to say this: The Coroner has asked my advice with respect to certain testimony presented in an alleged interview between Mr. Edwards, William E. Edwards and Lillian Jones at the Central Police Station, 9:00 P. M. Monday, August 28, 1939 [the previous evening]. I have examined this document and it is my opinion, and I have so advised the Coroner, that it has no bearing at all on this inquest and will not be received as testimony therein." After reading Section 2856 of the General Code, essentially spelling out the circumstances under which an inquest should be convened and what kind of testimony can be regarded as legally permissible, Danaceau concluded: "There is nothing in this interview which has any bearing on that [the death of Frank Dolezal], and it will not be received." He then turned to Gerber. "Is that a fact, Mr. Coroner?" "That is right," Gerber replied. After tidying up a few minor details, the coroner made a final announcement before calling for adjournment. "As soon as we have all of the reports from the laboratory and we get all the statements from the reporter, I will then give—draw up a conclusion, either at the end of this week or the first part of next week, and up until that time the inquest is closed." The nature of the interview to which Danaceau referred was not clarified; and, theoretically, in light of Gerber's formal adjournment at 11:00, that should have been the end of the matter. Yet, forty-five minutes later the inquest was suddenly reconvened solely to hear the testimony that Danaceau had earlier deemed to have "no bearing at all on this inquest" and get it on the official record. (At first blush, there is some confusion about the time element in the inquest transcript. Page 201 of the record concludes with the statement, "Thereupon at 11:00 P. M. [on August 29] the hearing was concluded." Page 202 begins with "PROCEEDINGS 11:45 A. M. TUESDAY, AUGUST 29, 1939." The official reporters clearly made a mistake when they recorded that the initial morning session ended at "11:00 *P.M.*" instead of "11:00 *A. M.*")

Why would Gerber adjourn the inquest at 11:00 only to reconvene it forty-five minutes later? Forty-five minutes is hardly enough time for those in charge—Gerber and Danaceau—to change their collective minds about the admissibility of this mysterious testimony, round up the two court reporters who had just been dismissed, and chase down the witnesses involved. The only logical explanation is that Danaceau and Gerber had planned this maneuver beforehand. The 11:00 adjournment was apparently just a clever ploy to clear the room of the sheriff, his deputies, and the gentlemen of the press corps so the testimony in question could be added to the official record in relative secrecy. O'Donnell was clearly present at the close of the initial morning session; before calling for adjournment at 11:00, Gerber addresses him. "Now if there is nothing else—Sheriff, do you have anything?" Danaceau was correct. The evidence provided by Lillian Jones and her sister Ruby Lee, two black women, had absolutely nothing to do with Frank Dolezal's death on August 24; and in a strictly legal sense, it probably would have never been admissible in court, since most of it was hearsay. But their testimony was explosive and damning, and the sheriff would have objected vehemently to both its veracity and its inclusion in the official transcript.

Gerber: Well, do you know any reason why Frank Dolezal should commit suicide?

Lillian Jones: Did I know?

Gerber: Do you know any reason why?

Lillian Jones: Because they were worrying him to death, and they were punching him and beating him and everything like that.

Gerber: How do you know that?

Lillian Jones: I heard a conversation.

Gerber: You don't have any actual knowledge of it? You just heard a conversation, is that right? . . . Now, you say that you heard that they were abusing him, is that the word you used?

Lillian Jones: Yes, I heard that.

Gerber: Who did you hear talk?

Lillian Jones: A white lady and a white fellow talking in front of me at County Jail.

Gerber: A white lady and white fellow talked in front of you?

Lillian Jones: Yes.

Gerber: Do you know their names?

Lillian Jones: No, I don't.

Gerber: When was this, you heard it?

Lillian Jones: I guess it was a week before [August 17?], it was about a week before he did this.

Gerber: You mean by "this" the suicide?

Lillian Jones: Yes.

Whether or not Frank Dolezal committed suicide, Lillian Jones's testimony provides independent verification from a disinterested party that he was, indeed, being severely abused while in the sheriff's custody. The testimony offered by her sister proved far more damning.

Danaceau: Did he [Pat Lyons] say anything at any other time about Frank Dolezal?

Ruby Lee: Yes. He wasn't talking to me, though, but he was talking to another girl.

Danaceau: Did you hear him?

Ruby Lee: Yes, I heard him, and he told the other girl, he said—I told the other girl, I said, "Ask him is Frank Dolezal the man," and he said, "Sure, we got the right man," and he said, "He might—" I asked him was he going to all get the Chair, and he said, "No, he going to get the 'hot seat.'

He will never come out of the County Jail alive." He said, "He will never walk out of the County Jail."

Gerber: Was this before or after Frank Dolezal died? [Note that the word "suicide" has been replaced by "died."]

Ruby Lee: Just before he died, a week.

Danaceau: He said he was going to get the "hot seat"?

Ruby Lee: Yes.

Gerber: Did he say anything about abusing Frank Dolezal?

Ruby Lee: Yes, he said, yes, they were beating him to death, making him say he was the man. They was making him say he was the man, he said, whether he is or not.

Gerber: You heard that?

Ruby Lee: Yes, I heard it.

Lillian and Ruby Lee Jones, as well as a third woman, had been arrested in connection with a robbery on Friday, August 25. Somehow, William Edwards got wind of this arrest and took the opportunity to question Lillian further. Perhaps he remembered that she was the woman who told reporters that she had once been in Frank Dolezal's apartment and had been forced to jump through a window to safety when he came at her with a knife. As the lead investigator in the torso murders, Detective Peter Merylo was assigned to accompany Edwards during his meeting with the Jones sisters in the evening of Monday, August 28; and he included an abbreviated version of their story in his special report to Eliot Ness dated April 2, 1940. Responding to questions and, no doubt, pressure from the two men, Lillian immediately retracted the lurid tale she had shared with the press back in July, insisting it was something she made up to satisfy Pat Lyons and get him off her back. (Lillian and Lyons frequented some of the same dives, and she apparently regarded him as something of a nuisance.)

At the conclusion of the Jones sisters' testimony, Edwards asked to be officially sworn in as a witness and proceeded to make the following statement. To be completely fair, I have reproduced that section of Edwards's statement in its entirety.

I first talked to Lillian Jones, whose transcript you have or, rather, whose testimony you have, and after that talked to this present witness, Ruby Lee Jones. I found her, at the outset, very reluctant to talk about the case at all. After a short time I ascertained what her difficulty was. In the first place she, at least, subjectively speaking, seems to have some concern about her welfare if she did talk. Secondly, and being of paramount importance, apparently, the fact that she was scared to death of a dead body. [The inquest was held at the county morgue.] You have my word for it that she was only asked to tell the truth and invited to come down here and tell the truth here, and, then, of course, there were no measures of persuasion other than to get her over this idea of coming down to where dead people were kept, and my only appeal to her was if she would come down and speak the truth, as she related it to me.

During this second morning session, the combined testimony of the Jones sisters and William Edwards covers seventeen pages in the official inquest transcript (202–19), and it certainly couldn't have taken more than a half an hour to an hour to get it recorded. At the end of his testimony, Edwards asks, "If we may go off the record for a moment?" To which Gerber responds, "Yes, off the record." These are the last four words spoken in the transcript. Yet Gerber did not officially bring proceedings to a close until 8:30 P.M. Could there actually have been an off-the-record discussion that went on for the rest of the day, for virtually eight hours? Even assuming they took breaks, what could they possibly be talking about for such an extended period? It is pure conjecture on my part, but it would seem likely that they wrestled with, among other things, the vexing dilemma of how to handle—officially—the testimony offered by the Jones sisters, how to incorporate the information they provided into the record while protecting them from possible reprisals. Just possibly, they also considered the full implications of that testimony when seen in the light of all the allegations of mistreatment presented during the inquest. If they suspected foul play, they may have deliberated on whether to go public with those suspicions.

This was heady stuff—contradictory testimony, personal agendas, frayed tempers, a near fistfight, all culminating in a procedural maneuver that resulted in a secret session. It was all very intoxicating, disturbing, perplexing, exciting, and a little frightening. It was obvious that, at the very least, Frank Dolezal's death was far more complicated than the sheriff's official version implied. Armed with our cache of photographs and the inquest testimony, Mark and I stood ready to rewrite history. But the real world of criminal investigation and forensic analysis requires far more exactness and specificity than TV's fantasy crime-solving arena. It also gradually became clear to us that those historical revisions could only come at a very high price for some Cleveland families. Questions over Frank Dolezal's guilt and death may have been an integral part of Kingsbury Run murder lore for close to seventy some years, but to prove with anything approaching scientific certainty that he had been murdered would automatically raise the question "By whom?" And to pursue that question would inevitably lead to other equally explosive issues. Was it an accident—an interrogation that got out of hand—or had it been a premeditated act? If premeditated, why had that drastic course of action been deemed necessary? Who had made the decision? Who had set the wheels in motion? How many people were involved? How many knew the truth; what, indeed, was the truth? Was there any kind of official cover-up, and, if so, how deep did its roots go and to how high a level of authority did the branches reach? Political warfare and posturing had been an ugly component of the official investigation of the Kingsbury Run murders virtually from the beginning, and one did not have to dig into the murders very deeply to uncover a tangle of political alliances and agendas infiltrating every aspect of the case, including the questionable death of Frank Dolezal.

None of these questions could be explored without casting deep suspicions on the character and integrity of men long dead—some in public life—but whose children, grandchildren, and other relatives still lived in and around Cleveland. The lure of potentially having uncovered a conspiracy to commit murder shined undeniably brilliantly and attractively, but we had to proceed slowly, and with tremendous caution. On the one hand, reputations were, after all, at stake. On the other hand, members of Frank Dolezal's family also still lived in the area; and they had quietly endured the stain on the family name for almost seventy years. The public sometimes tends to forget that a murder is not a clean, swift bolt of lightning striking down a lone individual; it is a continuing storm that wounds or destroys other lives in its wake. And, indeed, the summer 1939 events and their aftermath had punished the Dolezals for decades and had blasted their family tree to splinters.

† † †

Mark and I were certainly no casting director's dream of the ideal cold case unit or CSI team. Forget the glamor! We simply did not possess the necessary training and experience to adequately judge what we were seeing. We could count ourselves skilled researchers from an academic point of view. Beyond that, with two successful true crime books behind me, I knew my way around police reports and autopsy protocols; and experience had prepared me for working through and around the inevitable vagaries and occasional outright inaccuracies of public documents. But we were not forensic experts. We knew nothing about analyzing photographs of soft tissue damage or of a healed bone fracture, and we skated on very thin ice when it came to judging in-depth medical testimony. And, however fiercely our enthusiasm and dedication may have burned, we were, after all, just amateur sleuths looking at very old and fragmentary evidence with amateur eyes. We needed minds and eyes far more trained in the science and art of forensics than our own to pore over the huge pile of photographs and documents unearthed and pulled together by the archivist at the Cuyahoga County morgue. And perhaps it would be best if those minds and eyes were fresh and unburdened by the heavy baggage of Cleveland history.

There was at least one well-publicized precedent for the sort of cold case forensic reexamination we were proposing. In 2000, popular author Patricia Cornwell—armed with her stint in the Richmond, Virginia, crime lab; her experience as a crime reporter for the *Charlotte Observer;* and several million dollars of her own money—aimed the entire arsenal of modern forensics at the surviving Jack the Ripper evidence, including the infamous letters that may or may not have come from the perpetrator's hand, in hopes of finding and proving the identity of the world's most notorious slasher. For whatever reason, however, Cornwell chose to go solo. She did not consult or work with any of the long-standing experts in the established Ripperology community, and her defiant, in-your-face attitude toward them guaranteed her enemies from the start. When she fingered noted Victorian painter Walter Sickert as the culprit, the Ripper world merely shrugged its collective shoulders and rolled its eyes. Not only had Sickert been tried in other, older theories of the crimes, Cornwell had, so ran the arguments, ignored facts that did not fit her thesis. (Apparently, the determined author also had not bothered to consult anyone conversant with the biographical details of Walter Sickert's life.) Unfortunately, the resulting brouhaha of charges and countercharges in the media, national and international, obscured the significance of what Cornwell had attempted. For one of the first times in modern history, high-tech forensic tools and well-educated professional minds had been marshaled in the bright glare of the public arena to work on crime evidence over a century old.

May 26, 2004: a comfortable, sunny day—spring blooming rapidly into summer. On that pleasant morning, Mark and I helped Dave Brodowski load all his camera equipment into a rented van for our drive to Mercyhurst College in Erie, Pennsylvania, where we would present our collection of diverse material to a team of forensic experts. Now we continued in earnest the journey that had started in 1999, when Rebecca McFarland and Andrew Schug first looked at Frank Dolezal's autopsy photos. Every so often, life presents an opportunity to live out a well-worn cliché: on that morning our journey into our personal cold case truly began; and we had no idea where it would ultimately take us.

Note

The complete transcript of the coroner's inquest and all the photographs referred to in the text are on file at the Cuyahoga County Coroner's Office.

Chapter 7
CSI MERCYHURST AND BEYOND

For beleaguered Clevelanders smarting from national jokes about the city that have arisen from a plethora of local civic issues—the river that caught fire, the Howdy Doody lookalike mayor who steered the city into default, the mayoral spouse who allegedly turned down a presidential invitation to visit the White House because it conflicted with her bowling night—nearby Erie, Pennsylvania, seemed a godsend: a convenient whipping boy whose regional reputation ranked lower than our own. "Dreary Erie: The mistake on the lake!" About the city itself, I cannot comment since we saw so little of it on our drive to Mercyhurst College. The campus, however, would be a jewel in any city's crown: beautifully and spaciously laid out with no glaring clashes of architectural style. But it wasn't the palpable sense of collegiate nostalgia that brought Mark, Dave, and me here; the institution's applied forensic sciences department had been glowingly recommended by forensic anthropologists at the Smithsonian in Washington, D.C.; and after some preliminary phone and e-mail discussions, members of the faculty agreed to look over our material.

The notion that something was amiss with the official explanation of Frank Dolezal's death has been, of course, an integral part of the Kingsbury Run story since 1939. But it could not be explored beyond the contemporary newspaper coverage and a few bits of unverifiable oral legend until 1999, when the Cuyahoga County morgue archivist pulled the original autopsy photographs from the files where they had lain undisturbed for sixty years. Other significant pieces of the puzzle soon followed: Detective Peter Merylo's memoirs and official reports, Pat Lyons's memoirs and other miscellaneous papers, the complete record of Charles Dolezal's two lawsuits against the sheriff and his office, depositions taken at the time of Frank Dolezal's death, and, perhaps, the most crucial piece of all—the full transcript of the inquest proceedings.

We steered the department-provided cart, loaded with heavy TV camera equipment, down the well-scrubbed hallways, passed all the usual signs of modern college life—posters advertising up-coming events, all sorts of colorful messages from campus organizations, neatly arranged lounge chairs, a succession of office doors. When I glanced down at one of the cart's rattling wheels, I noticed for the first time the label placed on the cart's edge with its grim magic-marker message: "For Human Remains Only." As we entered the elevator to descend to the forensic department on the building's bottom floor, I entertained a whole series of pop culture–CSI notions: images of highly trained and attractive professionals who use the microscope and the test tube to solve heinous crimes in their always dark, space-age laboratories, all aglow with intriguing lights and outfitted with bright, shiny devices representing the last word in crime-solving technology. When the elevator doors opened, all those fantasy high-tech images vanished in the face of a long, brightly lit corridor lined with specimen display cases decidedly more reminiscent of a natural history museum than TV-land's glittering laboratories.

We were met by the director of the applied forensic sciences department, Dr. Dennis C. Dirkmaat—his striking professorial demeanor leavened by an affable smile and a pair of well-worn blue jeans. A highly regarded forensic anthropologist, his impressive resume includes working with coroners, medical examiners, and state police all through the Pennsylvania–Ohio–West Virginia area, as well as the FBI. On this visit, Dennis had graciously—and bravely—consented to sit down with me and allow his initial gut, though obviously learned, reactions to our pile of troubling photographs and other documents to be videotaped and recorded in their entirety.

Though we had e-mailed him copies of the crucial photos earlier, given him an overview of the entire Dolezal story, and spelled out our misgivings about Gerber's official verdict, this was the first time he was seeing much of the relevant material. As the camera hovered above us and rolled silently, he examined one photo after the next—constantly asking me questions about the contexts and circumstances surrounding what he was seeing, sometimes looking up to respond to one of Mark's inquiries, occasionally offering guardedly cautious comments. He carefully studied the two pre-autopsy morgue photographs showing the wound on Frank Dolezal's neck. His brow knitted somewhat when he encountered the various shots of the bulky length of rags, the alleged instrument of the suicide: a stone-faced Sam Gerber holding the cloth up for newspaper photographers at the morgue, a lengthy piece of the same material dangling from the clothes hook in the cell where the death allegedly occurred, the tangled pile of cloth on the chest of Frank Dolezal's corpse. And, of course, the final photo clearly showed curled in with the rags or sheeting the telltale piece of rope—whose presence was never questioned or explained back in 1939. In every sense of the term, this was a crap-shoot. Would Dirkmaat's highly trained and experienced eyes pick up on the discrepancies in the official version of events that we thought we had uncovered? Would he find any reason to question Sam Gerber's sixty-five-year-old suicide verdict, anything that could prompt a deeper, more detailed analysis on his part? If not, the adventure was over; and we might as well pack up our material and equipment and head back to Cleveland. For nearly an hour, the camera hovered silently over the pile of photographs as we rummaged through them and moved slowly between Dirkmaat and me as the microphones pinned to our shirts caught the stray bits of conversation, the comments, and the questions. Finally, Mark broached the crucial issue: "First impressions?" "Yes, first impressions," Dirkmaat responded as he raised his eyes from the material scattered on the table before us. "I think there are a lot of issues that have to be addressed. You know, it could turn out that all these things are legitimate; but there are enough questions here to have to do a little more research." Our suspicions were validated; the journey would continue.

Over the next several months, we would push that cart of TV equipment down the hallway—past the shelves lined with human skulls and the banks of cabinet drawers containing bones—twice more. On the second visit, August 31, 2004, Dirkmaat again sat before the camera and poured out his thoughts. By then, he had gone through the inquest thoroughly several times over and studied the photos in detail, comparing what he saw in them with the recorded testimony in the inquest. It became quickly apparent he was more interested in discussing the inquest testimony than in commenting on the photographs; this was understandable. A picture may be worth a thousand words, but in this case—no matter how big and clear they might be—they were, after all, no substitute for the actual presence of the physical body. "I hate two-dimensional evidence," roared James Starrs, professor of law and forensic science at George Washington University, when I showed him the same pictures after he had spoken at a Jack the Ripper conference in Baltimore.

Our third visit to Mercyhurst, on March 3, 2005, however, turned out to be the most fascinating and productive by far. On this occasion, we were met by Dr. Steven A. Symes—a tall, Lincolnesque professor sporting an impressive resume of teaching experience, professional accomplishments, research activities, and job-related interests. Dirkmaat and Symes had agreed to turn the questions about Frank Dolezal's death into a hands-on exercise for two of their classes in forensics. In late morning, I gave the small group of students a brief overview of the Kingsbury Run murders and a fairly detailed accounting of the Dolezal chapter. I stuck to the facts, keeping my narrative as neutral and objective as possible so as not to prejudice anyone before they had had a chance to examine the material. After Mark and I had handed out all the photographs and other official documents relating to Dolezal's death, we left them to their own devices and went off to lunch with Symes at the school cafeteria. An hour later, we returned to the classroom, suggested they might want to pick a spokesperson, and then—in spite of the intimidating presence of the TV camera—asked for their reactions. In the afternoon, we repeated the process, with one major difference, with a more advanced class. I told them nothing; we simply gave them the material, then asked them to look it over and offer up their conclusions. After downing a couple cups of coffee, we returned and repeated the morning taping process.

Realistically, we did not expect any grand, decisive "Eureka!" moments to come from this relatively brief period of study; the evidence was simply too fragmentary. In fact, one of the first lessons we learned was exactly how incomplete and fragmentary it was. "Unless there's a tremendous amount of other documentation," mused Dennis Donovan, adjunct professor in the Department of Applied Forensic Sciences and retired Pennsylvania State Police sergeant, "this is a very, very poorly documented case. Very poor! But considering, again, the historical context, I'm not sure what the normal procedure and protocol would have been seventy years ago either." And we did not have the body. (We had, indeed, tossed around the "E" word—exhumation—somewhat darkly and rather cavalierly, but that was never a realistic option. I knew Mary, as a next of kin, would readily grant family permission for the procedure, but the cost would be prohibitive and the probable results even less than inconclusive. "I've seen exhumed bodies that have been buried for only a few years show marked decomposition," Donovan remarked. Frank Dolezal had been in the ground for almost seventy years, and it remains doubtful that his family could have afforded the best undertaking services available.) But, at the very least, with the help of the best and the brightest among Mercyhurst faculty and students, we hoped to detect any small hints that would validate our misgivings about the official explanation of Frank Dolezal's death. And thanks to their learned assessment of our rather meager pile of documentation—all of it preserved on tape—our suspicions were confirmed. We can now say with absolute certainty that, at the very least, the official version of Dolezal's death—put forward and sworn to by Sheriff O'Donnell and his deputies, and, in part, supported by Coroner Gerber's suicide verdict—is simply not accurate, that both the official manner of death and the circumstances surrounding it are far more than simply questionable. "It stinks to high heaven," grumbled Donovan.

In spite of a number of witnesses and a lot of verbiage, the inquest testimony failed to resolve satisfactorily one of the most crucial issues in the case:

the injuries to Dolezal's face and trunk; all that testimony simply added up to a classic "he-said, he-said" standoff between the Dolezal camp and the sheriff's office. But in spite of all the fervid denials of mistreatment on the part of the sheriff and his staff, there can be no doubt that Frank Dolezal had been severely abused physically by his captors. Though he admitted to Father Zlamal that he had, indeed, tried to take his life twice, the injuries he had sustained—especially the broken ribs—could not have resulted from falls to the floor or on to the bench in his cell when his makeshift nooses failed. The damage was simply too great. "The issue is whether falling two or three or four feet to the ground—whether you would fracture all those ribs, and that's very unlikely," insisted Dirkmaat during August 31 taping. "This was a fairly robust individual," he continued. "He wasn't just skin and bones. He had fractured these ribs. There's one shot [a morgue photograph of what appears to be a section of a rib taken during the autopsy]—it's rather inconclusive; there's no scale or anything—but [it] appears that the ribs are fractured and, in fact, displaced a bit; and there's a little healing going on. So that's a pretty traumatic fracture. . . . These were significant fractures, and it's very unlikely that it was from a fall and from that distance. . . . But one or two falls: you're not going to have that amount of damage to the body." But, of course, that sort of damage could result from a swift, hard, sharp blow—a good, strong kick, for example. "I'm sure in that day and age, prisoners weren't treated as they are today," Dirkmaat reflected. "The fact that they were beaten and coerced to give information was not uncommon. From all the different angles to the evidence, it seems that he [Frank Dolezal] was. . . . From my point of view: high-profile case; they bring in somebody; they want to solve it; they want to look good. So they get a confession. They get a confession by beating him up. I don't know how they found this guy. I didn't really look into that. But they had somebody that they could pin it on."

There are also clear discrepancies in the inquest testimony as to who was where and when he was there. "In many respects, stories [presented by the sheriff and his deputies] changed and sequences were mixed around," reflected Dirkmaat,

> Part of that might be explained away by the fact that a lot is happening, and so the memories of exact details are a little fuzzy. But upon reading, for example, when people get into elevators and who they're seeing and who's in the elevators with them . . . you should remember those facts. But when you recount, or relate, that you got into the elevator [and] you told somebody to come in with you; you went up to a particular floor, and you went out. It's [the elevator] not stopping. But then you

have other accounts saying, "I stepped into the elevator, and these guys were here. They took me up." So there were a lot of discrepancies there. . . . When Crawford found Dolezal, he told the woman up there [Catherine Krial]—who was in the stockroom—to call down to Burns. And so Burns almost immediately went up; and then, all of a sudden, the sheriff was there. Whereas Smart doesn't describe the sheriff getting on [the elevator] at all; Burns doesn't describe him getting on. But the sheriff says that he got on, and here's Burns but not Smart. You think something like that would stick out in your mind. I'm going up in the elevator. Who's with me and where did we go?

Donovan's similar observation was more brutally succinct. "Some of the statements were just flat out contradictory."

There is virtually unanimous agreement that the mark on Frank Dolezal's neck is not consistent with either the cloth noose or the amount of time he reportedly was left hanging before being cut down. "No brainer!" smirked one of the students after a casual glance at the photographs. Asphyxiation by hanging with a cloth ligature can, indeed, occur within a few minutes—as the sheriff and his deputies alleged, but the mark left on the neck would be rather faint and would disappear in a couple of hours. The injury on Dolezal's neck is clearly visible in the two pre-autopsy photographs, and they were taken eighteen hours after his death. The mark is also far too narrow (one centimeter wide, according to Gerber's autopsy protocol) and far too deep to have been caused by a cloth ligature. "In my opinion, from what I've seen in my career," observed Greg Olson (a staff sergeant with the York Regional Police in Canada, and one of the older students) as he pointed to the mark on Dolezal's neck, "using cloth—unless it's wound real tight, and the circumference is very small—I don't think it would cause something like that. But I'm not a medical examiner; I base it on what I've done in the past as an investigator." Symes concurred: "The photographs, to me right now, don't seem consistent with the story being told." "All the descriptions [at the inquest] are of these muslin dust cloths," commented Dirkmaat. "And that's what's shown in the pictures; that's what's shown hanging from the hook. But then when you look at the pictures at [the] autopsy," he continued, "it is a very thin, one-centimeter-in-size line—which is not really possible for that cloth to create. So something else was going on. . . . So something is amiss there. If it was part of the hanging, and the description is only of these cloths, then that doesn't make sense at all. That doesn't seem to be the truth."

During the inquest, Sheriff O'Donnell and Deputies Clarence Smart, Hugh Crawford, and Archie Burns testified that Burns used the sheriff's pocketknife

Mercyhurst College: The best and brightest. Above left: Dr. Dennis C. Dirkmaat, Mercyhurst Anthropological Institute; above right: Dr. Steven A. Symes, Department of Applied Forensic Sciences; right: Sgt. Dennis Donovan, Pennsylvania State Police, retired, and adjunct professor of applied forensic sciences. Images courtesy of Storytellers Media Group.

to cut through the cloth ligature when they were unable to work the knot loose. Assuming Burns was right-handed, he would have steadied the bunched noose with his left, while Smart and Crawford held Dolezal's body erect, and cut or sawed through the cloth. (Admittedly, a lot would depend on the sharpness of the sheriff's knife.) If the noose had been cut this way, however, one would expect to see very sharp, jagged edges at the two points where the cloth had been severed; but none of the existing photographs show this. In all the photos, the edges look frayed and worn—not freshly cut. But if the cloth ligature, so loudly trumpeted in both the Cleveland press and the inquest, did not cause Dolezal's death, what did? The twine visible in one of the photos taken in the county jail is obviously far more consistent with the thin, deep mark on his neck. But why would the sheriff's men leave it with the body to be photographed? If the twine were somehow wrapped in with or tied to the length of cloth, it would be extremely difficult to disentangle the whole affair before photographers arrived on the scene. "I don't know if

The afternoon session at Mercyhurst College. Image courtesy of Storytellers Media Group.

we can attribute that particular ligature mark to that twine," mused Dirkmaat. Thus, in what may be one of the supreme ironies in the entire case, the length of rope that first began to call into doubt the official suicide verdict may not actually have been the instrument of death.

Does all this learned assessment and analysis add up to a definitive conclusion that Frank Dolezal was killed, either accidentally or on purpose, by one or more of his captors? The experts at Mercyhurst who studied the bits of surviving evidence have one of society's most serious and demanding jobs. They deal with death, the end of life—what causes it and what happens to the physical remains under a wide range of environmental circumstances once life has ceased. They treated the whole issue of Dolezal's death with the serious caution of seasoned professionals preparing to testify in court, and they had obviously passed that seriousness of purpose on to their students. Whatever casual comments they may have let slip during the period of examination, they all stopped short of making such a definitive, one might even say naked, pronouncement for the record. In spite of such understandable reticence, however, it would seem that no other conclusion is possible. There is no other reasonable scenario that can explain away all the discrepancies, the charges and countercharges, and the obvious maneuvering recorded in the inquest.

"Again, the best explanation is that he was done in by some individuals," pondered Dirkmaat, "that it wasn't just a hanging." "It's pretty clear," he went on, "that something was going on to cover somebody's tracks. Let's say he did commit suicide and did hang himself. . . . But if that were the case, then the witnesses should line up somehow as to the sequence of events. And none of them do." (One would logically assume, of course, that if there was a concerted effort to cover up a crime, the parties involved would have done a better job of coordinating their stories. But Gerber convened the inquest less than forty-eight hours after Dolezal's death—enough time for the subpoenaed deputies to agree on the general outline of their story, but wholly insufficient to satisfactorily nail down all the pesky details.) "From what I can see in the photographic evidence and the documented evidence, it does not truly appear to me that the individual [Frank Dolezal] died as a result of a suicide," concurred Donovan. "There's some inconsistencies, both physical and in the documentation, that would lead me to think that the cause of death might have been other."

† † †

Serendipity will always play its inevitable, unpredictable role in this sort of cold case research, and that elusive quality made a grand entrance one day over the faculty lunch table when Marge Geiger, one of my English department colleagues, casually announced that she had gone to college with Patricia Cornwell's fictional medical examiner, Kay Scarpetta. Dr. Marcella Fierro, former medical examiner for the Commonwealth of Virginia, had

Dr. Marcella F. Fierro, former chief medical examiner for the Commonwealth of Virginia. Courtesy of Marcella Fierro.

supposedly served as a model for Cornwell's popular crime solving forensic detective; and, with the path to her old classmate cleared by Geiger, Fierro consented to look at some of the evidence surrounding Frank Dolezal's death, primarily the pre-autopsy photographs and Gerber's formal verdict; and her succinct judgment provided a wonderfully satisfying coda to our Mercyhurst experience. "A cloth ligature would not leave a 1 cm mark on his neck. It was caused by something else"—she determined and then subsequently clarified. "A cloth ligature like a sheet (unless it was wound very tight and he had hung for hours) would leave a faint mark that would fade. Any narrow discrete mark would have to be from something else."

Thanks to Frank Dolezal's "timely" death, the cloud of guilt that had hung over him since his arrest early in July 1939 was never resolved legally and, therefore, literally became frozen in time; he would be forever known as the man who was arrested for the Kingsbury Run murders, who may or may not have been guilty and who may or may not have committed suicide to avoid prosecution. Thanks to the willing cooperation of a host of highly educated individuals, Mark and I had come as close as we possibly could to verifying that he was murdered. But that sense of accomplishment proved short-lived and oddly unfulfilling. It seems a truism of cold case research that hard-fought-for answers only lead to more questions. And so it was with the death of Frank Dolezal. Assuming he was murdered, who did it? And why? Granted, the already shaky case against him would have probably collapsed entirely when the Grand Jury scrutinized closely in September 1939 what little evidence that existed—an eventuality that would leave the sheriff with egg on his face and send local law enforcement off on yet another determined quest for the real perpetrator. Obviously, such a scenario would be embarrassing in the extreme to both O'Donnell and his office if it had occurred; but is avoiding public embarrassment in a high-profile case a sufficient reason for committing a murder? The "who" will most likely always remain a mystery, but the "why" is another matter. If one looks closely at the accumulated tangle of Kingsbury Run fact and legend, it is possible to discern vague hints of a plausible motive for Dolezal's death. There is a dark presence, silent and ominous, looming behind the bricklayer's vacant stare—the shadow of another man. Our journey was still not over; there were more chapters that needed to be written.

NOTES

All the quotations attributed to Mercyhurst faculty and students have been culled from the three sessions taped by Dave Brodowski.

Marcella Fierro's judgment is from one of her e-mails to me in winter 2008.

Part 3
RECKONING

Chapter 8
ALL IN THE FAMILY

When Eliot Ness died of a massive heart attack at his Pennsylvania home in 1957, he was a largely forgotten man in rather desperate financial circumstances. In the years just before his untimely death at the age of fifty-four, Cleveland's former safety director shared stories about his exploits in law enforcement with writer Oscar Fraley, a collaboration that ultimately resulted in Fraley's two books *The Untouchables* and *Four against the Mob*. During their wide-ranging conversations, Ness broke his silence on the twenty-year-old torso case and confided to Fraley that, while the very public police investigation was pressing forward largely under the guidance of Detective Peter Merylo, he had had his eye on man whom he felt was a viable—perhaps, the most viable—suspect in the officially unsolved murders, though exactly what led to these suspicions remains rather murky. At some undisclosed point in time, according to Ness, he had his operatives pick up the suspect and bring him in for questioning. Ness insisted that he administered a lie detector test that unequivocally pointed to his suspect's guilt, but he could do nothing due to the total lack of any supporting evidence. Once released from custody, the suspect entered a mental institution (where he subsequently died), a move that seemed to put him beyond the long arm of the law's reach. Ness called this mysterious figure Gaylord Sundheim: obviously not the suspect's real name and an extraordinarily curious pseudonym for a no-nonsense lawman like Ness to employ. Why not simply use the standard "John Doe"? Hovering over this entire cloak-and-dagger tale was the implication that the suspect was somehow connected to someone with political clout and that that connection, coupled with the facts that he was already institutionalized and the hard evidence against him was virtually nonexistent, ultimately saved him from the full wrath of the law. Over the years, variations of this intriguing tale, some of them embellished to the point of ridiculousness, have made the rounds in various true crime books.

At the time, Ness remained the only source for this curious coda to the city's most infamous murders; there seemed no other way to verify it. Some commentators insisted his story just did not add up. First of all, where did the lie detector come from? The East Cleveland Police Department owned the only polygraph in the Cuyahoga County area at the time; and, though Sheriff O'Donnell had—with great press fanfare—escorted Frank Dolezal there for a much ballyhooed test, there was no evidence that anyone else in city law enforcement, especially Safety Director Ness, had ever hauled out a suspect on a similar mission or that the East Cleveland Police Department had ever loaned the machine to Cleveland proper. And who would have administered the test? Certainly not Ness! His law enforcement credentials did not include polygraph expertise. For decades, the story remained either a plausible but unverifiable explanation for the Kingsbury Run horror or an imaginative flight of fancy on the part of the man who had once been the country's most famous law enforcement officer.

† † †

To this day, Democratic congressman Martin L. Sweeney of the 20th District ranks as one of the most colorful political figures Cleveland has ever seen. He was always good press, and the city's three dailies loved him. With Martin

A young man on the way up. Martin L. Sweeney in the early years of his political career. *Cleveland Press* Archives, Cleveland State University.

Sweeney around, there was no such thing as a slow news day. In 1932 he had broken—very publicly and very noisily—with the county party organization and put together his own alliance of disaffected and independent-minded Democrats. From then on, he battled vigorously on two different political fronts: Cuyahoga County's traditional Democratic Party structure and the city's Republican administration. His deep and obvious affection for his Irish forebears and their country was coupled with a predictable, virulent, and equally obvious hatred of the British. He was a noisy populist who prided himself on standing up for the working man. Every year he hosted a Cuyahoga River–Lake Erie excursion on the *Goodtime* for his rebel band of cronies and loyalists. Rather like Orson Welles's famous newspaper czar, Charles Foster Kane, Congressman Sweeney took a well-defined position on every public and party issue that came his way. It would not be an exaggeration to say that he personified "marching to the beat of a different drummer." The torso murders obviously provided him with the most potent and deadly political hand grenades any opposition party politician could ask for; and the seeming inability of Harold Burton's Republican administration, specifically Safety Director Eliot Ness, to make any real headway in solving the case ensured the maverick congressman an endless supply of fiery missiles to lob at city hall. Never one to turn away from a political brawl, time and again Sweeney railed at the Burton-Ness regime for wasting valuable time, manpower, and tax dollars on what he saw as relatively insignificant problems, such as the occasional city cop who might accept a dollar or two under the table to turn a blind eye to some bit of minor local corruption when a still unidentified murderer was raging through the decaying inner city, leaving behind human body parts as calling cards. In a typically virulent diatribe before the League of Independent Voter Clubs on March 6, 1937, he blasted Eliot Ness as Mayor Harold Burton's "alter ego." "We don't need 'Ness men' or yes men in City Hall," he raged in the *Press* on August 16. Over the months and years, Sweeney no doubt watched the endless parade of suspects hauled in by the police for interrogation with as much interest as any other Clevelander: the mentally deranged, the down-and-out, the violent and dangerous, the low-level criminals, the boozers and brawlers, those around whom any rumors of bizarre behavior swirled. There is no extant document of any sort or any bit of oral legend to confirm the discovery; but somehow, somewhere, sometime Congressman Martin L. Sweeney must have learned that Eliot Ness had his eye on a secret suspect in the grisly series of decapitation murders, and that man was not Frank Dolezal or anyone like him. The man upon whom Ness was focusing his attention and the full resources of his office, the man whom the safety director suspected had terrorized the city from the mid-1930s until the end of the decade was Sweeney's own cousin—the son of his father's younger brother—Dr. Francis Edward Sweeney.

Cleveland has always been a melting pot, boasting of one of the largest and most diverse immigrant populations in the country, perhaps second only to New York. The first Irish began to trickle into the city during the early 1820s; abandoning the traditional agrarian occupations of their homeland, many found work in the steel mills or as laborers building the Ohio & Erie Canal. However, it was not until the great potato famine of the 1840s that the Irish began settling along the southern shore of Lake Erie in substantial numbers. The exact genealogical history of the Sweeney family (or families) in Cleveland remains almost impossible for an outsider to untangle. As is the case for most common laborers of no particular civic distinction in the nineteenth century, very few traces of them survive in public records; the army of census enumerators, city directory compilers, and other public officials also commit a host of errors involving birth dates, ages, addresses, places of birth, and the proper spelling of names. A relatively small handful of first names, such as John, Joseph, Martin, Francis, Mary, occur over and over again. Middle names or initials that could help to distinguish one "John" from another are rare; and there are even variant spellings of the name Sweeney—"Sweeny" being the most common, "Swaany" the most creatively botched. (The "Swaany" version appears on the record of Francis Edward's birth. The name would have been provided by Francis's parents, and it is easy to imagine that, when uttered with a thick Irish brogue, "Sweeney" could easily have sounded like "Swaany" to whomever was recording the information.)

The grandparents of both Congressman Martin L. and Dr. Francis E. Sweeney were John and Catherine (née Mehan or Mahon) Sweeney. Burial records at St. Joseph Cemetery, detailing ages at and dates of death, suggest that the couple may have been the first Sweeneys from that particular branch of the family to emigrate from Ireland to northern Ohio, perhaps sometime in the 1840s or even earlier. At least two of their children turn up near downtown Cleveland during the final quarter of the nineteenth century: Dominic, owner and operator of a bar on Broadway (born 1850 or 1851) and Martin J. (Joseph), listed in city directories alternately as a laborer or teamster—born sometime between 1861 and 1863. Dominic's first wife, Winifred (née Callery or Collery), died at twenty-nine in 1881 after bearing three children and only seven years of marriage. Dominic married his second wife, Anna (née Cleary) two years later, a union that produced four additional children, including the future congressman Martin L. (born in 1885). Brother Martin J.'s sole marriage, to Delia O'Mara—or, possibly, simply Mara—resulted in six children, five of whom survived into adulthood. Francis Edward, the man who would potentially become his cousin Martin L.'s greatest political liability, was born in 1894. Dominic Sweeney died of pneumonia in 1897 at only forty-seven years of age; his brother Martin J. survived into his sixty-second year, dying in 1923. In an ominous foreshadowing of the lethal and destructive mental disease that would ultimately overwhelm his son Francis, Martin J. Sweeney spent the final years of his life in the mental hospital on Turney Road in Garfield Heights, one of Cleveland's older suburbs, southeast of the city proper. His death was attributed to "Apoplexy," with "Psychosis and cerebral Arterial Sclerosis" listed as contributing causes.

Though nine years separated Martin L. from his younger cousin Francis Edward, their lives took remarkably similar paths until the fourth decade of the twentieth century. Both suffered the devastating loss of a parent early in their lives. In 1897 the death of his father, Dominic, forced Martin L., then just twelve years old, to find a job to support himself and his widowed mother while he attended St. Bridget's Parochial School; when Delia Sweeney died of heart failure in 1903, her son Francis was barely ten years old. By 1910, his father, Martin J., had been committed to Sunny Acres Hospital with tuberculosis; thus, when he was still in his teens, Francis also found himself thrown suddenly into a very unforgiving adult world. Both men were obviously intelligent, tenacious, and determined; both struggled hard to rise above their working-class backgrounds and achieve some version of the classic American dream: for Martin L., the ultimate goal was law and politics; for Francis Edward, pharmacology and medicine. But the roads were rocky and included stints in blue-collar jobs. In the early years of his adulthood, Francis became an apprentice electrician, while Martin L. worked as a longshoreman and attended Cleveland Law School part-time.

In 1914, Martin L. passed the bar and—after serving a one-year term in the Ohio legislature (1913–14)—entered private practice. In 1917, Francis joined the U.S. Army and was sent to Europe, where he worked in medical supply for the remainder of World War I. The army granted him an honorable discharge with the cessation of hostilities in 1919. Somehow he received an unspecified, non-combat-related injury—serious enough to officially designate him as 25 percent disabled and render him eligible for an adjusted compensation certificate, apparently a monetary payment (or payments) similar to modern VA benefits. When he returned to civilian life, he served as vice chairman of the County Council of the American Legion. But a dark cloud had appeared on the horizon. Already suffering with tuberculosis, Francis's father, Martin J., began slipping into some sort of ill-defined mental disorder that forced him into the Turney Road mental hospital in Garfield Heights. The exact nature of his impairment remains impossible to determine; it may have been alcohol-related or even congenital.

The tenacity and sweat of the two Sweeney cousins began to pay off handsomely; both men stood on the brink of successful careers in their respective chosen fields. In 1922, Francis graduated from the Western Reserve University School of Pharmacy; in 1923, Martin L. was elected a Cleveland Municipal Court judge. That same year, Francis enrolled at John Carroll University, apparently to buttress his science background; for the following year, he enrolled in the medical school of St. Louis University, distinguishing himself as class president in his sophomore year.

During the 1920s, both men married and started families. Martin L. married Marie Carlin in 1921; Francis wedded Mary Josephine Sokol—a New York native working as a nurse at Cleveland's Charity Hospital—in 1927. The latter ceremony was performed by the Reverend Dominic J. Sweeney—Francis's cousin and brother of Martin L.—a circumstance that suggests that relations between the two branches of the family were at least cordial, if not particularly close. Francis completed the four-year medical school regimen at St. Louis University and graduated in 1928; he then returned to Cleveland to serve his internship at St. Alexis Hospital in the Broadway–East 55th neighborhood, close to where his older sister and her husband lived on East 65th. Francis and Mary settled in Garfield Heights, relatively close to St. Alexis Hospital by car or public transportation, and, coincidentally, also close to the mental institution where Francis's father had died only six years before. The Ohio State Medical Board granted him his certificate to practice medicine and surgery in 1929. The few surviving scraps of testimony relating to Francis Sweeney from his internship at St. Alexis and the early years of his medical practice paint a portrait of a dedicated, talented physician with a good sense of humor.

The 1929 stock market crash devastated Cleveland, as it had every other major American industrial center. The fiscal collapse left city fathers wrestling with a host of erupting socioeconomic catastrophes that were only exacerbated by the subsequent Depression. The early 1930s were, therefore, a pivotal period in Cleveland history. It was also a crucial time in the lives of the Sweeney cousins, for the courses of their respective lives began to diverge radically. In 1931, Martin L. successfully ran for the congressional seat left vacant by the sudden death of Charles A. Mooney of the 20th District. He launched his government career in the House of Representatives by lambasting his senior colleagues as "a lot of old women" in his inaugural speech—the sort of fiery diatribe that got him noticed, made him enemies, and became the hallmark of his oratorical style. A year later, the Cuyahoga County Democratic machine named Martin L. a delegate to the party's national convention and sent him off pledged to support Al Smith's bid for the presidential nomination. When he unexpectedly bucked the party bosses back home by switching his allegiance to Franklin D. Roosevelt, he precipitated a deep rift in the local Democratic Party structure, which festered for years. From that time on, Martin L. Sweeney was rarely out of the newspapers and never out of the public spotlight. The life of Francis Sweeney, however, was unraveling, though layers of family secrecy masked his precipitous downward spiral. In a twist of fate, Francis Edward, though he remained anonymous and was not identified publicly as a Butcher suspect, might have also dominated city newspapers during the latter half of the 1930s and was never out of the public's awareness.

The evidentiary traces of Francis Edward Sweeney's initial descent into the chaos of alcoholism and drug abuse survive only in the divorce and civil appearance docket records in the archives of the Cuyahoga County Probate Court. The first documented sign of trouble appears on December 1, 1933, when Mary Sweeney filed a complaint in Judge Nelson J. Brewer's court, questioning her husband's sanity. After the formal inquest the following day, an arrest warrant was duly issued and executed on December 5, which landed Dr. Francis E. Sweeney in a "Detention Hospital" for observation. (Civil Appearance Docket No. 250 does not specify the exact nature of Mary's complaint, but subsequent divorce papers, filed in 1934 and 1936, paint a deeply troubling picture of alcoholism, violence, and erratic behavior.) The facility in which Sweeney was temporarily incarcerated was City Hospital, on the near west side. Ironically, Edward Andrassy—killed in late September 1935 and usually designated the Butcher's first official victim—had been employed on and off as an orderly in the psychiatric ward of the hospital over an eight-year period, beginning in 1925, when he was nineteen. If there had ever been any contact between the two men, the initial meeting would have most likely occurred during Sweeney's period of observation in early December 1933. (Francis Sweeney remained at the hospital for a month. Whether this period of confinement overlapped with Andrassy's final weeks and days as an orderly at the facility is impossible to say; the hospital's employment records from that period do not survive.) On January 3, 1934, consulting psychiatrists K. S. West and C. W. Stone must have judged Francis Sweeney sane, for he was discharged into his wife's custody and care. Within ten days Mary was back in court standing before Judge Brewer a second time and filing another complaint. After three additional weeks at the hospital, the court system again discharged Francis.

During the first half of 1934 and into the fall months, Francis Sweeney's mental state undoubtedly continued to deteriorate, and his behavior became more violent and erratic. Life in the Sweeney household undoubtedly grew frighteningly unpredictable for Mary and her two boys—James Anthony, age three, and Francis Edward Jr., age five—at least during those periods when Francis was home. On September 11, 1934, Mary Sokol Sweeney filed for divorce, custody of her children, and the restoration of her maiden name—all of which the court granted in 1936. Though her first petition does not provide any specifics, the document does preserve a deeply disturbing portrait of a man sinking into a profound psychological disturbance. He would disappear from the family home frequently, for extended periods, without providing any explanation of where he was going or what he was doing. "She further states," reads the petition, "that he has upon many occasions humiliated her before her friends and has been abusive to her and their children both physically and mentally." Mary's second petition, filed in 1936, repeats these allegations and adds an extreme case of "Habitual Drunkenness" and "Gross Neglect" to the troubling mix. "The defendant became intoxicated almost continually beginning about two years after his marriage to this plaintiff, and remained in that condition practically all of the time until his separation from this plaintiff, which occurred in September, 1934."

On August 23, 1938—four years after separation from his wife and two years after his divorce—Francis Sweeney made application and was formally admitted to the Ohio Soldiers' and Sailors' Home in Sandusky, a few hours west of Cleveland. The date is significant on three counts. First, a week before, on August 16, three black scrap collectors and dealers uncovered the remains of victims nos. 11 and 12—the final two officially recognized torso victims—in a dump at the corner of East 9th and Lake Shore Drive. Second, on August 18, Eliot Ness led a highly publicized and heavily criticized raid of the shantytown sprawl in the Flats and Kingsbury Run that resulted in the arrest or incarceration of the inhabitants and the total destruction by fire of the hobo jungles themselves. Ness defended the Draconian measure by insisting it deprived the Butcher of victims. That only two of the officially recognized victims had been positively identified led authorities to assume that the killer selected his targets from among the socially dispossessed who gathered in the shantytowns—people who would probably not be missed and would certainly remain difficult for the police to identify, especially cases in which the corpses were not fresh enough to yield useable fingerprints. Finally, Francis Sweeney passed through the local justice system two additional times in the months leading up to his August 23 application for admission to the Soldiers' and Sailors' Home. On February 11, 1938, Dr. Leonard F. Prendergast, a dentist and probable friend, or at least acquaintance, of Francis Sweeney's, filed a complaint in Judge Nelson Brewer's court, questioning his sanity. This was the third time such a legal action against Sweeney had been undertaken in Judge Brewer's court. On February 28, the complaint was dismissed. On April 12, Francis's older sister, Mary, dragged her brother before Judge Brewer, only to have her complaint dismissed on April 25.

In her 1936 divorce petition, Mary Sokol Sweeney marked the onset of her husband's excessive drinking and subsequent mental decline at roughly mid-1929. The initial changes in his mood and behavior were most likely slight, so it's probably safe to assume that she either did not notice or deliberately ignored the first signs of looming trouble. Obviously, the situation had reached critical mass by December 1933, when she made her first complaint against him in probate court, an extraordinary action for the time in a domestic relations case, which resulted in his arrest and a one-month observation period in City Hospital. Just how conversant were relatives on either side of the family with the troubling details of the unfolding drama in the Sweeney-Sokol household? There is simply no way of knowing for sure. If Mary confided in anyone, she would have most likely done so with other members of the immediate Sokol family also living in the Cleveland area, not with her Sweeney in-laws. (There is evidence that the Sokols maintained close family ties: Mary and the two boys moved in with her sister's family on East Boulevard after she filed for divorce.) By the early 1930s, only three of Francis Sweeney's five siblings were still living—two married sisters (Mary older, Agnes younger), and an older brother, Martin J. Jr. (One of his two older brothers did not live beyond his third year, while the other, John Sweeney, died in 1912 of uremia.) What was the relationship dynamic among the surviving children of Martin J. and Delia Sweeney during the late 1920s and early 1930s? Again, there is, unfortunately, no way to know. But three of the four, including both sisters, were married and had children of their own, so there must have been some sort of interaction among the three families—certainly enough to make the two sisters aware of Francis's increasingly aberrant and dangerous behavior. No doubt the immediate Sweeney clan would have circled the wagons and done their best to keep the news of their brother's decline from escaping the immediate family. But would any murmurings of this evolving family tragedy have reached the ears of Martin L. Sweeney? And even if they did, would the congressman have taken much notice when he was deeply embroiled in his own local political wars? Just how much, if any, resonance would his cousin's precipitous decline have with him? Even if he knew about the brewing chaos, would he have regarded it as a sad but personal family nuisance or a potential political liability? Obviously, Sweeney's political career would not have been helped by public knowledge that he may have had a dangerous, alcoholic, mentally ill blood relative hidden away in the extended family closet. But in the early 1930s, that was not a pressing problem for Congressman Martin L. Sweeney; that dilemma was reserved for the future.

In his official application for admission into the Sandusky facility, Francis Sweeney enumerated "mitral insufficiency" and herniated discs among his medical problems and disabilities. (An attending physician added obesity and disease of the heart valves.) In a clear sign that his mind was unraveling, Sweeney wrote: "Life & its—stresses. Have contributed—to—the, total—toll, superimposed upon:" in the space where the admission form asked for comment on any "complications of case." Since his commitment to the institution was voluntary, he could—theoretically—come and go as he pleased; and the fragments of documentary evidence that survive in the archives at the Ohio Soldiers' and Sailors' Home show that he was in and out of the facility a number of times over the next seventeen years. According to records, he was "Discharged (Dropped)" in July 1940, only to be readmitted in February 1941. (An FBI document also places him in the Veterans Administration Hospital at Fort Custer, Michigan, during this seven-month period.) Discharged again from the facility in January 1942, he was back in December 1946. Hospital records also reveal he was unceremoniously booted from the home in 1951 by the administration; under the date of discharge, June 12, the letters "OC" appear—hospital code for "On Charges," meaning he was asked to leave for some unspecified reason—according to current staff members, most likely alcohol abuse. Sweeney's September 1953 petition for readmission was denied.

In the years between 1938 and 1951, there is little doubt as to where Francis Sweeney was, at least during his residencies at the Sandusky Ohio Soldiers' and Sailors' Home; but when his final stay at the facility ended in June 1951, he literally drops from the radar. In 1963, however, Dr. B. J. Chazin—chief of the Domiciliary Medical Service at the Veterans Administration Center in Dayton, Ohio—summarized both Francis Sweeney's physical condition and mental state, while also providing the clearest recounting of his winding odyssey through the VA system.

Francis Sweeney has been here in the Domiciliary on and off since 1946 [clearly establishing that he bounced back and forth between Dayton and Cleveland between 1946 and 1951]. In 1956 he was hospitalized. He was in Chillicothe Veterans Administration Hospital and returned from there with the diagnoses of schizoid personality, heart disease and cardiac enlargement. Since then he had numerous admissions to

The card showing Frank Sweeney's record of admissions and discharges from the Ohio Soldiers' and Sailors' Home in Sandusky. The "OC" written under the date 6-12-51 stands for "On Charges," indicating that he was asked to leave for an unspecified reason, most likely alcoholism. Courtesy of the Ohio Soldiers' and Sailors' Home, Sandusky, Ohio.

Brown Hospital [also in Dayton], mostly with the diagnoses of alcohol intoxication (he is being treated for it now on our Psychiatric Service). He is also a known drug addict with addiction to barbiturates. His most recent diagnoses are: acute brain syndrome due to alcoholism and chronic brain syndrome. He is considered incompetent by the Veterans Administration. [According to records at the Ohio State Medical Board, the assessment of incompetence was initially made in 1956 and substantiated by numerous subsequent examinations.]

Francis Edward Sweeney died in the Dayton VA facility on July 9, 1964. Family members had his body returned to Cleveland, where he was quietly buried in an unmarked grave in Calvary Cemetery. When Sheriff Martin L. O'Donnell had Frank Dolezal arrested in July 1939 for his alleged involvement in the torso murders, Francis Sweeney had officially been a resident at the Ohio Soldiers' and Sailors' Home for slightly less than a year. His movements around Cleveland after his return to the city from medical school in St. Louis in 1928 until his wife, Mary, sued for divorce in 1934 are easily established through city directories. But his whereabouts from late 1934 until his admission to the Sandusky home on August 25, 1938—an obviously crucial four-year span—remain a total mystery. Where was he? And, far more important, what was he doing?

Even for a highly trained investigator, the tangle of Sweeney genealogy stubbornly resists unraveling. In 1991–92, Sergeant John Fransen (since retired) of the Cleveland Police Homicide Unit received orders from then chief Edward Kovacic to explore a possible connection between the Kingsbury Run murders and the infamous Black Dahlia murder-bisection in 1947 Los Angeles, which ultimately led him to consider Francis Sweeney as the most likely suspect in the Cleveland killings. In his lengthy final report to his superiors, Fransen noted, "While reviewing the Directories, the names of MARTIN and JOHN SWEENEY appear multiple times. It cannot be determined if any though are brothers or if any were related in some manner to Francis E. Sweeney."

To twist the branches of the family tree to an even greater degree, public records indicate that Dominic and Martin J. Sweeney (the fathers of Martin L. and Francis E.) seem to have had a close relative, perhaps even a brother, named Myles (or Miles). The clearest indications of this are marriage records from the year 1874 and records from St. Joseph Cemetery. Dominic Sweeney married his first wife, Winifred Callery, on August 31; on August 17, Myles Sweeney had married Honora Callery. At first blush, this would seem to be a matter of two brothers courting and wedding two sisters. Records at St. Joseph Cemetery also show that Dominic and Myles Sweeney, along with "S. Marah" (a variation of Mara or O'Mara, the family into which Martin J. Sweeney married?), jointly bought about a dozen plots on September 28, 1881, the precipitating cause clearly being the death of John Sweeney (the father of Dominic and Martin J. and perhaps Myles) at the age of seventy-two. The last names of those interred in this substantial grouping of plots—Cullely [sic] (a probable perversion of Callery), Mehan, Mara, Colb, Hugger, and, of course, Sweeney—all occur in the genealogical record stemming directly from Dominic Sweeney and his two wives. The final burial in the family plots occurred in 1944. Although the name Mara appears in cemetery records in connection with this series of graves (probable relatives of Martin J.'s wife, Delia), there is no trace of Martin J. Sweeney, his wife, or any of their children in this grouping of family plots at St. Joseph; rather, in 1903, upon the death of his wife, Martin J. Sweeney bought a similar group of plots, some of which remain unused to this day, in Calvary Cemetery. Why did he choose a final resting place for himself and his immediate family in a different cemetery, away from his parents and Delia's relatives? Is there a simple, innocent explanation for his decision, or did it signal something decidedly more significant, such as a serious rupture in family relations? There is simply no way to know. Other than a rather pointed and nasty comment about excessive drinking, aimed at some distant members of the clan, the very few pieces of Sweeney family lore I have managed to uncover from this early period do not provide a satisfactory answer.

NOTES

When John Fransen turned in to his superiors his final report on Dr. Francis Edward Sweeney, he also submitted an impressively substantial dossier of related documents culled from a variety of sources, including the Ohio State Medical Board, the Montgomery County Medical Society, the Cleveland Probate Court system, and the Veterans Administration. This voluminous collection of official correspondence and other documents relating to Frank Sweeney's life and career is currently housed in the archives of the Cleveland Police Department.

The account of Martin L. Sweeney's early life and career is drawn from *The Encyclopedia of Cleveland History,* edited by David D. Van Tassel and John J. Grabowski. The congressman's subsequent public career is fully covered by Cleveland's three daily newspapers from the period.

The surviving records of Francis Sweeney's residencies at the Ohio Soldiers' and Sailors' Home are in the facility's archives.

Former Clevelander Marilyn Bardsley was the first researcher to breach the wall of secrecy that had been so carefully erected around Eliot Ness's fabled "secret suspect" and identify him as Dr. Francis Edward Sweeney. She obtained the FBI document briefly alluded to in the text through the Freedom of Information Act.

See the bibliography for a fuller description of these sources.

Chapter 9
CONSPIRACY AND COVER-UP

Conspiracy theories in public affairs have always been insidiously attractive—in part because a belief in nefarious plots protects us from having to confront the disturbing possibility of utter randomness in human affairs; in part because a good, meaty conspiracy appeals to some universal streak of paranoia in the human psyche—the disturbing yet, for some, curiously comforting notion that dark forces are forever working away behind the scenes, chipping relentlessly at society's security and peace of mind. When politics and fame are wed with high crimes and misdemeanors, conspiracy theories grow with the alarming rapidity of mold in a wet basement. The bigger and more complex the theory, the more attractive it becomes to the potential true believer. John Fitzgerald Kennedy's assassination actually grew out of the evil machinations of a gigantic international cabal of individuals and agencies, official and otherwise, including the CIA, the KGB, the Mafia, and the entire island nation of Cuba! But, as Benjamin Franklin once so wryly observed, three may keep a secret if two of them are dead: grand conspiracies invariably require the implausible cooperation of an enormous number of people—far, far too many to maintain a code of silence over time. Human nature being what it is, someone, sometime, somewhere is going to start leaking the details. In his book *The Cases That Haunt Us* former FBI profiler John Douglas notes that every case has its anomalies, those pesky details that don't seem to quite fit as neatly as we would like. And, as Vincent Bugliosi argues in both *Outrage: Five Reasons Why O. J. Simpson Got Away with Murder* and *Reclaiming History: The Assassination of President John F. Kennedy,* those who concoct and put forth theories about infamous crimes that are utterly at odds with the accepted wisdom of the official versions usually base their assertions on a couple of nuggets of information, those pieces of the puzzle that stubbornly refuse to fit comfortably with the rest, those anomalies that John Douglas says are a feature of virtually every case. These become the grains of sand discretely embedded in the oyster's shell, around which the theory's proponents form their pearls. Aspects of the case that do not fit the theory are twisted out of shape or—even worse—blithely ignored all together. Queen Victoria's grandson the Duke of Wales was really Jack the Ripper; Charles Lindbergh accidentally killed his own young son while playing a sick joke on his wife.

In the immediate aftermath of the torso murders and in the years that followed, the poisonous seeds of potentially alluring conspiracies were planted deeply and liberally watered. Actually, there are two separate alleged conspiracies in the history of Kingsbury Run, each accompanied by its own attendant rumor of cover-up. First, a troubled bricklayer by the name of Frank Dolezal had been charged in the murder-dismemberments but died under very questionable circumstances while in the sheriff's custody before he could go on trial. Was he murdered, and was there a concerted effort on the parts of everyone in the sheriff's office to conceal the crime and pass it off as a suicide? Second, Eliot Ness revealed that he had once had a secret suspect who may have been the elusive Mad Butcher, someone who may have escaped the justice system due to some sort of unspecified connection. There was a local doctor in town named Francis Edward Sweeney who, after a promising start in life, had tumbled into the abyss of drug addiction, alcoholism, and madness. And that doctor was, indeed, connected; his cousin was the colorful congressman from Cleveland's 20th Congressional District, Martin L. Sweeney. Could Ness's suspect and Sweeney be one and the same, and was there some sort of agreement among the elements of Cleveland's law enforcement community to keep Sweeney's name under wraps as long as he was safely hidden away in a mental institution? And if these two murky cover-ups could be linked, the result would be one of the grandest and most alluring conspiracies of all. In other words, is there enough surviving evidence to say with any certainty that there was a link between Ness's focus on Francis Sweeney and the tragic fate of the bricklayer while in the hands of Sheriff O'Donnell? A determined conspiracy buff could easily take the established facts and the documented events of the Dolezal affair and the Sweeney question and—by applying a little creative imagination and adopting a casual approach to connecting the dots—create a wonderfully complex theory as lurid and fascinating as any ever hatched by a Hollywood scriptwriter or penned by a veteran crime novelist. It would read something like this: after a couple years of pummeling the city's Republican administration with its failure to solve the Kingsbury Run murders, Congressman Martin L. Sweeney suddenly becomes aware that Dr. Francis Edward Sweeney, his own cousin, is Eliot Ness's prime suspect in the gruesome killings. To protect both the family name and his own career in public life, the congressman forges a desperate deal with his political enemies, Mayor Harold Burton and Safety Director Ness, to keep his errant relative's guilt secret, as long as the mentally unbalanced and murderous doctor is safely tucked away in an institution where he can do no further harm. A very public arrest and trial would accomplish little, save the humiliation of Francis's immediate family, his siblings, and their families. Since any formal proceedings would most likely result in Francis's institutionalization anyway, why not bypass the lurid spectacle of an official trial and send him straight to a mental hospital? That way everyone wins: the public is protected because the murderer is off the street; Francis's family is spared extreme embarrassment; and Martin L. Sweeney saves both family name and his reputation. But the murderer has never been identified publicly, and the populace still clamors for closure. So, to deflect any potential lingering or growing suspicion from his cousin, with his good friend and political ally Sheriff O'Donnell, Martin L. hatches an insidious plot to offer up a plausible alternative. Conveniently, special sheriff's deputy Pat Lyons has just fingered Frank Dolezal—an alcoholic, probably homosexual bricklayer with a shady past and a suspicious lifestyle, who is already known to, and at one time suspected by, the police—as a likely candidate in the brutal series of murder-dismemberments. Hence, Dolezal is arrested by the sheriff's office. But the fragile circumstantial case against him starts to unravel almost immediately after his arrest, and he also stubbornly refuses to confess to anything. A series of beatings administered over time by O'Donnell's deputies finally convinces Dolezal to make a trio of confessions, none of which holds up well under press scrutiny. If Frank Dolezal goes to trial, the entire case against him will likely collapse like the proverbial house of cards; the press will reexamine the circumstances surrounding his arrest with even greater intensity; and the City of Cleveland will look elsewhere for the actual perpetrator. To prevent this scenario from playing out, Sweeney and O'Donnell plot to have the bricklayer murdered and pass the death off as a suicide. That way the notion of Frank Dolezal's guilt will still be firmly lodged in the public mind, and O'Donnell can reinforce it by arguing that his suicide was a virtual admission from a man too frightened and guilt-ridden to face the rigors of the justice system.

Conspiracy theories, like stereotypes, don't just grow from nothing. There is always a grain (or grains) of truth around which the other elements of the case coalesce. Those may be so blown out of shape as to be unrecognizable, have far more weight heaped on them than they can support, be linked in ways that simply defy logic, or be focused on to the exclusion of other pertinent facts; but they are always there. Even though it was never articulated in any detail, a vague outline of the scenario presented here has hovered around the Kingsbury Run case for decades; and it is easy to see how such a tale could grow from the tangle of fact, rumor, and legend swirling through the city in the aftermath of the Kingsbury Run killings, Frank Dolezal's death, Eliot Ness's belatedly revealed tale of his unidentified suspect, and the relatively recent revelation that Francis Sweeney was that suspect.

The name "Dr. Francis Edward Sweeney" first rose out of the murky swamp of Kingsbury Run fact and legend in the early 1970s. Former Clevelander Marilyn Bardsley succumbed to the sheer allure of the city's most infamous and gruesome unsolved murder cycle and began a doggedly determined search for answers. Some of the major players in the drama—Sam Gerber, David Cowles, and Cuyahoga County psychiatrist Royal Grossman—were still living and willing to talk, but only up to a certain point. The wall of secrecy that Ness had put up around his suspect's identity thirty years before still held strong. Bardsley coaxed out verbal verification of the interrogation that Ness discussed with Oscar Fraley. (Why keep that part of the story secret? Ness had already broken his silence.) But the suspect's identity remained stubbornly elusive. The name "Dr. Francis Edward Sweeney" ultimately surfaced thanks to relentless digging on her part, coupled with a series of serendipitous circumstances. With a possible identity in tow, she was then able to pry some extremely reluctant grumbles of confirmation from a few of Eliot Ness's surviving associates. But that is as far as matters went. Save for a few public records documenting Francis Sweeney's mental decline, divorce, and admission to the Sandusky facility, there was nothing tangible, nothing that anyone could point to that would link the Sweeney name to the torso killings. Mental disease and alcoholism do not automatically translate into murder and mutilation. And, she further reasoned, publicly throwing around a name so prominent in Cleveland political and legal circles with virtually no backing would probably not be wise.

Matters changed significantly in 1977. Eliot and Elizabeth (his third wife) Ness were never able to have any children biologically, so they adopted a young boy, whom they named Robert Eliot Ness. Sadly, Robert died of leukemia on August 31, 1976. About a year later, Robert's widow, Sharon, donated a treasure trove of her late father-in-law's scrapbooks and papers to the Western Reserve Historical Society library in her husband's name. It would take a long time to sort through all this material, but during the process of examination and cataloguing some very odd, disturbing documents surfaced: five loose postcards and an incoherent letter, all sent from Dayton, Ohio, in the early 1950s and addressed, in an incredibly bizarre fashion, to Eliot Ness—"*Eliot-Am-Big-U-ous-Ness*," "*Eliot-Direct-Um Ness*," "*Eliot* (Es*op*hogotic) *Ness*," and, perhaps, most revealingly, *"Eliot (Head Man) Ness."* Each of the exceedingly weird postcards contains disjointed pronouncements and messages that literally seem to joke and taunt at the same time. The writer underlines words and individual letters seemingly at random and sprinkles everything with a liberal supply of dashes. Dayton's Deeds Carillon, a tall, thin structure resembling a knife blade, appears on the picture side of one card with a cryptic pronouncement on the message side. *"In- das- Freudiology | this-organ-has-the-eminence-of-a-reamer. | Whether-the-chimes | peal-the-note-for | bell-ringing-effect | or-not-is* the / Macbethean-question." This torturous illusion to Shakespeare's tragedy most likely refers to Macbeth's famous lines in act II, scene II: "Is this a dagger which I see before me, / The handle before my hand?" The references to Freud and the Bard indicate a certain amount of erudition breaking through the utter chaos of the writer's thought. And so it was with all five of the postcards: disjointed jokes, wild and sometimes incoherent pronouncements, and seeming taunts. Two things, however, were clear: the writer was suffering from some sort of severe mental disorder and was obviously obsessed with Eliot Ness. The Western Reserve Historical Society eventually duplicated the cards and occasionally put them on display—with the name of the apparent sender discreetly concealed.

Cleveland writer and journalist Fred McGunagle was the first to break the story of the mysterious postcards in print. In a March 9, 1989, article in the now-defunct *Cleveland Edition*, McGunagle provided an overview of the entire case and reiterated in detail Eliot Ness's then relatively familiar story of his secret suspect. He then took his readers along with him on a fascinating trip to the Western Reserve Historical Society library in Cleveland's University Circle. We sat with him at one of the tables while he waited. "I waited while a page searched and finally emerged with a carton of scrapbooks and folders," he wrote. "Impatiently, I leafed through them. There they were—the postcards." Though he described the five cards in detail, McGunagle did not disclose the name that appears on three of them; rather he left his readers hanging with a tantalizing, almost taunting coda. "There is a name on three of the cards which could be that of the sender or an allusion to a legendary mass murderer. Or both." He then added cryptically, "It's a common Cleveland name and it was—and is—a highly electable name. It may or not be the name of the murderer. Whether it is or not, I believe the cards I held in my hand came from the hand of the Mad Butcher of Kingsbury Run. It's as close to him as I care to have come." The "common" and "electable" "Cleveland name" that McGunagle so coyly avoided revealing was, of course, Sweeney. *"A-Signatur | The* Sweeney *Boy | R-member"* appears on one card; *"Good Cheer | The-American | Sweeney"* graces another. McGunagle quite rightly wondered if this later greeting might be a rather sly but obvious reference to Sweeney Todd, the infamous demon barber of Fleet Street who sent his customers tumbling into his basement where they were summarily dispatched, butchered, and turned into meat pies. On the third card to bear the Sweeney name, the sender clearly identifies himself as, "*F. E. Sweeney-M.D. / Paranoidal Nemesis.*" The obviously deranged doctor seems utterly consumed with Cleveland's onetime safety director and clearly must have derived some sort of ghoulish pleasure from taunting him with his stream of cryptic jabs. But what led to this fixation, and why would he describe himself as Ness's "Paranoidal Nemesis"? Was he just some kind of nut taunting a famous public official for his own incomprehensibly twisted reasons, or did he and Ness share a history so secret that virtually no one outside the very tight circle of trusted Ness associates knew about it?

Chapter 10

FEARFUL SYMMETRIES AND DAMNING COINCIDENCES

Eliot Ness really knew the identity of the Mad Butcher of Kingsbury Run, but, because of the perpetrator's "connections," he was forced to hold his tongue while the suspect's family hid him safely away in a mental institution and an innocent man met a cruel and unjust fate in the county jail. Murder, secrecy, dramatis personae in high places, a miscarriage of justice, and a cover-up: it's a tale to warm the heart and stir the blood of the most dedicated conspiracy buff. And if one merely takes a casual glance at this chain of assumptions, it does make sense. In fact, the outline of this scenario has been a persistent element of the Kingsbury Run saga for the last few decades. But is any of it even remotely true? To arrive at the truth in this morass of fact and assumption—assuming that is even entirely possible, given the amount of time that has passed and the quantity of information that has been lost—this lingering conspiratorial tangle must be pulled apart and each element in it analyzed for verifiability and reasonableness; further, the established facts, the interpretation of them, and the sensible assumptions based on them—the dots, in other words—need to be connected with enormous care and caution, always keeping in mind writer-profiler John Douglas's warning that every case has its anomalies. Things will never add up with the precision of an accountant's ledger.

WAS DR. FRANCIS EDWARD SWEENEY ELIOT NESS'S PRIME SUSPECT?

There is only one surviving official document that actually links Sweeney by name to the Kingsbury Run murders and the investigation: a police report submitted by Detective Peter Merylo on February 6, 1940. At the beginning of the two-page report, Merylo writes, "Dr. Sweeney was referred to us [Merylo and his partner Martin Zalewski] by Superintendent [David] Cowles of the

Scientific Bureau of Identification for a further check up, as it was believed that Dr. Sweeney might be a good suspect in the Torso Murders." The date of the report coincides with the first of Sweeney's on-again, off-again residencies at the Sandusky Solders' and Sailors' Home. Merylo notes that the doctor had come to stay with his older sister, Mary, on East 65th (the same sister who took him to court in April 1938 to question his sanity) while his niece underwent a surgical procedure at St. Alexis Hospital, where, ironically, he had served his internship. That it was David Cowles who dispatched Merylo and partner Martin Zalewski to the East 65th address is extremely significant. During Eliot Ness's Cleveland years, Cowles was a trusted member of the inner circle and one of the very few individuals close enough to the safety director to know precisely what steps his office was taking in the hunt for the Mad Butcher. Further, Cowles was obviously an active participant in Ness's largely behind-the-scenes maneuvering during the investigation. That Cowles knew to send Merylo and Zalewski to East 65th on February 5 shows clearly that someone from the Ness office was keeping Sweeney under constant surveillance and that that individual, or those individuals, reported back either to David Cowles or, perhaps, Eliot Ness himself. After the hotel-room interrogation in May 1938, the Ness office most likely always knew where Francis Sweeney was and what he was doing.

Unfortunately, there is little left of Sweeney's records in the archives of the Soldiers' and Sailors' Home; and what does remain has been transferred to microfilm, some of it virtually unreadable. In the 1970s, however, his file contained a note stating Cleveland police were to be notified if he left the facility. Unfortunately, the note—which has since disappeared—was not dated, so it is virtually impossible to ascertain exactly when official surveillance began. Had it been initiated at the time of Sweeney's admission to the home on August 25, 1938, or did it commence later, or earlier?

Arnold Sagalyn, a onetime assistant to Eliot Ness, remains the only other source to link Sweeney's name to the investigation in general and Eliot Ness in particular. Andrew Schug—a member of my research team and former trustee on the board of the Cleveland Police Historical Society—and I interviewed Sagalyn, then seventy-nine years old, by phone in October 1997. Immediately after his graduation from Oberlin College in 1939, Sagalyn became a trusted Ness associate who worked with him professionally and socialized with him personally both in Cleveland and later in Washington, D.C. Although he could not be certain of the time frame, Sagalyn remembered clearly that Sweeney was being kept under relatively constant surveillance by the Ness office. On one particularly memorable day, the designated tail was apparently indisposed, and Sagalyn drew the last-minute assignment of trailing the doctor around in his various wanderings around the city and keeping an eye on him. Incredibly, Sweeney knew he was being followed and turned the whole affair into a wildly elaborate cat-and-mouse game, jumping on and off street cars to see if poor Sagalyn could keep up with him. Surveillance was apparently not Arnold Sagalyn's forte, and Sweeney easily lost him in the crowds of downtown Cleveland. In a wicked display of his warped sense of humor, Sweeney later called the police—presumably the central station on Payne Avenue—and announced that he found his tail for the day sadly wanting in tracking skills and if the poor fellow should want to meet up with him later, he would be at Higbee's department store on Public Square around 2:00 in the afternoon.

The only other surviving document from a primary source that deals with Ness's suspect in depth is a taped interview with David Cowles conducted by Florence Schwein and police lieutenant Tom Brown on September 6, 1983. The then eighty-six-year-old Cowles provided a wide-ranging oral history of his days as head of the Cleveland Police Department's Scientific Investigation Bureau. When he turned his attention to the Kingsbury Run murders, he described Eliot Ness's prime suspect in minute detail, and there can be absolutely no doubt as to whom he is referring.

> There was a suspect in those murders. I won't mention any names. He was born and raised as a boy on the edge of the run [Jessie Avenue, now East 79th]. He later went into the service; in the service, he was in the Medical Corps. He came back, and he went to college [Western Reserve and John Carroll Universities] and went through medical school [St. Louis University's School of Medicine] and became an M.D. Married a nurse [Mary Josephine Sokol working at Charity Hospital]. Came back, did his internship at St. Alexis Hospital out on Broadway and finally kept going down and down and down with the booze. . . . We played on him for a long time. . . . A relative of his was a congressman [cousin Martin L. Sweeney]. And he [Eliot Ness] had to be very careful how we handled him.

Significantly, Cowles says, "There was a suspect in those murders." One suspect! A single, important suspect; not just one among many others! And, perhaps, by implication, he makes it clear that the Ness office did not regard Frank Dolezal as a viable candidate.

Though not as blatantly obvious as the Cowles description, there are a few other references that clearly point to Francis Sweeney. Perhaps the most remarkable came over the radio from legendary newsman Walter Winchell one Sunday evening in October 1938. "Attention Cleveland, Ohio," he trumpeted in his familiar "I've got a scoop!" manner. "The unsolved torso murders, more than a dozen of them in Cleveland, may result one day in the apprehension of one of Cleveland's outstanding citizens. . . . A fanatic, a medical man with great skill is allegedly responsible for the gruesome crimes in which all the murdered were dismembered." (The Winchell broadcast demonstrates how easily the details of a story can get warped in the retelling. Francis Sweeney was certainly "a medical man with great skill" but hardly "one of Cleveland's outstanding citizens.") The same elusive medical man to whom Winchell referred had previously made a brief but tantalizing appearance in the pages of the *Cleveland News* on April 9, 1938. "A once-prominent Clevelander, described as a physician in disrepute with his profession, is under suspicion in Cleveland's 11 unsolved torso murders. The man, said to have discontinued his practice [a charge made by Mary Sokol Sweeney in her petitions for divorce], is middle-aged [Francis Sweeney was forty-four in 1938], has some surgical skill and is described as being a powerfully built, chronic alcoholic [also one of Mary Sokol Sweeney's allegations] with apparent sadistic tendencies." Both Ness assistant Robert Chamberlin and Coroner Sam Gerber verified the *News* story, and Gerber obligingly added the rather startling revelation that the unidentified physician had been a suspect for about two years—in other words roughly since early 1936. Former county coroner A. J. Pearce had convened his torso clinic on September 15, 1936. The deliberations at that groundbreaking profiling session clearly pointed to someone with anatomical knowledge and surgical skill; and though the attendees seemed to go out of their way to avoid labeling the Butcher a doctor, the notion that Cleveland's infamous killer could be a deranged physician was soon abroad in the land. But if Gerber's assertion about the time element is correct, Frank Sweeney had attracted official attention several months before the clinic ever took place. As David Cowles reflected in 1983, "We played on him for a long time."

The years 1984–89 marked the fiftieth anniversary of Cleveland's notorious period of horror, and a number of "celebratory" retrospective pieces appeared in the local press to mark the occasion. An article by former *Plain Dealer* columnist George Condon appeared in the March 1984 issue of *Cleveland Magazine*. Coroner Sam Gerber was not only still living but was—incredibly— still on the job after forty-eight years. While researching his article, Condon confronted Gerber with a description of the killer that the coroner had given to the press forty-five years before: the Kingsbury Run murderer was a "broken-down doctor who becomes frenzied with drugs or liquor." The ever-combative Gerber denied he had ever said any such thing and insisted that "the newspapers made up that stuff." Cleveland journalistic standards may have been a tad looser in the 1930s and 1940s than they are today, but it still strains credulity to believe any reporter would make up something that specific without support or manage to manufacture a description that just happened to be exactly on target.

In 1988–89, then *Plain Dealer* staff writer Brian Albrecht published a similar retrospective piece and, in the process, became the resident local expert on the Kingsbury Run atrocities. By then, Gerber was gone. (He had retired in 1986 and died the following year.) But Albrecht was able to talk to David Kerr, the retired head of the homicide unit. (James Hogan had held that position during the Butcher's reign of terror, and Kerr was his immediate successor.) Kerr remembered, in Albrecht's words, that rumors about a renegade physician "related to a well-known political family, who had fallen into disrepute after receiving treatment in an insane asylum," still swirled through the Cleveland Police Department long after the killings had passed into history and "that police had focused their search on a once prominent, middle-aged physician said to be powerfully built and a chronic alcoholic with sadistic tendencies." Again, some of the details have become mangled. Francis Sweeney was not particularly prominent in the social sense; and he had fallen into disrepute, at least with his own family, long before he ever saw the insides of an institution. But, as with Gerber's alleged description of the killer, the specifics clearly point to him. In 2004, Thomas G. Matowitz Sr. (son of George J. Matowitz, Cleveland chief of police during the Ness years) recalled those same departmental rumors. "They had, I think, a very strong suspicion as to who was doing it. And they realized that they couldn't really prove it beyond a reasonable doubt. He [George Matowitz? Eliot Ness?] felt . . . that it was this doctor . . . who was doing it who apparently had gone around the bend. In fact, he wound up in a rubber room, I think, in some institution, if I remember correctly."

In late 1991 or early 1992, then Cleveland chief of police Edward Kovacic received an intriguing and rather strange request from the Los Angeles Police Department: investigate a possible link between the Kingsbury Run murders and the infamous 1947 murder-mutilation of Elizabeth Short, the Black Dahlia, in Los Angeles. (There had been a flurry of speculation in the popular media, primarily on television, that the torso killings could be related to the Short murder, and this may have prompted the official request.) Kovacic turned this plum assignment over to Sergeant John Fransen, now retired, of the Homicide Unit. It didn't take long for Fransen to decide that, though the notion of a link remained undeniably intriguing, there was no connection between the Black Dahlia and the Kingsbury Run victims. (The modi operandi of the respective perpetrators were significantly different. Though her face had been viciously mutilated, Elizabeth Short's killer left her head attached to the upper trunk. Whatever other indignities the Butcher may have visited upon the corpses of his victims, he always removed the heads. Decapitation, more than anything else, remained his signature—hence one of his sobriquets, the Head Hunter of Kingsbury Run. Also, though Elizabeth Short had been neatly bisected roughly at the waist—as had some of the Cleveland victims, the other mutilations to her corpse did not match the Butcher's methods. Last, the Dahlia had obviously been tortured before her grisly death. With the possible exception of victim no. 1, Edward Andrassy, who bore rope burns on his wrists, all of the Kingsbury Run victims seemed to have been dispatched quickly.)

As a savvy cop with a lot of investigative experience behind him, Fransen quickly picked up the vague remnants of Francis Sweeney's then fifty-some-year-old trail. The Kingsbury Run murders may rank among the very coldest of cold cases, but it is still officially open. As an investigator working on an infamous open case with the full weight of the Cleveland Police Department behind him, Fransen could compel the cooperation of official agencies far more readily than a layman might and compile an impressively substantial dossier on Dr. Francis Sweeney from a variety of sources, including the local probate court, the Cleveland Catholic diocese, the Western Reserve Historical Society, the University of St. Louis's School of Medicine, and the State Medical Board of Ohio. When he submitted his final report to his superiors, along with all the corroborating documentation he had amassed, Fransen harbored no doubts that the tale about his secret suspect that Eliot Ness had shared with Oscar Fraley was entirely true and that the man he described was Dr. Francis Edward Sweeney.

On May 6, 2003, the family of Officer James M. Limber donated to the Cleveland Police Historical Society Museum material relating to Kingsbury Run from his estate. The documents include several snapshot-sized photographs attached to individual pages, obviously removed from a small six-ringed notebook measuring approximately six-and-one-half by four inches. A brief, typed caption appears under each picture. Most of the photos are relatively neutral—shots of Kingsbury Run, the surrounding area, and piles of trash. Among these grim landscape studies, however, is a formal portrait of Francis Sweeney, the caption beneath it reading "Doctor X." The photographs are obviously not official police material; the format is too small, the mounting too casual, and the captions personal rather than officially formal. It would be easy to miss the importance of this small collection of material. Since Limber did not join the force until 1937 (toward the end of

Doctor X

the Butcher's activities) and his name does not appear in any of the extant police reports, it would seem logical to assume that whatever contact he may have had with the investigation remained strictly tangential. Yet this small collection of photographs constitutes one of the more significant pieces in the vast Kingsbury Run puzzle.

Sometime after former coroner Pearce's torso clinic, David Cowles put together a handpicked team of eight operatives, culled from the ranks of the police and low-level criminals, to work behind the scenes on the torso murders. Since Cowles controlled every aspect of their activities, nothing was known about this top-secret group until Cowles broke his silence during his 1983 interview with Florence Schwein and Tom Brown. When James Limber and a second officer, Tommy Whelan, graduated from the police academy in 1937, they were immediately assigned to work under Cowles. Since no one knew they were police officers, Cowles used them freely in undercover assignments related to the Kingsbury Run investigation. The Limber photographs (including the portrait of Francis Sweeney), therefore, come from the highest investigative levels, from the very heart of the search for the Mad Butcher.

Finally, there is that strange pseudonym "Gaylord Sundheim" that Eliot Ness used with Oscar Fraley to identify his prime suspect. It remains an extraordinarily curious concoction for a no-nonsense lawman like Ness to come up with. "Gaylord" was English slang for homosexual (there were suggestions that Sweeney might be gay); and "Sundheim" could be read as a rather elitist joke created by combining the two German nouns "die Sünde" (sin, misdeed, transgression) and "das Heim" (home): Gaylord Sundheim—Homosexual (or Gay) Home of Sin. It's all too convoluted and obscure for someone such as Eliot Ness to use, but it is right in line with the bizarre taunting and fractured phraseology that Francis Sweeney employed on the five surviving postcards he sent Cleveland's former safety director in the early 1950s. Gaylord Sundheim: a private joke Sweeney may have enjoyed with himself, perhaps something he shouted out at some point during the marathon interrogation of May 1938. Admittedly, this remains speculation; there is no way to know for sure.

Facing page: The photograph of Dr. Francis Edward Sweeney donated to the Cleveland Police Historical Society Museum by the family of Officer James M. Limber (dates of service, 1937–74). This is one of a series of pictures related to the Kingsbury Run investigation. It is shown here as mounted on a page taken from a small, ringed notebook. The "Doctor X" caption beneath the photo is part of the original document. It is obviously a formal portrait. Courtesy of the Cleveland Police Historical Society Museum.

The rumors about the secret suspect, the legendary but unidentified individual who enjoyed some sort of connections, the man who apparently wound up in an institution, had been swirling around in the Cleveland Police Department since at least the 1940s. Eliot Ness himself first went public in leaking the tale of his mysterious suspect to Oscar Fraley, and both David Cowles and Royal Grossman later added their own personal bits and pieces to the story. Was Dr. Francis Edward Sweeney Eliot Ness's legendary secret suspect? Emphatically, yes! Given all the evidence presented here, there can be no doubt that he was.

IS ELIOT NESS'S ACCOUNT OF A SECRET INTERROGATION INVOLVING A LIE DETECTOR TEST VERIFIABLE?

Again, the 1983 Florence Schwein–Tom Brown interview with David Cowles remains the most significant and informative surviving document. Since the Cowles account is the only existing hard-copy source of testimony about the entire episode (other than Ness's account as recorded by Oscar Fraley), it is worth quoting at length: "I was telling you about the fella that lived on the edge of the Run and became a doctor, etc. A relative of his was a congressman. He [Eliot Ness] had to be very careful how he handled it. However, we had a detail on him and picked him up. He had been drinking heavy too. We didn't bring him to jail but brought him to the Cleveland Hotel [now the Renaissance on Public Square]. Ray Oldag and I worked with him eight hours a day."

In response to Florence Schwein's question as to how long this all lasted, Cowles replied: "Possibly a week or two. We had Keeler come in with his lie detector from Chicago and examined him. When Keeler got through, he said he was the man, no question about it. 'I may as well throw my machine out the window if I say anything else.' We had some other man who worked in the courts in Detroit, and he gave us the same opinion." Commonly regarded as the father of the modern polygraph machine, Leonard Keeler of Northwestern University reigned as the ultimate authority on the device in the late 1930s— its use and the interpretation of the results. He reportedly had never found an innocent man guilty and had refined his interrogation technique over a lengthy period of testing, during which he had conducted literally thousands of interviews. Ness apparently knew Keeler from his Chicago days and was, no doubt, responsible for bringing him to Cleveland to question Francis Sweeney in secret. Ness always played his cards very close to his chest when it came to talking about potential suspects. Arnold Sagalyn does not remember Ness saying anything specifically about Francis Sweeney's possible guilt, beyond the comment that he found him "interesting." But Keeler's presence in that hotel room testifies to just how seriously Ness regarded Sweeney as a viable suspect and the sheer importance he attached to the entire operation.

It is an extraordinary tale of behind-the-scenes, cloak-and-dagger maneuvering worthy of any first-rate spy drama. The entire operation would require—indeed, demand—extremely careful and detailed planning; the coordination would have to be meticulously precise. Arrangements would have to be made with hotel management for a room—a place where those involved could come and go in relative secrecy, and guards of some sort could keep watch outside the door without attracting undue attention from hotel guests. Since an evening of dancing in one of downtown's many elegant ballrooms was one of the safety director's favorite pastimes, Ness probably established and maintained close relations with hotel managements throughout the city; so making arrangements for a place to conduct a secret, off-the-books interrogation session would be fairly easy. Obviously, the room could not be in a high traffic area; it would have to be in a corner somewhere or at the end of a relatively out-of-the-way hotel corridor where few employees and guests were likely to wander. It's unlikely Ness's operatives escorted the inebriated physician through the lobby, passed the registration desk to a hotel elevator, and then down a corridor to the waiting room in broad daylight. All of this must have involved spiriting Sweeney in through a back entrance and up or down a little-used stairway or elevator late at night or early in the morning. Obviously, Sweeney would have to be fed. After all, Cowles said this interrogation lasted anywhere from one to two weeks. This would mean, presumably, a steady stream of meals from the kitchen delivered to the room by hotel staff. Or did Ness arrange for food to be brought in from the outside? Surely, hotel staffers must have wondered and whispered about the strange goings-on—or was this something they were relatively used to? A man like Eliot Ness, accustomed to careful planning and comfortable working in secrecy, may have arranged for a room to be placed permanently at his disposal for contingencies just such as this. Plans would also have to be made to bring Leonard Keeler and his polygraph to Cleveland in relative secrecy; and once here, he would have to stay somewhere. The whole story provides a window to an age when the rules governing law enforcement personnel were considerably more lax than they are today. A modern-day civil libertarian would be horrified: one to two weeks of eight-hour-a-day grilling with, obviously, no Miranda rights having been read and no attorney present!

The only other accounts of this hotel-room episode are anecdotal and would probably be regarded as hearsay in today's legal environment. When, in the early 1970s, former Clevelander Marilyn Bardsley began digging into the Kingsbury Run mystery, her probings eventually attracted the attention of Royal H. Grossman, a practicing psychiatrist working for Cuyahoga County, who had been among the chosen few present at Sweeney's interrogation. Without naming the suspect, Grossman broke three decades of silence on the case and described the hotel-room scene in detail. He fixed the month of the marathon interrogation session as May 1938, and some of the specifics he supplied corroborate the details in David Cowles's oral account. Cowles maintained, for example, that Sweeney had "been drinking heavy"; Grossman alleged that the doctor was so intoxicated that it took them three days just to dry him out sufficiently for questioning. Elizabeth Ness also shared what she remembered from her husband's recounting of the session and added a fascinating detail of her own. At one point, Sweeney glared at Ness with such intense hatred and barely suppressed rage that the safety director stepped back toward the room door in case he needed assistance from those on watch outside in the corridor. But no one was there; the official changing of the guard had not yet been completed. Ness confided to his wife that he experienced a moment of genuine panic when he realized he was utterly alone with his unpredictable, possibly, exceedingly dangerous, quarry. A really startling admission, considering the dangers Ness had faced and the bullets he had dodged in his career!

Cowles's authoritative recounting of the entire hotel-room episode—recollected at the age of eighty-six and twenty-five years after the fact—may not be as precise and detailed as one could wish; but his story is solid; and it also addresses, in passing, the most nagging questions generated by Ness's account: where the lie detector had come from and who had conducted the examination. In the face of Cowles's testimony, there can be no serious doubts that both the nonstop interrogation and the lie detector examination did take place. Today, the old hotel, now refurbished, is one of Cleveland's most glamorous and glitzy establishments. Somewhere, though, in this spacious, glittering, upscale world from a bygone age there is a corridor where ghosts still hover; somewhere there is a room where the voices of the country's most famous lawman and his mentally unbalanced, potentially dangerous nemesis still echo.

Was There a Deal to Keep Francis Sweeney's Name Secret? (Part 1)

Though the very concept of a deal would be implicit in any story or legend that involved protecting a suspect's identity because of his connections, there is no surviving hard evidence of any sort to support such a claim. Obviously, such an arrangement—if it even existed—would be the epitome of the proverbial secret, smoke-filled backroom agreement; there would be no contract on file anywhere that anyone could point to. But, besides Francis, the only person in Cleveland who would benefit from any such backroom shenanigans was Martin L. Sweeney; the public revelation that the Mad Butcher of Kingsbury Run was his own cousin would not only utterly destroy his political career but splinter his coalition of rebel Democrats as well. But the reputation of maverick Democratic congressman Sweeney was probably the last thing on earth the leaders of Cleveland's Republican administration would care to protect—especially since Sweeney had attacked Mayor Burton and Ness so vociferously over a host of issues, notably their inability to catch or even identify the city's most notorious killer.

The issue of how much Congressman Sweeney actually knew about his cousin's predicaments and the nature of Ness's investigation is central to the whole notion of a secret deal; or, to repeat the famous question about President Richard Nixon from the days of the Watergate scandal in the 1970s with a slight variation, "How much did Martin L. Sweeney know, and when did he know it?" The *Cleveland News* story that pegged a degenerate physician plagued by alcoholism as a central suspect in the murders appeared on April 9, 1938; in the same story, Gerber acknowledged the existence of the mysterious medical man and added that law enforcement had been watching him, among others, for almost two years. Though Martin Sweeney undoubtedly knew Francis's life and medical career were unraveling, would he have guessed the unnamed suspect of the *Cleveland News* story was his cousin? As a good, loyal Democrat, would Gerber have alerted his fellow party member to that fact? Gerber's position was extremely delicate, difficult, even dangerous—his loyalties potentially divided sharply between his political party, on the one hand, and his duties to law enforcement, on the other. Walter Winchell's radio story about the potentially imminent arrest of "a medical man of great skill" hit Cleveland one Sunday evening in the middle of October 1938. Assuming Martin Sweeney heard the broadcast, would he have recognized the suspect Winchell described as his cousin? The *Cleveland News* and Walter Winchell stories are perhaps the only two accounts describing the unidentified renegade physician that have survived from the April–October 1938 period. How many other similar stories may there have been swirling through the city at the time, tales that an astute politician such as Martin Sweeney—with one ear to the ground, the other cocked to the wind, and surrounded by well-positioned cronies—would hear? It is probably safe to assume that by the middle of 1938, Cleveland's colorful congressman knew that his dissolute cousin had attracted the ever-watchful eye of the city's safety director. Ness's secret interrogation of Francis Sweeney occurred in May 1938—between the *Cleveland News* story and the Winchell announcement. Did Congressman Sweeney know about it? Probably not. It would be helpful at this point to recall David Cowles's statement from the 1983 interview: "I was telling you about the fella that lived on the edge of the Run and became a doctor, etc. A relative of his was a congressman. *He* [Ness] *had to be very careful how he handled it"* (my italics). The entire hotel-room episode had been the most carefully planned and secret element in the long-running hunt for the Butcher, so it is probably equally safe to assume that Ness and company successfully kept any news of it away from the public in general and Martin Sweeney in particular.

After the marathon interrogation, because of a total lack of hard evidence against him, save for Leonard Keeler's polygraph examination, Ness was forced to release Francis. There was simply nothing with which to charge him. In August 1938, neither Congressman Sweeney nor Safety Director Ness possessed the necessary ammunition to force a deal. Ness had nothing he could take to court, and he was far too much the straight-arrow lawman to allow malicious leaks about Francis Sweeney to escape his office. And unless there was at least the threat of some sort of public move on Francis, Martin Sweeney would have had nothing to react to. The two political adversaries most likely camped in their respective corners and glared at each other in stony silence.

Politics does, indeed, make strange bedfellows. On October 21, 1938—two months after the discovery of victims nos. 11 and 12, Ness's shantytown raid, and Francis Sweeney's admission to the Sandusky Soldiers' and Sailors' Home—two sworn political enemies, Mayor Harold Burton and Congressman Martin L. Sweeney, appeared together before the Veterans Administration in Washington, D.C., to lobby for the construction of a new VA hospital in Cleveland. The timing of this unlikely alliance will no doubt tweak the noses of the conspiratorially minded, prompting them to catch the faintest whiff of a deal. Why, they will ask, would Martin Sweeney cooperate with Harold Burton unless he were forced to somehow? But the motivation behind this uneasy partnership could conceivably be far more innocent. Those hearings had most likely been set up months in advance—long before the events of August 1938; no doubt both men saw the potential for their own personal political gain and the city's economic gain in such a rapprochement. It was a win-win situation; after all, who could possibly object to a project that would benefit the country's servicemen? If there was a deal to keep suspicions about Francis Sweeney quiet, it was most likely not struck in August of 1938.

Was Frank Dolezal Arrested and Charged to
Deflect Attention from Francis Sweeney?

The only set of circumstances that would support such an allegation is the apparent desperation on the part of Sheriff O'Donnell and his office to get a confession out of Dolezal and have him officially charged as quickly as possible once he had been arrested, in July 1939. But there had to be a reason for this haste; something would have had to have happened in spring or summer 1939 that would have provoked the need for a scapegoat. There is, however, no surviving evidence that there was such a trigger. Francis Sweeney had been safely tucked away in Sandusky for almost a year and would not be discharged until July 30, 1940; if he left on his own, he would be shadowed by the Ness office; there had not been any new torso victims for almost a year—since August 1938. The Butcher had never allowed a gap that long to lapse between victims—save for the period between the Lady of the Lake, assuming she was one of the Butcher's targets (September 1934), and the deaths of Edward Andrassy and his never-identified companion (September 1935). What reason would there be for a scapegoat in July 1939? The *Plain Dealer* did resuscitate the Kingsbury Run story on April 2 of that year, with a full-page piece, complete with pictures, exploring the question of what type of person the perpetrator must be; but that retrospective rumination hardly seems sufficient in itself to provoke the Dolezal affair a couple months later. There had to be something else.

Pat Lyons began digging into Kingsbury Run independently of the sheriff's office and the Cleveland Police Department around April 1938; and, according to his own written account, he did not have any contact with Sheriff O'Donnell or identify Frank Dolezal as a potentially viable suspect until sometime after January 1939. Exactly when did Martin L. Sweeney learn that his down-and-out cousin was Eliot Ness's prime suspect? If that decidedly unpleasant revelation dawned on the congressman sometime during the first six months of 1939, it could possibly serve as the event that triggered a determinedly desperate hunt for a suitable patsy. If such were the case, that Pat Lyons was independently offering up Frank Dolezal as the Mad Butcher during the same period, it would be among the very happiest of coincidences. And all the surviving evidence suggests it was, indeed, a coincidence. Lyons's papers make it clear that he considered a wide range of potential suspects; his notes give no sense that he was zeroing in on Dolezal or anyone else because of outside pressure. The evolution of his interest in the bricklayer clearly grows out of his own investigation. The notion, however, of possible collusion between two high-ranking public officials such as Sweeney and

O'Donnell to take advantage of a possible suspect—conveniently fingered at just the right moment by an independent investigator—for the sole purpose of protecting a relative is certainly the sort of insidious plot that whets the appetite of the most determined conspiracy buff. But there is no proof that anything like this scenario actually took place. It would be just as easy, and perhaps more logical, to argue that Sheriff O'Donnell, a Democrat, latched on to Frank Dolezal because he saw an opportunity to score major political points against Republican rivals Mayor Harold Burton and Safety Director Eliot Ness. During the 1930s, the sheriff's office was not seriously involved with criminal investigations, per se; its purview was running the county jail. It would, therefore, be seen as a stunning political victory if O'Donnell and company could succeed where Ness and the police department had failed.

And O'Donnell badly needed a public victory in the early months of 1939. He had won election to the sheriff's office in 1936 (previously, he had been mayor of Garfield Heights); and in less than two years, he suffered two major public relations disasters. In September 1937, he endured a savage lambasting in city papers over what the *Press* termed "Cleveland's worst prison break." On September 23, in an editorial titled "Sheriff O'Donnell's Carelessness," the paper reported that three bank robbers and an accused murderer armed with guns, apparently smuggled to them by family members and friends during totally unsupervised visits, broke out of the county jail. "The desperados capture five deputies, lock them up and get out of the modern, well-equipped jail without a shot being fired by deputies or guards on duty," raged the city daily. "They jump into automobiles, begin a mad dash through congested downtown streets, manhandle a city judge, take his car from him, [and] run down a woman waiting for a street car in a safety zone." The revelation that the bank robbers had already broken out of one prison and that the sheriff had been warned they would likely try it again only compounded the embarrassment.

Already sporting one black eye, the sheriff acquired another in late 1938. From the very beginning of his administration, O'Donnell let it be known publicly that he was a staunch believer in home rule when it came to matters of law enforcement. The practical implications of this rather vague but innocuous-sounding legal philosophy, however, put him and his office on a direct collision course with the Cleveland Crime Commission and its operating director, William E. Edwards. O'Donnell adopted a hands-off policy when it came to enforcing gambling laws in Cuyahoga County, believing that any crackdown on known illegal gambling establishments should come from the local municipalities in which they operated, not the sheriff's office. Fed up with O'Donnell's apparent refusal to move against entrenched gambling interests in the county, the Crime Commission launched a petition drive to have him ousted from office in early June 1938—a move that enjoyed the active vocal support of both County Prosecutor Frank T. Cullitan and Safety Director Eliot Ness. Within a week of the commission's action, the Federation of Women's Clubs and the Steel Workers' Organizing Committee joined the crusade; by August, Labor's Non-Partisan League also threw its support behind the ouster movement. The entire gambling issue, coupled with the ouster drive, grew so contentious that it wound up on the agenda of the fourth annual meeting of the Interstate Commission on Crime—an organization that included attorneys general from thirty-five states—held at the Hotel Cleveland in early July. By the end of August, organizers behind the drive, growing more and more confident that their attempt to boot the sheriff out of office would be ultimately successful, were even planning an "ouster O'Donnell" rally at Public Hall. In early September, however, the entire movement fizzled when organizers proved unable to secure the necessary twenty-five thousand petition signatures to force the issue.

By the end of 1938, O'Donnell had endured three months of intense, relentless battering in city newspapers. When Pat Lyons approached him in January 1939 with his carefully worked out plans to finally apprehend the elusive Mad Butcher, the beleaguered sheriff—no doubt still smarting from negative press coverage—leapt at the chance to both score a major triumph in the city and rehabilitate his badly damaged public image. And, indeed, in the heady early days after Frank Dolezal's arrest on July 5, 1939, the sheriff's image shone brightly with a renewed luster, only to tarnish again when questions over Dolezal's arrest, treatment, and death mushroomed over the next month.

In late March 1940, in probate court, Charles Dolezal filed his two lawsuits against O'Donnell and his deputies over his brother's death—an event that may have been a major catalyst in the rebirth of the ouster drive in early May. Headed by the Cleveland Bar Association, a coalition of various organizations and individuals again banded together and dedicated itself to forcing Martin O'Donnell out of office. The scrappy sheriff shot back by threatening to subpoena every individual who signed an ouster petition. The entire legal brouhaha ended suddenly in June 1941 when O'Donnell died of a massive heart attack.

WAS FRANK DOLEZAL MURDERED?

"Isn't it convenient that he should kill himself just before going on trial?" mused the high-ranking official in the Cleveland Police Department—who asked for, indeed demanded, anonymity—when Mark Stone and I consulted with him. In fact, as he lounged back in his chair and allowed a knowing smile to wander across his face, he said it again. "Isn't it convenient that he should take his own life before going to trial?" And that, of course, is precisely the issue. It seems too convenient that Dolezal should commit suicide about a week before his case was to be presented to the Grand Jury, especially since the case against him had been in a state of collapse almost since his arrest on July 5. At the very least, it can be said with total certainty that his death remains highly suspicious and that it did not occur in the manner so meticulously laid out in the official record.

As I dealt with this question at length in chapter 6, here I will confine myself primarily to a brief review of the most pertinent facts that challenge the official version of events, as well as Coroner Gerber's suicide verdict. The time of death is at issue. Dolezal supposedly hanged himself around 1:55–2:00 P.M., yet Dr. Fried testified at the inquest that when he examined the body less than a half an hour later, "he was entirely cold. The entire body was cold." In response to Gerber's prompting, Fried even implied that rigor mortis had already set in. A corpse could not be "entirely cold" after only a half an hour—especially on the fourth floor of a building on an eighty-some-degree day, and full rigor would not occur for several hours. If Fried is correct, death occurred far earlier in the day than 2:00 P.M. Inquest testimony records that sheriff's deputies Hugh Crawford and Clarence Smart cut the noose around Dolezal's neck with a pocketknife provided by Sheriff O'Donnell. But none of the extant photos of the noose material show the kind of jagged edge that would result if the sheeting were cut in such a fashion. All visible ends of the cloth appear frayed and worn, not freshly cut. Inquest testimony from those deputies present also agrees that Dolezal was left hanging for only a few minutes—sufficient time to cause asphyxiation, perhaps, but nowhere near long enough to cause the deep mark on his neck visible in the pre-autopsy photographs taken eighteen hours later, which, in his official verdict, Gerber described as being one centimeter in width. According to Marcella F. Fierro's July 24, 2007, e-mail to me, "A cloth ligature would not leave a 1 cm mark on his neck. It was caused by something else"—something like the rope clearly visible in two of the extant photos, the existence of which is never referred to in any of the official documents dealing with Frank Dolezal's death.

Charles Dolezal filed his two petitions in the Court of Common Pleas on March 27, 1940, charging Sheriff O'Donnell and his deputies with gross misconduct in their handling of his brother Frank's arrest and incarceration. The first listed seven different causes of action—primarily false arrest and mistreatment—against O'Donnell, Pat Lyons, and four of the sheriff's deputies. The second accepts Gerber's suicide verdict for purely legal reasons and then charges O'Donnell with negligence for failing to prevent it, even though his prisoner had been reportedly placed on suicide watch following the two unsuccessful attempts on his own life. Within days of Dolezal's filing, Eliot Ness requested a formal report from Detective Peter Merylo detailing Pat Lyons's activities in the whole affair. (Ness would obviously be quite familiar with O'Donnell and the four deputies charged in the suits, but he may not have known anything about Pat Lyons and his role beyond what the newspapers had reported at the time of Frank Dolezal's arrest.) Clearly Ness was trying to put together an overall picture of the episode; after all, the reputations of some in law enforcement—indeed, the city itself and all of Cuyahoga County—were at stake. Merylo turned in his less-than-flattering report on Lyons's conduct—discussed at length in chapter 2—to the safety director on April 2, 1940. In June 1941, Sheriff Martin L. O'Donnell suddenly died of a heart attack. On March 28, 1942, the law offices of Minshall & Mosier contacted Pat Lyons by mail: "The above entitled case [the first of Charles Dolezal's suits] in which you are a party defendant has finally been adjusted satisfactorily. Will you please get in touch with me [partner W. E. Minshall] upon receipt of this letter so that I may discuss with you the expense involved in connection with this lawsuit?" Exactly what this summons means for Pat Lyons, especially from a financial point of view, is unclear; but the final pages of the paperwork for both of Charles Dolezal's suits contain the following: "settled and dismissed at defendants' cost." As county employees, O'Donnell and his deputies would have been covered financially by the Massachusetts Bonding and Insurance Company and the National Surety Corporation; but Pat Lyons's onetime status as a special deputy or agent to the sheriff may not have guaranteed him any such protection.

With Sheriff O'Donnell's death, a political obstacle had been conveniently removed; and the Cuyahoga County Commissioners cleaned house. "I think that what I can remember of the sheriff's department in those days," mused Thomas G. Matowitz Sr. (son of the then police chief George J. Matowitz), "it left a little bit to be desired." And the Dolezal affair was only the tip of the iceberg. Bad blood had been brewing between the sheriff's office and the county government for years, primarily over the issue of illegal gambling. On December 4, 1940, as part of a Grand Jury probe, Common Pleas judge Frank D. Lausche ordered the sheriff's office to search the Harvard Club in Newburgh Heights (an infamous gambling den already busted once by Eliot Ness) and seize any and all gambling equipment and devices. In an incredibly brazen act of defiance, sheriff's deputy Harry Brown entered the establishment, looked around for approximately sixty seconds, and left empty-handed. Absolutely furious over what he saw as obvious and deliberate disobedience, Judge Lausche ordered Brown to appear in court and explain why he had ignored a direct order from the bench. When Brown refused to show up, Lausche cited him for contempt. Thomas Matowitz characterized O'Donnell's deputies as political "hacks and thugs." The prevailing patronage system "just dragged them in, pinned a star on them, turned them loose." In the hunt for a new sheriff, commissioners turned to the Cleveland Police Department and appointed Inspector Joseph M. Sweeney (no relation to Martin L. and Francis) to the position—an action that signaled a real change in legal philosophy as to how the sheriff's office would be managed. O'Donnell had not been a lawman; he was a politician. And those who remember the sheriff's office in those days insist the real power in the county jail was Deputy Clarence Tylicki. All of this legal sparring, culminating in the settling of Charles Dolezal's two lawsuits in his favor and the commissioners' draconian move on the sheriff's office, adds up to a tacit admission on the part of county officialdom that the mess at the county jail had to be cleaned up and, at the very least, something was seriously amiss with the official version of Frank Dolezal's death.

Was Dolezal murdered? A preponderance of the existing evidence would suggest that he was—though precisely when, by whom, under what circumstances, and exactly why are difficult to say. At one end of the scale is the Grand Conspiracy Theory explanation: like a mafia don, Martin L. Sweeney put out a contract on Frank Dolezal, and Sheriff Martin L. O'Donnell passed the order down to his deputies, who then carried out their instructions with the ruthless efficiency of mob soldiers. By the end of August 1939, the case against Frank Dolezal was in deep trouble. The Grand Jury was scheduled to reconvene in September; Frank Dolezal's death occurred on August 24. That this alleged suicide should occur so close to his scheduled appearance before that august legal body suggests that someone was in a mighty hurry to resolve the entire affair—through either another confession or some other means—before the Grand Jury reconvened. At the other end of the spectrum stands the Accidental Death Theory: an attempt to extract a more definitive confession from him that would stand up under press and legal scrutiny simply got out of hand. The jailhouse personnel who daily dealt with their prisoner face-to-face were obviously the sheriff's deputies. Given Thomas Matowitz Sr.'s characterization of them as "hacks and thugs," it is not difficult to believe one or more of them took matters into their own hands, out of either frustration or sheer meanness. At the inquest, Gerber gave O'Donnell the chance to distance himself from his gang of deputies. After the sheriff asserted that his office "treated him [Dolezal] better than the average prisoner," Gerber asked, "Do you think it would have been possible, without your knowledge, for any Deputy to have taken advantage or disadvantage of your instructions?" Though he chose not to walk through the door that had just been opened for him, O'Donnell at least kept it ajar. "Do I think it is possible? Well, I can't say what goes on in there, but I know this, my Deputies do follow orders."

It would be both instructive and sobering at this point to recall the testimony provided by the Jones sisters on the final day of the inquest. "They were worrying him [Frank Dolezal] to death," Lillian declared, "and they were punching him and beating him and everything like that." And Ruby Lee insisted she overheard Pat Lyons say, "He will never come out of the County Jail alive. . . . He will never walk out of the County Jail." Why would Lyons make such an incriminating statement in public? Assuming he was not just blowing hot air, what was the basis for this damning pronouncement? It could have been a simple case of macho bravado. Gerber did not subpoena him to testify at the inquest—a clear indication that no one thought Lyons had anything directly to do with Frank Dolezal's death. Though he had been deeply involved in Dolezal's arrest and had been celebrated in the press for apparently cracking the case, he had had nothing to do with the interrogation or anything else that happened in the county jail after July 5—at least as far as that can be determined. Though he does appear in some of the photographs that show Dolezal being escorted to a waiting automobile, Lyons virtually disappears from newspaper coverage shortly after the July 5 arrest. He may, therefore, have been feeling marginalized; hence, his statement could be read as a boastful attempt to reinsert himself into the heart of the action—to appear "in the know" and more deeply involved in subsequent events than he actually was. Or perhaps he did know what was going on behind the closed jailhouse door; thus his damning pronouncement should be seen as a clear admission that Frank Dolezal's death was indeed deliberate and premeditated.

WAS THERE A DEAL? (PART 2)

The evidence is regrettably even less than scant; but if there was a deal of some sort, it was signed, sealed, and delivered after Frank Dolezal's death on August 24, 1939. The only way to approach this touchy issue seventy years after the fact is to look very carefully at what the people potentially and most likely involved did or did not do, what they did or did not say in response to unfolding events during the crucial three-year period between Dolezal's death and Eliot Ness's departure from Cleveland in 1942. "It'll Be Lonesome without Sweeney," read the lead to a *Press* story by politics editor Richard L. Maher in the September 14, 1939, issue of the city daily. Three weeks after the death of Frank Dolezal and slightly more than two after the inquest, "Congressman Martin L. Sweeney, the West Side Democrat who once led the insurgent legions of the local democracy will sit out the current mayoralty campaign." Citing the demands of his congressional seat in the nation's capital, "For the first time in years the congressman will watch the campaign parade go by and won't be marching along as he has in every campaign since 1931." Maher's piece was brief, but the announcement was startling: Cleveland's most colorful and noisy politician suddenly withdraws almost entirely from the local public arena! And that this dramatic move should occur less than three weeks after Dolezal's "suicide" and the subsequent inquest is obviously food for thought. Sweeney reveled in the local political scene with the gusto of a gourmand contemplating a five-course meal. Could his duties in the nation's capital really be so pressing that he would so readily vacate the Cleveland arena and the political fray? Or was there something else behind this announcement? Again, the possibility of some sort of deal rears its head. Was Sweeney's decision wholly his own and a mere coincidence in its timing, or was there a quid pro quo understanding with city administration that compelled him to remove himself from local politics, at least temporarily, to protect his cousin's identity? But, again, did either side have the necessary ammunition to force a deal? In the immediate aftermath of the secret May 1938 hotel-room interrogation, Eliot Ness had little or nothing that pointed to Francis Sweeney's guilt, save a polygraph examination conducted by the best in the business plus his personal suspicions. There was, however, nothing to support any kind of overt legal action against him; and, quite frankly, Martin Sweeney had nothing with which to bargain. What could he possibly threaten to do or say if the Burton-Ness regime didn't keep its suspicions about his cousin's potential guilt secret? It's hard to believe he would lower himself to beg for a favor from men he attacked and despised. Presumably, by August–September 1939, nothing had changed, in spite of the controversy surrounding Frank Dolezal's arrest and death. Given these circumstances, what sort of deal could possibly have been struck?

It's safe to assume that if there were enough solid evidence to arrest and try Francis Sweeney for murder, no one in city administration or law enforcement would sit still for a deal that would protect him in any way. Police Chief George Matowitz's son and grandson insist unequivocally that he would never accept any kind of arrangement that would shield a murderer whose guilt could be proven in court; and both of Detective Peter Merylo's daughters similarly maintain that their father, totally apolitical animal that he was, would never keep quiet in the face of any secret wheeling and dealing. Martin

A shotgun marriage or a simple case of political expediency? Cleveland mayor Harold Burton (left) and Congressman Martin L. Sweeney lobby the Veterans Administration in Washington, D.C., on October 21, 1938, for the construction of a new VA facility in Cleveland. The secret hotel-room interrogation and lie detector test involving Francis Sweeney had taken place in May of that year. Frank Dolezal would be arrested in July 1939. Although it is tempting to see this unlikely alliance as part of some sort of deal between the Burton administration and Congressman Sweeney, there is no surviving hard evidence that this was the case.

Sweeney may have been a huge thorn in the side of Cleveland's Republican administration; but he was, when all is said and done, a duly elected public official who—smoke-filled backroom shenanigans aside—had done nothing illegal. To tar and feather him with suspicions, however well founded, about his cousin's guilt in the city's four-year nightmare would amount to nothing more than character assassination—hardly the sort of behavior to be expected from straight arrows such as Eliot Ness and Mayor Burton. If some sort of "understanding" was reached between Martin Sweeney and the city administration, it would probably be more accurate to call it an arrangement or a gentlemen's agreement rather than a deal. The secret hotel-room interrogation and polygraph examination may have convinced Ness of Francis Sweeney's guilt; but because of the lack of any hard evidence to support this conclusion, there was little the Ness office could do but keep the doctor under constant surveillance, in the hope of a break. Perhaps, just perhaps, the message was somehow conveyed to Congressman Sweeney that his cousin was "a person of interest" and that his surveillance would continue, but discreetly. And in return for this promise of total discretion, the city administration expected him to behave himself on the local political stage and use whatever influence he may have with his deranged cousin and his family to keep the former safely off the street. The clearest indication that there must have been some sort of mutually agreed upon understanding that resulted in a shroud of secrecy around Francis Sweeney's name that lasted for decades lies in the subsequent words and actions of three men most deeply involved in the Kingsbury Run investigation: Eliot Ness, Royal Grossman, and David Cowles. When in the 1950s Ness broke his twenty-year silence about his suspect with Oscar Fraley, he opted for the odd pseudonym "Gaylord Sundheim" rather than the actual name, "Francis Edward Sweeney"; Grossman, citing a promise made to Ness, would not divulge the suspect's name to researcher Marilyn Bardsley in the early 1970s; and Cowles refused to use it when he talked about the case on tape in 1983. Three men who had been deeply involved in the clandestine hotel-room interrogation, arguably the most significant event in the Kingsbury Run murder investigation saga, all refused to use the suspect's name. At first blush, it certainly sounds like a deal. When Bardsley finally uncovered the Sweeney name on her own, she phoned Cowles (then living in Florida) and simply said, "Francis Edward Sweeney." The startled Cowles barked back at her, "Who gave you that name?"

WAS DR. FRANCIS EDWARD SWEENEY THE MAD BUTCHER OF KINGSBURY RUN?

Today, no hard evidence exists to support Francis E. Sweeney's guilt; and obviously there was none, or at least very little, seventy years ago. If there had been any solid proof, Ness would have had Sweeney arrested and brought up on charges immediately. However deep his suspicions may have been and in spite of what his gut may have told him, Ness was forced to turn the doctor loose after interrogation, because there was no solid evidence beyond Leonard Keeler's polygraph examination—which, of course, would not have been admissible in court. Unfortunately, Arnold Sagalyn's unsuccessful attempt to trail Sweeney around downtown Cleveland cannot be precisely dated; but as late as February 1940 (the date of Peter Merylo's encounter with him), the doctor was still being carefully watched. All of this ongoing surveillance suggests that Ness and his colleagues, in spite of Keeler's assertion, were not entirely convinced of Sweeney's guilt, still trying to build their case against him, or—at the very least—simply keeping an eye on him.

In the best of all investigative-forensic worlds, the accumulation and objective analysis of evidence should point to the most viable suspect. The process should not work the other way around; one should not pick a suspect and then try to fit the evidence to him. (For the Ripper killings and the Lizzie Borden case, veritable industries have grown around the practice of identifying a suspect—usually someone who, up until this posthumous coronation, had never attracted any attention—and then tailoring the body of known facts to fit him or her.) Unfortunately, with Kingsbury Run, there is no other way to proceed. In the many years since the murder-mutilations and the investigation into them, too much vital evidence has disappeared, too much of the official paperwork has been dispersed by the bureaucratic winds, and the names of too many other potential suspects have been lost. All of the numerous, compelling, but undeniable links between Francis Sweeney and the Kingsbury Run killings may remain purely circumstantial and coincidental. They are, however, numerous and compelling.

In her petitions for divorce, Mary Sokol Sweeney places the beginning of her husband's mental decline, alcoholism, aberrant behavior, and violence in 1929—two years after their marriage and roughly a year after the completion of his medical studies. She did not, however, file an affidavit questioning his sanity until December 1, 1933. It was an extraordinarily bold legal move for a wife and mother to take in the early 1930s, and one can only assume that life in the Sweeney household must have become unbearably difficult, perhaps even dangerous. Modern profiling theory holds that serial killers are propelled into their murderous activities by a stressor of some sort—something in their private lives that tips an already fragile and damaged psyche over the edge. After a month-long incarceration at City Hospital in December 1933, Francis Sweeney was discharged into his wife's custody. Within a week, she was back in court filing another affidavit. The first piece of the Lady of the Lake's body washed up on the shores of Lake Erie on September 5, 1934; but then Cuyahoga County coroner Arthur J. Pearce fixed the never-identified woman's time of death as March 1934. To this day it is still not entirely clear that the Lady of the Lake should be officially counted among the torso victims. Assuming, however, that she belongs in the Butcher's tally and that Sweeney was, indeed, her killer, it is possible to argue that Mary Sokol Sweeney's legal assaults on her husband's sanity in December 1933 and January 1934 were the necessary triggers that pushed him to murder for the first time. And, interestingly enough, this first victim was a woman. Had Francis Sweeney conveniently transferred his rage toward his wife to another target?

Two young boys discovered the body of the first officially recognized torso victim, Edward Andrassy, at the base of Jackass Hill on September 23, 1935. Andrassy's only reasonably steady job had been at City Hospital, where he had been employed as an orderly in the psychiatric ward. He seems to have left, or been fired from, the facility around the time Judge Nelson J. Brewer had Francis Sweeney arrested and committed to City Hospital for observation and psychiatric evaluation in response to Mary Sokol Sweeney's affidavit. Unfortunately, it is impossible to determine exactly when Andrassy lost his job at the hospital, but he could conceivably still have been working there during the period of Francis Sweeney's incarceration—thus affording an opportunity for the two men to meet and establish some sort of relationship. Andrassy reportedly used the ruse that he was a doctor specializing in female problems as a seduction tool, and investigating officers found medical books in his room at his parents' house after his death. Medical texts were expensive and not easy to come by; if the two men did become acquainted at the hospital in late 1933 or early 1934, Sweeney could easily have been the source of those books. Assuming this scenario is correct, why, then, would Francis Sweeney kill Andrassy almost two years later in September 1935? In response to another stressor or to something Sweeney perceived as a personal betrayal? The presence of rope burns on Andrassy's wrists suggests rage or some sort of payback; and as dismembered bodies accumulated over the next three years, those marks would remain an utterly unique feature. Whoever murdered Andrassy seems to have known him and apparently to have killed him out of anger.

In the months following Flo Polillo's murder-dismemberment in January 1936, Cleveland police ransacked her background and sorted through the seemingly unending tally of low-level criminals who moved in and out of her life. One individual of more than casual interest whom they were never able to track down was a mysterious man named "Al," who allegedly supplied her with drugs. There is at least one report that Francis Sweeney once introduced himself as Al. As a licensed physician, whether or not he was actually practicing, Sweeney could obviously write prescriptions for just about anything and trade them for money, booze, or other favors. The members of my research team always wondered how he managed to support himself financially between 1934, when his practice fell apart, and August 1938, when he entered the Sandusky Soldiers' and Sailors' Home. The obvious answer is that he trafficked in illegal medical favors—writing prescriptions, patching up hoodlums, perhaps even performing abortions. (During the investigation into the death of victim no. 7—a young woman—in February 1937, the whole issue of illegal abortions and "baby farms" came into play.)

There is substantial evidence, both documentary and anecdotal, that Francis Sweeney did, indeed, survive and feed his addictions to alcohol and drugs, both while on the street and during his various incarcerations, by writing prescriptions for himself and others. The dossier John Fransen compiled on him in 1991–92 contains a letter from Ray Q. Bumgarner, director of the Dayton, Ohio, Veterans Administration Center (dated January 11, 1962) addressed to Dr. H. M. Platter, secretary of the Ohio State Medical Board. "We have a veteran under care in our Domiciliary by the name of Frank E. Sweeney who is a licensed M.D.," Bumgarner writes. "Although he has been under care at a mental hospital as a psychotic and is still rated as incompetent by the Veterans Administration, we have a continuing problem with him in that he writes prescription[s] for barbiturates and tranquilizers in fictitious names for his own use." Bumgarner then petitions that Sweeney's medical license be revoked: "We believe it would be very helpful in caring for this veteran if it would be possible to get his license suspended while at this Center and this fact made known to the local pharmacists." John Fransen's dossier contains other pieces of similar correspondence dealing with the same issue dated right up to Frank Sweeney's death. An October 2, 1953, FBI report addressed to "Director, FBI" (presumably J. Edgar Hoover) contains the following: "Mr. HULL [Coubron Hull, Domiciliary Officer at the Veterans Administration Center in Dayton] stated further that SWEENEY is constantly in trouble at the Veterans Administration Center with the courts there, and has been charged ten times out of twenty appearances in court with being drunk." In 1938, during Francis Sweeney's initial residence at the Sandusky Soldiers' and Sailors' Home, the facility enjoyed a unique working relationship with the Ohio State Penitentiary in Mansfield. Honor prisoners were allowed to work at the home and live in one of the many cottages on the grounds. Among those so "honored" was Al (Alec or Alex) Archacki, serving a sentence for armed robbery. He had met Frank Sweeney a couple of years before, during a chance encounter in a downtown Cleveland restaurant or bar. (At that time, though Sweeney had bought him a drink, Archacki remained wary of any further contact with him because he sensed he was gay.) Now, in the fall months of 1938, the two men met again in the facility mess hall and immediately established an ideal working relationship: Sweeney wrote Archacki prescriptions for drugs, and Archacki reciprocated by supplying him with booze—just perhaps, the sort of mutually beneficial alliance Sweeney could have forged with Edward Andrassy at City Hospital in 1933–34 and with Flo Polillo in 1935.

There is also an intriguing chain of events and circumstances clustered around the discovery of victims nos. 11 and 12 on August 16, 1938, that would seem to point to Francis Sweeney, just three months after the marathon Ness–Keeler interrogation session. Now, two more victims popped up in a city dump on East 9th—in clear view of City Hall and (tauntingly?) right under Eliot Ness's nose. According to the autopsy protocols, the skeletal remains of no. 12 were about a year old; and very little evidence tied them to Kingsbury Run, save for the knife marks at the joints. But there were serious questions about victim no. 11 that never made the city papers and, in fact, remained undisclosed until the Cowles interview of 1983. County pathologist Reuben Straus performed the examination of the badly decomposed pieces of the corpse and judged the unidentified female one of the Butcher's victims. The woman's remains were then turned over to the Western Reserve Medical School anatomist T. Windgate Todd, one of the principal participants in coroner A. J. Pearce's torso clinic, declared them the pieces of a body that had already been embalmed—not a legitimate torso victim! By phone, Todd immediately summoned David Cowles to his office and—indicating the remains—angrily told the startled Ness associate that they definitely did not belong to a legitimate torso victim; these were pieces of a body that had already been embalmed!

The Erasmus V. Raus & Sons funeral home stood across the street from St. Alexis Hospital (where Sweeney interned) on the north side of Broadway. The Raus establishment handled all of Cleveland's indigent bodies and stood close to the building that housed the offices of Doctors Edward Peterka and Francis Edward Sweeney in the mid-1930s. "It's a known fact; we had people who testified, who would testify to it," Cowles explains in the 1983 interview, "that across the street from the hospital [St. Alexis] was an undertaker who buried all the indigent bodies. And it was a known fact that he'd [Sweeney] go over there and would amputate, or just remove, the way these bodies were found, exactly the same way he would do with unknown bodies in the war." Unfortunately, Cowles's statement is hardly a model of clarity, but the potential implications of it are stunningly clear. Sweeney enjoyed some sort of privilege at the Raus funeral establishment that allowed him, apparently, to practice surgical techniques or indulge himself in anatomical study on the unclaimed indigent bodies. Assuming that Sweeney was responsible for depositing the disarticulated remains of an already embalmed body at the East 9th dump site, the motivation and subsequent chain of events might read something like this: Filled with rage and booze over his one-to-two-week ordeal with Ness and company at the Cleveland Hotel, but also boiling over with elation that the safety director and his forces could not charge him with anything in spite of Keeler and his polygraph, Sweeney desperately looked for a way to vent his anger and defiantly thumb his nose at his tormentor. Since he knew the Ness men were watching him carefully, committing another murder-dismemberment was out of the question. So he opted for the next best thing. He disarticulated an embalmed corpse of an unidentified female at the Raus funeral home without the director's knowledge and somehow managed to spirit the pieces to the East 9th trash heaps, where he dumped them in full view of Eliot Ness's office—the ultimate "Take that Mr. Ness! Catch me if you can!" (Just how the skeletal remains of no. 12 might fit into this scenario is difficult to say.) Two days after the August 16 discovery of the remains, the safety director led his heavily criticized raid of the shantytown complex sprawling through the Flats and into Kingsbury Run. The dispossessed and otherwise homeless residents were rounded up by the police, and their dilapidated hovels were razed and torched. On August 23, perhaps feeling the heat in more ways than one, Francis Sweeney formally petitioned the Sandusky Soldiers' and Sailors' Home for admission. Two days later, he officially took up residence.

Two other chapters from the Kingsbury Run saga are relevant in forging a possible, though circumstantial, link between Francis Sweeney and the killings. In late August 1938, a onetime homeless drifter by the name of Emil Fronek—then working in Chicago as a longshoreman—shared a lurid, potentially valuable tale with Cleveland's law enforcement and press establishments. In late 1934, Fronek had been wandering aimlessly up Broadway one dark evening toward the East 55th intersection. Unemployed, alone, hungry, and desperate, he somehow managed to wind up on the second floor of a Broadway office building, where he found himself loitering outside a doctor's office. The affable physician took pity on him and graciously offered him a meal and a badly needed new pair of shoes. Halfway through his simple repast, he began to feel woozy, and, fearing his benefactor had drugged him, bolted from the office and ran down Broadway toward Kingsbury Run, with the doctor in hot pursuit. Fighting desperately to hold on to his senses, Fronek finally managed to lose his pursuer in the sprawling blackness of the Run. Three days later a couple of transients roused him from his deep, drug induced, and comalike slumber. If true, his narrative could have served as a valuable blueprint for how the Butcher overpowered his prey, but Cleveland law enforcement tended to dismiss his undeniably fascinating tale—in part because Fronek could not locate the office four years after the fact, in part because in late 1938 city officialdom believed the Butcher's lair lay much closer to the center of the city than the Broadway–East 55th intersection. The office (or offices) that Sweeney shared with Edward Peterka were, of course, situated on Broadway, across from St. Alexis Hospital, close to East 55th. Assuming Sweeney had actually been Fronek's would-be attacker, the later history of the Kingsbury Run murders might have unfolded far differently if the onetime drifter could have led Cleveland police directly to the doctor's former office door.

On July 22, 1950, a couple of residents from the Wayfarer's Lodge on Lakeside out for an afternoon stroll happened upon the badly decomposed disarticulated remains of a white male at Norris Brothers, a moving company on Davenport Avenue. Sickening odors had been permeating the area for some time, but apparently no one could pinpoint exactly from where they were coming. The dismemberments had been carried out with a familiar and frightening skill not seen in Cleveland since the Mad Butcher left the remains of his last two officially recognized victims in a dump site at the corner of East 9th and Lakeside twelve years before. "Was he back?" asked nervous city residents. Eventually identified as Robert Robertson, a drifter and resident of the Wayfarer's Lodge, the unfortunate man dominated city papers for weeks as private citizens and public officials alike wrestled with the disturbing notion that the horror of the 1930s had returned. Interestingly, in the weeks before Robertson's remains had turned up, Norris Brothers employees had watched in bemused incredulity as a heavyset man in his fifties with thinning gray hair had ascended a pile of steel girders stored on the west end of company property on a daily basis for about twenty minutes of sunbathing. After six weeks of this bizarre ritual, the sunbather, as he was known to Norris Brothers workers, suddenly ceased his regular visits—just about the time the unpleasantly oppressive odors began to circulate through company grounds.

In July 1950 Francis Sweeney still resided at the Soldiers' and Sailors' Home. It would be another year before facility administrators summarily booted him out, apparently due to his alcoholism. The admittedly vague description of the mysterious sunbather provided by Norris Brothers Company employees eerily matches what Sweeney would probably have looked like in mid-1950. At fifty-six years of age and with his hair, indeed, thinning, he was severely overweight. In his official police report of February 5, 1940, Merylo labeled him "fat and soft"; and Sweeney's surviving medical records actually use the word "obese" in describing his physical condition. The VA would not officially judge Sweeney incompetent until the mid-1950s; and since his residencies in Sandusky were voluntary, he could have left facility grounds whenever he felt like it. Conceivably, he could still haunt the Cleveland area at will, staying, perhaps, with his older sister as he had in 1940 while his niece underwent surgery at St. Alexis. The entire six-week sunbathing ritual, virtually on top of the dismembered remains of a corpse, smacks of the taunting and the twisted humor that characterized Francis Sweeney's bits of "correspondence" and his antics when he knew he was being watched. Though he had clearly been under close surveillance by the police through the late 1930s and very early 1940s, there is simply no way to know whether that had continued after Eliot Ness left Cleveland in 1942.

Was Dr. Francis Edward Sweeney the Mad Butcher of Kingsbury Run? He clearly fits the profile worked out in Coroner A. J. Pearce's torso clinic. He possessed both the necessary familiarity with the Run to move through it easily while avoiding detection and the requisite surgical skills to perform the expert dismemberments. As someone who had once been a practicing physician, he may have owned an automobile or at least had access to one, thus transporting the remains of his victims would not have been a problem. According to the very few existing physical descriptions, he was big and strong enough to have done the job. His documented mental disease, alcoholism, and drug abuse could easily serve as the catalysts for those brutal bursts of murder and mutilation. The progressive nature of his mental and physical afflictions could explain the relative sloppiness in the dissection Gerber noted in some of the later victims. His deterioration over time could also explain the curious shift from the careful staging of the earlier crime scenes (no. 4's head rolled up in his pants, parts of Flo Polillo's body neatly packed in produce baskets, et cetera) to the seemingly casual dumping of later victims in the Cuyahoga River or Lake Erie. And insofar as Sweeney's movements can be traced, it can be said that over and over again, he was more or less in the right place at the right time. He was clearly the primary focus of Ness's investigative efforts; the safety director kept him under relatively constant and tight surveillance for at least the three-year period 1938–40. Unfortunately, it is now impossible to determine how many other serious suspects the safety director may have considered and who they may have been. Several physicians crop up in the extant official police reports, many of them named. Some, such as a certain "Dr. Kerr" appear more than once, but none of these leads seems to have panned out. Ness also believed strongly enough in the possibility of Sweeney's guilt that he went to the considerable trouble of arranging the secret hotel-room interrogation and polygraph examination of May 1938, an extraordinary, well-planned operation as detailed and intricate as any dreamed up by a Hollywood scriptwriter, and not the sort of initiative Ness would have undertaken lightly.

Peter Merylo remained the only prominent figure in local law enforcement deeply involved in the Kingsbury Run investigation who seems not to have accepted Sweeney's guilt—or, at the very least, to have entertained serious doubts. Although he left the Cleveland Police force in 1943, he pushed forward his own investigation into the torso killings and pursued other suspects he considered viable until his death in 1958. A dedicated lawman like Merylo would never have wasted his time and energy in such a fashion if he were convinced that Sweeney was the Butcher.

At some undetermined time, Sweeney began sending his nemesis Eliot Ness jeering cards and letters, though it is difficult to tell whether he was simply venting his rage at the individual who, in his mind, unfairly tormented him or taunting the most famous lawman in the country for not being able to build a case against him—perhaps both. (In 1948, his growing obsessions with the safety director even prompted a rambling and incoherent four-page missive to J. Edgar Hoover complaining of "Nessism"—an action that triggered a minor FBI investigation into who he was and whether his communications to the bureau should be taken seriously.) But no matter how twisted and unhinged his logic became during his various rants at Eliot Ness, Sweeney always remained clever enough to never admit anything openly. He slipped only once—and even that seeming admission is subject to interpretation. If he was, indeed, referring to Sweeney Todd, the demon barber of Fleet Street, when he identified himself as *"The-American / Sweeney"* on one of his post-cards to Ness, then this is as close as he comes to a confession.

With any cold case, especially one this old, a researcher-commentator is going to be limited by the material that has survived. Usually, there is simply no way of telling how much potential evidence may have been lost and what the nature of that evidence may have been. Though an investigator must always be mindful that the body of extant fact and evidence—simply by the luck of the draw—may produce a somewhat skewed picture of events, he should not, indeed, cannot, build castles in the air by speculating about what is not there to be analyzed. In cold case research, the dots must be connected conservatively and with extraordinary caution. Jack the Ripper still remains the best known and most infamous serial murderer in history, and the vast catalogue of books detailing his crimes and searching for his identity run the gamut from lurid, tabloid sensationalism to carefully reasoned scholarship. Donald Rumbelow, however, one of the most renowned Ripper scholars, confesses that students of the crimes are occasionally haunted by the notion that when Jack's true identity is finally revealed in the hereafter, all the Ripperologists will stare blankly at each other and mumble, "Who?" Is it similarly conceivable that the Butcher could turn out to be someone of whom no one has ever heard or just a name buried in a corner of an obscure police report? Cleveland's official search for the Butcher was certainly not perfect, and law enforcement personnel may not have fully understood the serial killer dynamic; but by the standards of the day, the investigation—the most massive and intense in city history—was professional and thorough. Though possible, it is difficult to believe that the perpetrator could pass so completely unnoticed with so many trained professionals searching for him. As of this writing, most of the existing evidence—circumstantial though some if it may be—and all the accumulated Kingsbury Run legends point, fairly or unfairly, to a single individual: Dr. Francis Edward Sweeney.

NOTES

The Merylo report of February 6, 1940, describing his and partner Martin Zalewski's interrogation of Francis Sweeney is among the detective's collection of reports, papers, and manuscripts. See the bibliography for a fuller description.

The taped interview with David Cowles and the transcripts of that interview are both on file at the Cleveland Police Historical Society Museum.

The account of the Walter Winchell announcement concerning the imminent arrest of a suspect in the torso murders appears in the unpublished manuscript Peter Merylo coauthored with *Cleveland News* staff writer Frank Otwell. It is a part of the collection referred to above.

Thomas Matowitz's quotations are from an interview conducted by Mark stone on June 10, 2004.

John Fransen's dossier on Francis Edward Sweeney is on file at the Cleveland Police Department.

The letter to Pat Lyons from the law firm of Minshall & Mosier is in his collection of documents. See the bibliography for a fuller description.

Mary Sokol Sweeney's two divorce petitions are in the Cuyahoga County Probate Court Archives.

Marilyn Bardsley provided me the account of Al Archacki's encounters with Frank Sweeney.

Marilyn Bardsley obtained the FBI documents relevant to Frank Sweeney through the Freedom of Information Act. See the bibliography for a more detailed breakdown.

Chapter 11
CONCLUSIONS, FRAGMENTS, AND LOOSE ENDS

All the recoverable pieces of the huge puzzle have been gathered and arranged as carefully as possible. From newspaper accounts, police reports, and other documents—both public and private—it is clear that certain events took place, that certain statements were made. From those same sources it can be inferred that some things apparently did not happen or seem not to have been said. Silences and inactivity assume significance through timing. If common sense dictates or suggests that a particular player in the drama would most likely respond in some way to a single occurrence or chain of events, and that individual remains inactive or silent, then that lack of response becomes at least interesting and, perhaps, significant. Does all this add up to a premeditated murder as part of a grand conspiracy and cover-up to shield the identity of a suspected killer? A tabloid journalist would undoubtedly scream "yes"; but I can only say, "Murder, apparently; cover-up, obviously; conspiracy, perhaps!"

† † †

At first blush, Eliot Ness's almost total silence during the period of Frank Dolezal's arrest, incarceration, and death seems strangely uncharacteristic of a man who enjoyed such a glowing reputation for honesty and incorruptibility. If the safety director knew—or, at least, suspected—that Francis Sweeney was guilty of the Kingsbury Run murders, why would he sit idly by while the local press meticulously raked over and reported every lurid detail, charge, and countercharge in the unfolding Dolezal saga? Wouldn't the country's most famous G-man, the straight shooter sporting a Boy Scout reputation, have intervened in some way, especially when it became clear to him that Dolezal's rights under the law were being so seriously violated that the ACLU had to ride to the rescue? But, realistically speaking, what could Eliot Ness have done? The only avenue open to him would have been a legal one; and as safety director of the City of Cleveland, he did not have the authority to wield any control over the sheriff of Cuyahoga County. When Detective Peter Merylo stormed into Chief of Police George Matowitz's office after Dolezal's arrest, loudly declaring that his own careful investigation had cleared the man of any involvement, his boss counseled him that political realities in the city were such that the sheriff must be allowed to build his own case without any interference from other law enforcement agencies. Presumably, those same political realities would have constrained Eliot Ness as well.

Peter Merylo, however, was something of a bull in a china shop. He would never have allowed political considerations to interfere with the apprehension and prosecution of criminals; for him, a guilty man was a guilty man. It isn't clear from his memoirs whether the press came to him, seeking his opinions, or he went to them. Either way, Merylo became the Deep Throat of the entire Dolezal affair. As long as reporters respected his anonymity, he exposed the holes in Dolezal's trio of confessions and the sheriff's case to the eager gentlemen of the press establishment who dutifully repeated every nugget of information he gave them. Did Ness know of the veteran cop's behind-the-scenes maneuvering? I suspect he did; thanks to his group of secret operatives, sometimes referred to as the Unknowns, there was very little going on in the underbelly and back alleys of Cleveland that the safety director didn't know about. The working relationship between Ness and Merylo was professional but strained. Merylo didn't particularly care for the safety director, but he did outwardly respect the lines of authority. I also suspect Ness would have turned a blind eye to Merylo's activities because, at the very least, the detective's anonymous whistle-blowing was a way of challenging the sheriff's office without violating some code of public political decorum.

The case against Frank Dolezal had been unraveling in fits and starts almost from the day he was arrested, July 5. By the end of the month, almost all of the allegations concerning his guilt in the Kingsbury Run murders had evaporated, leaving behind a single charge of manslaughter in the death of Flo Polillo. As Merylo watched from the sidelines, he probably reasoned the entire case would collapse completely when presented to the Grand Jury in September and Dolezal would be released, an assumption probably shared by Eliot Ness. There was, therefore, no need to publicly intervene on his behalf; the slow grinding of justice's wheels would ultimately solve the whole problem. It must have come as a very nasty surprise to both men when, on August 24, Dolezal turned up dead. Peter Merylo's daughter Winifred Buebe remembers that Dolezal's unexpected death left her father deeply disheartened. As one who believed in the system of American law enforcement and had worked in that field most of his professional life, he found it hard to understand and impossible to accept that such a glaring miscarriage of justice could be allowed to happen.

Eliot Ness did not attend the inquest Gerber convened on August 26. It's questionable he even had the legal right to do so, but it is probably safe to assume someone there reported back to him. In January 1942, Francis Sweeney was discharged from the Sandusky Soldiers' and Sailors' Home; and at the end of April Ness resigned his position as safety director and left Cleveland for Washington, D.C. Whether he was still having his operatives track the doctor's movements during this brief period is impossible to say now; but there can be little doubt that any lingering interest in keeping Sweeney under surveillance would have faded rapidly after Ness's departure.

"Ya know what you get when you cross a scientist with a prostitute?" grumbled a burly ex-cop in spring 2004. "A fuckin' know-it-all! And that was Sam Gerber. Everyone hated the guy." Samuel R. Gerber was a Cleveland institution and celebrity, indeed, a veritable monument. He served as Cuyahoga County coroner for fifty years. Until his 1986 retirement, the man and the office were inseparable in the minds of most county residents. And he did have his detractors and enemies. He could be haughty, combative, arrogant, and protective of his turf—as his high-handed behavior during the Sheppard murder case of 1954 clearly demonstrated. But he was also a highly respected author and lecturer on forensic matters. He had, and continues to have, a legion of loyal supporters and admirers, some still employed at the coroner's office.

Accurately assessing Gerber's behavior and determining the exact nature of the role he played in the Dolezal affair and Ness's suspicions about Francis Sweeney are at once difficult and illuminating. In 1936, when Gerber was elected coroner of Cuyahoga County, the official body count in the torso murders stood at six—seven if the Lady of the Lake is included. His predecessor, Arthur J. Pearce, had handled those first victims and had been the guiding force behind the groundbreaking torso clinic. No doubt Pearce's shadow loomed oppressively over the new coroner as he assumed his responsibilities, and Gerber was quick to put his own stamp on the forensic side of the investigation largely through statements to the press. At the time of Dolezal's death, he was a few months shy of his third year into his tenure. When he arrived at the jail on August 24, he probably made a snap judgment about the cause of death, based on a cursory glance at the scene and what he heard from the sheriff and his deputies: a dead body with a wound on the neck, the remnants of a noose hanging from the hook in the cell, and assurances from everyone present that Dolezal had been found hanging. It all added up to a suicide.

If Gerber experienced any sort of epiphany, any moment of startling clarity as to exactly what had happened to Frank Dolezal, it undoubtedly occurred during the autopsy in the early morning hours of August 25. When the chest was opened and he saw those broken, partly healed ribs on both sides of the rib cage, he very likely realized that Dolezal had, indeed, been severely beaten, that those press rumors about mistreatment were true, in spite of the sheriff's office's official claims to the contrary. Gerber would then have found himself in an extraordinarily difficult, perhaps even dangerous, position. He had already unofficially declared the death a suicide. To equivocate now, to raise the mere possibility that there may have been more to the death than initially met the eye, would be to publicly cast doubts on his own professional judgment (not something he would do lightly) and to incur the wrath of the sheriff—one of the most politically powerful men in the county. Now wrestling with some very real doubts about Dolezal's death, he would have to convene and officially preside over an inquest the next day (August 26) under the exceedingly stern and watchful eye of Sheriff Martin L. O'Donnell.

"He [Gerber] didn't really point out any discrepancies at all, which is interesting," reflected Dennis Dirkmaat after studying the inquest transcript. "Maybe, it's just . . . you can attribute that to not being totally prepared or a more cynical thing that's going on—that he's trying not to get too much out in the open." Time and again, discrepancies arise in the testimony; and, as Dirkmaat correctly observed, Gerber simply allows them to bloom (or fester) without comment. But was Gerber deliberately trying to conceal information, or was he doing his best to ensure that some of the more significant contradictions in the testimony at least made it to the official record? Assuming he harbored any nagging doubts about Frank Dolezal's death, the coroner was truly picking his way across a minefield during the entire inquest. The sheriff and the deputies who had been on the scene had already "told" him what had happened; he had been given the "correct" version of events when he arrived at the jail; he had already made a determination that the death was a suicide—all he had to do at the inquest was allow the entire story to be officially confirmed. The most significant moments in the proceedings, of course, occur at the end of the second day's testimony, when Gerber officially adjourned, only to reconvene forty-five minutes later for the sole purpose of getting the extraordinarily damning testimony of the Jones sisters into the official record. The adjournment was obviously a ploy to get O'Donnell, as well as any of his deputies who may also have been present, out of the room so the testimony could be taken without the sheriff's knowledge and free from any worries or questions about intimidation. If Gerber's conduct during the entire inquest is judged in the light of this very obvious maneuver to ensure at least some secrecy, then it becomes clear that all through the proceedings he was doing his best to make sure the discrepancies in the testimony were at least on the official record, even if he never tried to have them resolved. Mindful that O'Donnell was looking on, Gerber pushed matters as far as he dared. He worked fairly diligently to establish through sworn testimony that Frank Dolezal had no prior injuries and that the damage to his ribs and the bruising on his face had to have occurred while he was in the sheriff's custody. Similarly, he unsuccessfully tried to badger an exceedingly reluctant Dr. L. J. Sternicki into making some kind of statement as to Dolezal's mental condition.

Finally, there is the matter of that elegantly bound volume of the inquest testimony, as well as those huge photographs documenting Frank Dolezal's corpse in the county jail and on the autopsy table. Today, personnel at the morgue—including those who worked under Gerber—confirm that it was not standard procedure in the 1930s to take pictures of such monstrous size, nor was it common practice to lavish such elaborate care on the preservation of inquest testimony. Gerber only gave such extra attention to high-profile cases that he regarded as special. As Mark and I worked our way through the box of material in the morgue relating to Dolezal's death, we both experienced the somewhat eerie feeling that we were walking a path that had already been laid out for us. On August 24, 1939, Coroner Sam Gerber made a snap judgment about the cause of Dolezal's death, based on what he saw in the county jail and was told by the sheriff and his deputies. One day later, Dolezal's chest was opened during the formal autopsy; Geber could see the broken ribs— perhaps realizing for the first time that the charges of abuse that had been persistently made in the press were true and that his initial suicide verdict, made on the scene, may not have been accurate. But the damage had been done. Mindful that he could not retract that informal pronouncement of suicide without calling into question his own professional judgment and, at the same time, publicly challenging the sheriff and his office, he bowed to political realities and dutifully wrote a formal verdict that would conform to the "official" version of events. But he left enough signposts behind to ensure that someone, sometime, could follow and set the record straight.

Assessing what Gerber may have known or suspected about Francis Edward Sweeney's potential guilt in the torso murders is equally problematic. *Cleveland News* reporter Howard Beaufait and his wife, Doris, knew Gerber well and socialized with him frequently. In recent years, Doris O'Donnell

Beaufait—herself, a crack reporter on the local scene—has remained some-what dubious about the notion that Sweeney may have been the Butcher. "If Sam Gerber had known anything, he would have told Howard," she insists. Yet there is no doubt that the coroner knew who the derelict phy-sician was and was fully aware of his status as a prime suspect. When the *Cleveland News* announced on April 9, 1938, that police had their sights on "a once-prominent Clevelander, described as a physician in disrepute with his profession" who "is middle-aged, has some surgical skill and is described as being a powerfully built, chronic alcoholic," Gerber verified the story and declared, "We are watching him, as well as two or three others." In 1984, when former *Plain Dealer* columnist George Condon was preparing a retrospective piece on the murders for *Cleveland Magazine,* he reminded the coroner that he had once described the killer as a "broken-down doctor who becomes frenzied with drugs or liquor." Though Gerber indignantly denied he had ever said such a thing, it is interesting to note that this brief portrait Condon alleges he painted matches Frank Sweeney perfectly. Exactly why Gerber would have maintained his silence about Sweeney for the rest of his life is difficult to say. The coroner was not part of Ness's inner circle of associates and confidants. Royal Grossman and David Cowles may have kept quiet for years about the identity of Ness's prime suspect out of loyalty to the former safety director, but such considerations would not have restrained Gerber. Could his silence be attributed to loyalty to the Democratic Party in general or to Martin L. Sweeney in particular? There is simply no way to know. And, of course, it must be remembered that there was no hard evidence against Francis Sweeney: only an elaborate web of circumstances and coincidences, an inadmissible-in-court lie detector test, and the suspicions of Eliot Ness. As a public official, Gerber may have refrained from casually dropping any unguarded comments about a suspect in Cleveland's most notorious string of killings simply out of his sense of professional ethics.

Accurately assessing the conduct of both Congressman Martin L. Sweeney and Sheriff Martin L. O'Donnell during the period of the Frank Dolezal affair, from arrest to inquest, remains an extraordinarily difficult proposition. If city papers accurately reflect the congressman's behavior while these events were unfolding, Sweeney remained uncharacteristically silent. Considering that he rarely passed up an opportunity to make political hay on the lo-cal scene, and realizing that Sheriff O'Donnell was both political ally and friend, the congressman's silence seems absolutely deafening and utterly perplexing—especially when the case against Dolezal began to publicly unravel and the sheriff came under increased fire from the local press, the courts, and the ACLU. Why would Sweeney allow a close political ally to twist slowly in the wind without coming to his defense? If one is willing to give any credence to the notion that Sweeney may have come to some sort of gentleman's agreement with city administration (protection of his cousin Francis's identity in exchange for his good conduct on the local political stage), then his silence becomes understandable and reasonable. He was simply sticking by his word and keeping his nose clean.

Sheriff O'Donnell obviously had a huge personal, professional, and political stake in Frank Dolezal's guilt, so it is hardly surprising that he would fight hard to establish it and strike back with a vengeance at those who would tear down his case. Once he committed himself and publicly bought into that notion of Dolezal's guilt, he would have found it increasingly difficult and embarrassing—perhaps, totally impossible—to back off when circumstances turned against him. Though the conspiratorially inclined would love to believe that the sheriff was deeply involved in every aspect of Dolezal's death, from planning to execution, it is just as likely that some of his more aggressive deputies did the deed without his knowledge or consent, thus putting him in the undeniably difficult position of having to clean up a terrible mess left by others.

† † †

Francis Sweeney's future wife, Mary Josephine Sokol, moved to Cleveland with her family sometime just prior to 1920 and settled in the large working-class Hungarian neighborhood on the city's east side. She trained and worked as a nurse at St. Vincent's Charity Hospital, an institution in the midst of several significant Kingsbury Run sites: the area in which Frank Dolezal lived, where the initial set of Flo Polillo's remains were discovered, near the bar on the corner of East 20th and Central Avenue where the few officially identified players in the Kingsbury Run drama often drank. When her firstborn son, Francis Edward Sweeney Jr., of the U.S. Marine Corps, was killed in an automobile accident at a Cleveland railroad crossing in 1947, she was living in New York State. At the time, her younger son, James, was still residing in Cleveland, most likely with his mother's relatives, while he finished high school. In 1949, Mary apparently moved as far away from Cleveland as she could possibly get; in that year St. Vincent's transferred all her educational and professional records to the State Medical Board in California. Did James follow his mother to the West Coast upon graduation from high school, the same year? A likely scenario, perhaps, but there is no way to know. At the time, Francis Sweeney would have still been a resident at the Ohio Soldiers' and Sailors' Home. Did his ex-wife and surviving son know anything about his possible involvement in Cleveland's most gruesome series of murders? Probably, but, again, it is impossible to know. There is a single photograph of Mary Josephine Sokol's 1926 graduating class in nursing in the archives of St. Vincent's Charity Hospital. No one in the formal picture is identified, however; so there is no accurate way of picking her out from the sea of fresh, serious, eager faces.

On September 21, 1939, almost exactly one month after the death of Frank Dolezal, Francis Sweeney's sole surviving brother, Martin Joseph Jr., died of internal injuries sustained when he fell from the roof of a house at 2674 East 53rd. The house was not his, nor did he even live there as a renter. (The death certificate states he was living with his sister Mary on East 65th.) The house belonged to Angelo and Mary DeCaro—wine dealers, according to the city directory. Just what Martin Joseph was doing on the roof of a house in which he did not live is anyone's guess. That the owners had something to do with wine sales could explain why he was there in the first place. Francis wrestled unsuccessfully with the demons of alcohol; perhaps Martin Joseph fought similar battles. In fact, one of my research partners initially attributed his deadly plunge to the "Irish disease."

Was his death an accident or something more sinister? He could easily have been doing something completely innocent, such as repairing the roof. He was, after all, a common laborer and seems to have spent most of the 1930s without steady employment. Odd jobs would be one way to survive. A photograph of the house at the Cuyahoga County archives shows the pitch of the roof to be uncommonly steep, so it is easy to believe he simply lost his footing. But that his deadly fall so closely followed the death of Frank Dolezal does, at the very least, raise an eyebrow. Conspiracy aficionados would love to allege that Martin Joseph knew or suspected something, either about his younger brother Francis's involvement in Kingsbury Run or perhaps even Frank Dolezal's death and had decided to cash in on his suspicions through blackmail. But he underestimated the brutality and determined efficiency of his potential targets. Rather than buying his silence, someone with an agenda simply decided to end the whole matter by arranging an "accident." An engaging and attractive conspiracy, indeed, and one whose timing would dovetail precisely with the broader theory of Eliot Ness's secret suspect! But there is not a shred of hard evidence to support it. Having identified Francis Sweeney as a viable suspect, Ness would have thoroughly investigated his background. He would, therefore, have been familiar with Francis's siblings—their names, employment circumstances, family situations, and so forth. Ness would certainly have known who Martin Joseph Sweeney Jr. was. There is, however, no surviving evidence to suggest that the safety director saw anything suspicious in the death of Frank Sweeney's brother. However, there is nothing that proves he didn't. We just don't know. All one can say with certainty is that Martin Joseph's demise, coming so soon after the death of Frank Dolezal, is a bizarre, perhaps, even a convenient, coincidence.

When I first met Mary Dolezal in 1999, I was aware of the significant pieces of the family genealogy: Frank Dolezal's brother Charles had married Louise Vorell, and Louise's brother Frank Vorell was a Cleveland cop and one of the few people to visit Frank in jail. I was, however, not prepared for the almost virulent animosity the Dolezals harbored toward the Vorells, especially as there had apparently been no personal contact between the two branches of the family for years. As far as Mary knew then, the palpable hatred directed at the Vorells stemmed from an obscure Dolezal family legend that the Mad Butcher of Kingsbury Run was actually Frank Vorell's brother Charles. (It remains a little confusing to be dealing with two sets of brothers, both named Frank and Charles.) Those in the Dolezal clan who remembered Charles Vorell described him as a brutal, violent man who on two separate occasions had ordered Mary's father and his siblings to wash blood off the backseat of his car. According to family lore, Frank Vorell had allowed his brother-in-law Frank Dolezal to be arrested and murdered to shield his brother Charles Vorell from prosecution. The errant Vorell was packed off to the merchant marine during World War II, during which he was accidentally, and conveniently, washed overboard.

I initially informed Mary Dolezal in 1999 that her grandfather Charles had brought two separate causes of action against the sheriff and his deputies and that both those legal attacks had been settled in her grandfather's favor. At the time, she was surprised and confused. It seems that the Dolezals had hunkered down and built an impregnable wall of silence around themselves in reaction to the veritable explosion of negative publicity generated by Frank's arrest. No one in the family seemed to know about Charles's suits; and as far as anyone knew, no money had ever changed hands. It was not until 2007 that one of the older members of the family broke the code of silence in a fit of pique and alleged that money had, indeed, been paid to Charles Dolezal for his suits and that someone on the Vorell side of the family had tricked him out of it by taking advantage of his poor English and even poorer understanding of American legal procedures. The devious Vorell allegedly used the money to invest in real estate. (Mary asserts that her father worked for Frank Vorell as an apprentice in the late 1940s, when the latter built apartments either in Bedford or Bedford Heights.)

At the time of Frank Dolezal's incarceration and death, his family undoubtedly felt unfairly besieged by events; and there is an obvious, though wholly understandable, touch of paranoia in both tales. Unfortunately, given what little evidence remains, it is extremely difficult to verify or dispute either story. Frank Vorell did, indeed, have a brother Charles, seven years his junior; but the patrolman's recorded actions and words do not suggest that he was protecting anyone at the expense of his sister's beleaguered brother-in-law Frank Dolezal. He visited him in the county jail—the only family member to do so—and testified on his behalf at the inquest. In June 1940, acting on his long-held belief that the Butcher was a transient who rode the rails between Cleveland and other nearby industrial cities, Detective Peter Merylo finally got Chief of Police George Matowitz's permission to go underground as a "bum" in search of evidence that could point to the killer. Believing that Frank Vorell might want to avenge his relative's death and redeem his shattered reputation, Merylo asked the patrolman to ride the rails with him, a proposition to which Vorell readily agreed. None of his known actions suggest that Vorell was secretly maneuvering to focus potential attention away from his brother Charles at the expense of Frank or anyone else.

The question of whether money had been paid to Charles Dolezal as a result of his lawsuits against the sheriff and his office is more complex. The paperwork in probate court for both suits ends with the statement, "settled and dismissed at defendants' cost," but whether that meant that Charles Dolezal actually got the $125,000 for which he was asking is impossible to say. On March 28, 1942, however, the law firm of Minshall & Mosier wrote Pat Lyons—one of the named defendants—asking him to contact their office in order to discuss "the expense [to Lyons] involved in connection with this lawsuit." Both these evidentiary fragments suggest very strongly that money was somehow involved, though there is no way to verify it or ascertain how much. But the Dolezals remain adamant: Charles never saw a penny; and, though he did not exactly die in abject poverty, he was never financially well off. It remains, however, a huge leap in logic to insist that someone on the Vorell side of the family tricked him out of whatever money he may have been awarded.

Family legends of this sort, however, don't just grow from nothing; somewhere there is a grain of truth that gave birth to the story in the first place. Records in the Cuyahoga County Recorder's Office do show that between 1944 and 1950 there were fifteen real estate transactions involving the Vorells, eleven of them with either Frank Vorell or his wife, Lillian. Whatever the facts may be, there is no doubt that bad blood still festers between the two branches of the family descended from Charles and Louise (née Vorell) Dolezal; and whatever the causes, real or imagined, they clearly grew out of the tragic series of events that unfolded seventy years ago.

Today, the area—now known as Slavic Village—that borders the south side of Kingsbury Run and surrounds the Broadway and East 55th neighborhood struggles against the twin urban blights of general decay and crime. St. Alexis Hospital, where Francis Sweeney served his internship, was closed and eventually torn down—in spite of a lot of political noise and posturing; and the buildings that once housed the medical offices he shared with Dr. Edward Peterka and the Raus funeral home (where David Cowles alleges Sweeney practiced some sort of surgery or dissection on the corpses of unidentified indigents) have also been demolished. But if you spend enough time haunting the bars and hanging out on the streets in that old neighborhood, you can still pick up the vague remnants of a local legend that maintains—in some unknown or, perhaps, forgotten way—that the neighborhood had some sort of connection with the Mad Butcher of Kingsbury Run.

In early spring 2004, Mark Stone and I met with then Cuyahoga County coroner Elizabeth Balraj to discuss the Frank Dolezal affair. At that time, she saw no reason to question any of the official conclusions Sam Gerber—her immediate predecessor and mentor—had arrived at in 1939 concerning Dolezal's death.

Epilogue
THE TRAGIC STORY OF ANNA AND JOSEPH NIGRIN

Did Frank Dolezal murder his sister Anna Nigrin and perhaps even her son (his nephew), Joseph? The charge—or, at least, the suggestion—that he may have done so contributed to the swirl of ugly rumors and poisonous allegations that hung over his head at the time of his arrest. The only source for this damning charge came in a letter from Nettie Taylor of Wheaton, Illinois, a woman who identified herself as Frank Dolezal's sister-in-law. The document no longer exists, but it remains one of the more perplexing enigmas in the entire Dolezal affair. The first public reference to this mysterious piece of correspondence appeared on July 10, 1939, in a front-page article of the *Press*. Though there is no way to be certain, the letter had apparently been sent directly to Martin O'Donnell, for the sheriff showed the document in question to assembled reporters—presumably that day. We will never know for certain everything that letter contained; the *Press* account provides only the briefest summary of its contents: Frank Dolezal's sister, Anna Nigrin [wife of Gottlieb Nigrin], had been found dead—presumably murdered—on a Geauga County farm near Chardon in July 1931. Further, her twenty-two-year-old son, Joseph Allan Nigrin, had come to Cleveland in April 1938 to stay with his Uncle Frank while he cleared up his mother's affairs. Reportedly, Joseph was never seen again. O'Donnell verified some of the letter's basic allegations through Adam Crumpton, a printer and friend of Dolezal's, who resided on Wade Park Avenue. The *Press* quoted Crumpton on July 10 as having said, "One day [the exact time frame is not clarified] Dolezal came to me crying and said his sister had been found dead. He said her head had been cut off and he thought she had been murdered. He said he thought a farmhand did it." Whether the detail concerning decapitation actually appeared in the original Taylor letter or was added by Crumpton is not at all clear, but the damage was done. Once the trigger is pulled, the bullet cannot be recalled. Pat Lyons repeats the allegation in his notes that Anna Nigrin had, indeed, been murdered and decapitated: "Affidavid [*sic*] by person states Frank told him Frank's sister was murdered[:] had her head cut off. Mrs. Anna Nigrin in Geauga County near Chardon, July 1931." Now, almost seventy years after the fact, it is difficult to gauge exactly how much impact the Taylor letter may have had on public perceptions of Dolezal's guilt in the torso killings. The sheriff, however, obviously regarded it as a major link in the chain of evidence he was forging against his prisoner, and the allegation of decapitation would obviously have been seen as conspicuously damning under the circumstances.

But were any of these very serious charges true? Exactly who was Nettie Taylor? She identified herself as Frank Dolezal's sister-in-law, but the only set of circumstances that would explain such a relationship would be to assume she was one of Gottlieb Nigrin's (Frank Dolezal's brother-in-law) siblings. There is no doubt, however, that Anna Nigrin existed. She and her husband, Gottlieb, first appear in the 1919–20 Cleveland city directory at an East 79th address, and the census records for 1920 confirm this. Further, the 1930 Geauga County census places the family on a Geauga County farm in Huntsville Township. Husband and wife immigrated to the United States in 1903 or 1904 from Czechoslovakia. There is, however, no record in Cuyahoga County of any woman with the last name "Dolezal" being married to a man with a name even remotely close to Gottlieb Nigrin. (Public records, of course, are certainly not infallible; the 1920 census mistakenly enumerates him as "Kottlieb Negrin" and identifies his wife as "Annie.") The marriage obviously must have taken place out of state, possibly even in Europe. Their son, Joseph Allan, however, was born in Ohio in 1917.

When I first raised the entire Anna Nigrin story with Mary Dolezal in 1999, she met my enquiries with raised eyebrows, an uncomprehending stare, and a defiantly uttered "Who??" No one in her immediate family, not even her father, had ever heard of Anna Dolezal Nigrin. So far as they knew, of the ten Dolezal children, only Charles (Mary's grandfather) and Frank had come to the United States. When they learned the details of the Anna Nigrin story, Mary's entire family regarded it as a hoax, a vicious piece of slander concocted to further incriminate an innocent man. In late 2004, however, I conclusively verified the existence of the Nigrins through the 1930 census, so I raised the issue with Mary a second time. By then her father had died, and the only living relative she could approach who might know was her father's older brother, Al—a man from whom she was virtually estranged, since he had not taken kindly to his rebel niece digging around in the family's not-so-secret shame. The first line of Mary's subsequent e-mail to me virtually screamed from the computer screen: "Why didn't I know about these people?!" Uncle Al had, indeed, confirmed the existence of Anna Nigrin, but his explanation for her death proved far different from the allegations made in the Nettie Taylor letter and repeated in the *Press*. Supposedly, her son, Joseph—then fourteen—had simply discovered her dead body in the driveway of the family farm. There is no mention of murder or decapitation. Joseph, however, had apparently learned how to drive a car in 1925, at the age of eight, and those very few Dolezal family members who even knew the Nigrin story suspected he had accidentally run over his mother in July 1931. (Why Al had kept this rather lurid and compelling piece of family lore to himself all these years is almost impossible to explain, beyond the fact that it is yet another conspicuous example of the total, almost pathological, lack of communication that seems characteristic of Dolezal family relationships. Charles and Frank had minimal contact with each other after the former's 1920 marriage, and at the time of his arrest, Frank insisted to authorities that he had no siblings.) As it turns out, Al Dolezal's recounting of buried family legend is remarkably close to what actually happened. Fourteen-year-old Joseph Nigrin did kill his mother, Anna, when he ran over her with a car on July 3, 1931. (Reportedly, he did not see her.) Geauga County coroner Philip Pease attributed her death to a combination of internal injuries and a fractured skull caused by the accident; there was no murder and obviously no decapitation. Unlike the *Press*, the *Plain Dealer* got the details of the actual story straight on July 11, but the paper buried the revelation on the back pages, at the tail end of a very long story. The truth, if anyone even noticed it, seems to have had little or no impact on the much more lurid myth of mysterious death that had been born the day before.

On July 10, 1939, the *Press* reported that the sheriff's office in Chardon could not find any record for the death of Anna Nigrin in Geauga County. Very loud alarm bells should have sounded at that point for everyone involved. While it remains possible to accept that a death by natural causes might slip through the bureaucratic cracks of a rural area, it is simply inconceivable that a supposed murder, especially one that involved a decapitation, could pass by without some sort of official record. Certainly, no community of reasonable size and civic organization in mid-twentieth-century America could commit such a large bureaucratic blunder. If there was no death record, there had to be a reason; and the inability of the sheriff's men in Chardon to track down that reason casts very grave doubts on either their investigative abilities or their willingness to investigate in the first place. It would also seem that the Cuyahoga County sheriff's office was not all that interested in decisively nailing down all the details alleged in the Taylor letter; O'Donnell seems to have accepted with a mere shrug of his shoulders that his Geauga County counterparts could not find a death certificate. Anna Nigrin's husband,

Gottlieb, however, died in 1930 of diabetes; and there is record of his death in Geauga County. Obviously, a widow with a young son—then twelve or thirteen—would find it extremely difficult to manage a farm by herself; so, shortly after Gottlieb's death, Anna married her second husband, Charles Zak. (There is a record of the Nigrin-Zak marriage in Cuyahoga County.) The record of her accidental death is, therefore, to be found under "Zak," not "Nigrin." When the sheriff's men did not find a death certificate under Nigrin, they obviously looked no further.

The only part of the Nettie Taylor letter that Al Dolezal came close to confirming was the unknown fate of Anna's son, Joseph Allan Nigrin. Uncle Al had no idea what happened to him. Taylor alleges that Joseph came to Cleveland from Chicago in April 1938, planning to stay with his uncle Frank while he cleaned up his mother's affairs and that he had never been seen again. At least part of her account makes sense, even if it cannot be conclusively verified. Joseph would have been fourteen at the time of his mother's death and, therefore, incapable of clearing up anything connected to the family estate legally. That he would come to Cleveland from Chicago in 1938 at the age of twenty-two to do so is also clearly plausible. It is not much of a reach to assume that Joseph may have joined his father's relatives in Illinois, from where Nettie Taylor had mailed her letter, after the death of his mother. In 1938, he would have been at least twenty-one and thus in a position to act legally in regard to his parents' estate. But he did not, as Nettie Taylor alleges—and as Al Dolezal seems to confirm—vanish without a trace after April 1938. There was no mysterious disappearance that could be laid at his Uncle Frank's feet. The unspoken but clearly inferred allegation that Frank Dolezal had probably murdered his nephew is simply untrue. Joseph returned to Geauga County, though it is virtually impossible to ascertain when, and married Mildred Souvey. (If Joseph did have relatives living in Illinois, he seems to have severed his connections with them completely at this point for reasons unknown.) Joseph and Mildred Nigrin had two children: Gertrude Ann (dubbed Sue by relatives and friends, since her father called her Susie-Q), born in 1939, and Joseph Allan II, born in 1942. Sadly, Joseph Nigrin died of cancer in 1945, at the age of twenty-eight.

In the summer of 2004, I spoke to the absolutely flabbergasted Sue Nigrin Marks on the phone. Since she was only six when her father, Joseph, died, she remembered little about him; she knew virtually nothing of her grandparents Gottlieb and Anna Nigrin, beyond their names. She still harbored some extremely vague memories of the name "Dolezal" floating about in family lore, but the history of Frank (her great uncle) and his connection to the Kingsbury Run murders came as an utterly shocking surprise. I subsequently set up a phone meeting between Mary Dolezal and Sue Marks, and the two have eagerly—and with a certain sense of awe—traded family photos, names, and stories. In the 1930s, a series of tragedies had quite literally blasted their family tree apart. Now, almost three quarters of a century later, two women— neither of whom had known previously the other existed—gathered up the shattered branches.

No doubt, Nettie Taylor believed everything she wrote to the sheriff (What conceivable reasons could she have had for lying?), and O'Donnell, aided by the press, clearly used the contents of that letter to strengthen his case against Frank Dolezal. Nothing was ever stated publicly or directly, and no charges were ever leveled, but the inference was clear: Dolezal must be guilty of the torso killings, for he had allegedly murdered members of his own family in the same viciously gruesome manner. But the truth about the deaths of both Anna Nigrin and her son, Joseph, proved far more poignant than the surviving lurid myth of murder. A fourteen-year-old boy had accidentally hit his mother with an automobile, and he had to carry with him the impossibly heavy burden that he was responsible for her death until his own passing a mere fourteen years later.

Afterword

GAYLORD SUNDHEIM

CATHLEEN A. CERNY, M.D.

By now you are aware that Eliot Ness had a secret suspect in the torso killings investigation, a man by the name of Gaylord Sundheim. In his first book on the topic, *In the Wake of the Butcher: Cleveland's Torso Murders*, James Badal outlined how he concluded that Gaylord Sundheim and Francis E. Sweeney were one and the same. After establishing Sundheim was really Sweeney, the next question naturally is, "Was Francis Sweeney the Mad Butcher of Kingsbury Run?" It is a fascinating proposition, but not a question a forensic psychiatrist like me can answer. "Did Francis Sweeney suffer from a mental illness?" Yet another question I am unable to answer. "So why keep reading?" you are asking yourselves. "What does this psychiatrist have to offer?" I can explain a bit about forensic psychiatry and the usual roles of forensic psychiatrists in criminal contexts. I also hope to give some insights into the possible mental illness of Eliot Ness's secret suspect and whether his known history contains any indicators of violence risk.

I want to start with a disclaimer. Psychiatrists must practice in accordance with ethical guidelines and standards. The 2009 American Psychiatric Association's *The Principles of Medical Ethics with Annotations Especially Applicable to Psychiatry* provides the following instruction: "On occasion psychiatrists are asked for an opinion about an individual who is in the light of public attention or who has disclosed information about himself/herself through public media. In such circumstances, a psychiatrist may share with the public his or her expertise about psychiatric issues in general. However, it is unethical for a psychiatrist to offer a professional opinion unless he or she has conducted an examination and has been granted proper authorization for such a statement."

In a way, Francis Sweeney falls under this guideline. Through the writings of James Badal and others, Sweeney was brought into the public consciousness as a torso killer suspect. In fact, Sweeney is named as a suspect on a display at the National Museum of Crime and Punishment in Washington, D.C. He died more than ten years before my birth, so I've obviously never personally evaluated him. In addition, there are a limited number of historical documents for me to review. Medical records are especially scarce. It would, therefore, be unethical for me to offer any definitive mental health diagnoses here. That Sweeney is long deceased does provide some room to maneuver with regard to the ethical standards of my profession. It allows for "psychohistory," the application of psychological models in historical research.

There is also another ethical consideration. Sweeney has living descendents. Because of the stigma associated with mental illness, not to mention the stigma of being a suspect in one of the most notorious unsolved serial murder cases of all time, I want to be as sensitive to the remaining family members as possible. For that reason, I will create a little psychological distance from Francis E. Sweeney by using Eliot Ness's pseudonym, Gaylord Sundheim, for him.

For the purposes of this "analysis," I relied on the source material James J. Badal gathered during the writing of his books on the torso killer.[1] Badal obtained copies of actual historical documents, including birth certificates, death certificates, divorce proceedings, probate court papers, postcards from Francis Sweeney/Sundheim to Eliot Ness, and correspondence between individuals working for Ohio's Veterans Administration. I summarized all of the documents in the same way I would for a modern forensic assessment (see the appendix). If the copies or writing were unclear in any way, I've indicated so in the summary rather than guessing at the content. Evidence from these historical documents supports all of my statements about Sweeney/Sundheim.

A little background on forensic psychiatry will help you understand the limitations of what I can say about Gaylord Sundheim and give an appreciation for the work forensic psychiatrists do. I am not the world's foremost authority on forensic psychiatry. My intent is not to describe every aspect and nuance of the field but only to convey some general information about forensic psychiatry.

I am willing to bet that most of what you think you know about forensic psychiatry comes from the world of fiction. That's not a criticism! I was drawn to my career path by popular culture. More specifically, I wanted to be Clarice Starling from Thomas Harris's *Silence of the Lambs*. I had great visions of joining the FBI and using my knowledge of psychopathology to track down cunning serial killers. Even now, I watch *Law & Order: SVU* and long to be Dr. Emil Skoda or Dr. George Huang with their skillful criminal profiles and direct assistance to the police. Although the reality of forensic psychiatry and psychology is not nearly as glamorous and exciting as that seen on TV or in the movies (most of the time—there are exceptions!), it is a fascinating field and its practitioners provide valuable services.

According to the American Academy of Psychiatry and the Law, forensic psychiatry is "a medical subspecialty that includes research and clinical practice in the many areas in which psychiatry is applied to legal issues."[2] Forensic psychiatry can be further subdivided into many different areas. These include criminal (competency to stand trial and NGRI evaluations), civil (psychiatric malpractice, disability evaluations), and treatment (in a forensic hospital, in correctional institutions). This is not a complete list, and it is a simplistic one. Many forensic psychiatrists and psychologists wear multiple hats. For example, I used to work on an inpatient forensic unit at a state mental hospital. All of my patients were either NGRI or incompetent to stand trial. My job involved providing clinical care, writing reports for the court, testifying, and supervising forensic psychiatry trainees.

Individuals were practicing forensic psychiatry long before it was recognized as a unique field. However, the American Academy of Psychiatry and the Law was not founded until 1969. In 1992, the American Board of Psychiatry and Neurology established a Committee on Certification of Added Qualifications in Forensic Psychiatry, which made forensic psychiatry a specific subfield of the discipline. To sit for the board's examination provided by this committee and receive credentials as a board-certified forensic psychiatrist, an individual must complete a year-long forensic fellowship after four years of general adult psychiatry training. After passing the initial certification test, a maintenance-of-certification examination must be passed every ten years to maintain credentials. Board certification in forensic psychiatry is not a requirement for the practice of forensic psychiatry, however: many psychiatrists perform forensic evaluations and act as expert witnesses without specialized training. Having forensic credentials, however, may give a psychiatrist more credibility as an expert in the eyes of juries and servants of the court.

As I've already indicated, the reality of criminal forensic psychiatry *is* a little different from as-seen-on-TV. Most of us psychiatrists are not part of police interrogations or victim interviews during the investigation of a crime, although I am sure that there are some who work very directly with law enforcement. Our involvement with the criminal justice system usually begins after a suspect has been charged. A court might order a defendant to undergo an evaluation by a psychiatrist or psychologist for many reasons. If there are any concerns that the defendant's ability to understand court-related information or participate in his or her own defense is impaired by a mental condition, the court may order a Competence to Stand Trial evaluation. A Sanity at the Time of the Act evaluation is ordered when a defendant's mental status at the time of the alleged offense(s) may have affected his or her criminal responsibility. If a defendant has already been found guilty of the charges, the court could order a mitigation of penalty evaluation or request psychiatric recommendations for treatment. If a defendant is found not guilty by reason of insanity and is hospitalized, the court requires periodic evaluations to justify the need for continued hospitalization. A series of evaluations are also required before one of these patients can be discharged from the hospital.

In the 1930s, "insanity" meant something different than it does today. Essentially, it was used as a synonym for "mentally ill." At his inquests of lunacy, Gaylord Sundheim was said to be "insane" and in need of hospitalization. Today, "insane" is a specific legal finding: when someone is insane or not guilty by reason of insanity, under the applicable state insanity statute, a defendant has been found criminally non-responsible for his or her crime. In Ohio, "A person is 'Not Guilty by Reason of Insanity' if he proves that *at the time* of the commission of the offense, the person *did not know, as a result of severe mental disease or defect,* the *wrongfulness* of the person's acts."[3] Sanity statutes vary from state to state, and if the examiner applies the wrong one, her evaluation and final conclusions will be wrong, and her opinion will get torn apart on cross-examination. The insanity defense is rarely used and rarely successful. All persons found insane are mentally ill or mentally retarded, but not all defendants with mental illness are insane.

In an NGRI evaluation, once the evaluator understands the applicable law, the data collection and review begin. In a given case, this data can include clinical interview(s) with defendant; interviews of victims, witnesses, involved law enforcement, and attorneys; the defendant's medical and psychiatric records; and review of the prosecutor's case file. *Who* and *what* the psychiatric expert has access to may be determined by which side, prosecution or defense, hired him in accordance with the laws of evidence. Some states, Ohio among them, have designated forensic centers or court clinics. Evaluators who work for court psychiatric clinics are neutral, in the sense that they are not hired by either side. Regardless of whether the evaluator is employed by a neutral organization or was employed by the prosecution or defense, their final opinion should be based on an unbiased assessment of the data.

The clinical interview with the defendant must be thorough and free from leading questions. The purpose of the interview is to reconstruct the mental state of the defendant at the time of the act. Sanity is past-mental-state evaluation. The evaluator must always keep in mind that the person's present mental state can be vastly different from what it was at the time of the alleged acts.

Once the interviews are done and the paper records are reviewed, it is time to try and make sense of things. This is the truly fun and rewarding part of forensic psychiatry. It is a bit like a mind-challenge puzzle. Did the defendant have a severe mental disease at the time of the alleged act? Does the evidence suggest knowledge of wrongfulness at the time of the act, or does it imply the defendant did not know what he or she was doing was wrong? Did the defendant have a rational motive for doing what he or she did (i.e., revenge or profit) or was there a non-reality-based (delusional) motivation?

What qualifies as a "severe mental disease?" Schizophrenia, major depressive disorder, and bipolar disorder are pretty universally recognized as severe psychiatric illnesses. For the purposes of an insanity defense, some psychiatric disorders are controversial. These include post-traumatic stress disorder and dissociative identity disorder (DID, more commonly known as multiple personality disorder). Disorders of substance use do not qualify as severe mental disorders for the purposes of insanity. For example, an individual high on cocaine who commits an assault cannot claim insanity even if he is determined to suffer from *The Diagnostic and Statistical Manual of Mental Disorders, Version IV-TR (DSM-IV)* diagnosable cocaine dependence. Keep this in mind for the discussion of Sundheim's alcohol and barbiturate use.

Just because a defendant carries a historical diagnosis of schizophrenia (or bipolar disorder or . . .), he will not automatically be found insane for all criminal acts. It is entirely possible that his symptoms of mental illness were inactive or minor at the time of the alleged crime. The symptoms could also have been totally unrelated to the criminal acts. For example, if someone's schizophrenia causes him to believe his mother is trying to poison him and he goes out and kills the first person he sees, it does not follow that his act flowed from the delusional belief about his mother. However, if he had killed her because he genuinely believed it was the only way to preserve his own life, he *may* have a legitimate case for insanity. As a forensic psychiatrist, I ask myself: "If I accept the delusional belief or hallucination as being true in this mentally ill individual's reality, would that justify the offense committed?" A man's auditory hallucination that a woman he passed on the street called him "stupid" would not justify his killing her. However, if the man had a delusional belief that the woman was following him with the intent to kidnap and torture him for top-secret government information, this changes things a bit. If he further delusionally believed that this woman would torture his wife and children to get to him, well, you can see how this scenario *might* lead to a successful insanity defense, should he harm the woman.

Not guilty by reason of insanity is an affirmative defense. This means that the accused admits to doing the wrong act but is offering a justification for why she should not be held criminally responsible for it. Self-defense and duress are two other examples of affirmative defenses. If Gaylord Sundheim had admitted to being the torso killer during Eliot Ness's secret interrogation and we had some documentation of what was said during that meeting, it would be possible to do a very rudimentary insanity analysis. How fascinating that would be!

"Was Gaylord Sundheim insane? A lunatic? A psychopath? Or just plain crazy?" As a psychiatrist, I try to stay away from words like "crazy" and "lunatic." Those are nonspecific lay terms that only serve to foster stigma against the mentally ill. Before I suggest possible diagnoses for Sundheim, a few more definitions and explanations are called for. First, I will describe antisocial personality disorder and psychopathy.

Antisocial personality disorder is one of several personality disorders described in the *DSM-IV*. A personality disorder is a pattern of behavior and emotions that differs from cultural norms and manifests in several areas: cognition, emotional response, interpersonal functioning, and impulse control. The pattern is evident in many different areas of the individual's life. It is an inflexible way of seeing and responding to the world that starts in early adulthood. Perhaps most important, the pattern causes distress or impairment to the individual.[4] Notably for our assessment of Gaylord Sundheim, it cannot be due to the direct physiological effects of a substance or a medical condition.

The hallmarks of antisocial personality disorder are a disregard for and violation of the rights of others starting by age fifteen. The *DSM-IV* specifies that three or more of the following must be present to make the diagnosis: repeated breaking of the law, deceitfulness, impulsivity, aggression and fighting, recklessness, and remorseless irresponsibility.[5] The individual must also be at least eighteen years old at the time of diagnosis. Evidence of childhood conduct disorder must also be present. Unfortunately, we know next to nothing about Sundheim's childhood.

What can we conclude about antisocial personality disorder and the Mad Butcher of Kingsbury Run? If we look at the acts of the torso killer, we can identify many of these traits. The killer certainly did not conform to social norms. Murder is definitely a violation of the law. Beheading numerous human beings is certainly aggressive and shows disregard for safety. I think we can also infer that the killer must have used deceitfulness to lure his victims and hide from the law. Mrs. Sundheim clearly felt her husband demonstrated consistent irresponsibility in his roles as husband and father. With the caveat that we don't know anything about childhood conduct problems, we have more than enough criteria to make the diagnosis of antisocial personality disorder.

Popular culture is filled with examples of "psycho killers," but what exactly is a psychopath? The literature on psychopathy is complex and extensive. In some articles, psychopathy is said to be the old term for antisocial personality disorder. Many use the terms interchangeably. Still others consider psychopathy to be a broader concept than antisocial personality disorder. Not all psychopaths are criminals and not all criminals are psychopaths. Dr. Robert D. Hare is a firm believer that antisocial personality disorder and psychopathy are not the same thing. He devised the *Psychopathy Checklist-Revised* (*PCL-R*), which has been used to evaluate psychopathy in research settings. Put very briefly, two main factors are assessed by the *PCL-R*: callous, selfish, remorseless use of others and chronically unstable and antisocial lifestyle. It is also very important to state that psychopathy is not the same thing as psychosis. Fictional examples of psychopaths include Hannibal Lector from *Silence of the Lambs* and Alex from *A Clockwork Orange*. Real-life killers like Jeffrey Dahmer, Ted Bundy, and John Wayne Gacy have been described as psychopaths. Because of the gruesome nature of his murders and the way some of the bodies were disposed of, many would be quick to label the torso killer as a psychopath. However, even if we could prove Gaylord Sundheim was the Mad Butcher, it would be irresponsible to label him a psychopath on such limited data.

So what can we conclude about Gaylord Sundheim and still be on reasonably firm footing? With the obvious caveat, once more, that I did not conduct a personal evaluation of Sundheim, the available evidence most strongly supports a diagnosis of chemical dependence. Specifically, Sundheim appears to have suffered from alcohol dependence. The *DSM-IV* diagnosis of this disorder requires a maladaptive pattern of alcohol use leading to impairment or distress in at least three of these areas within the same twelve-month span: tolerance; withdrawal; using alcohol in larger amounts or over a longer period than was intended; persistent desire or unsuccessful efforts to cut down or control alcohol use; giving up or reducing important activities because of alcohol use; and continued alcohol use despite knowledge of a persistent or recurrent physical or psychological problem likely to have been caused or exacerbated by alcohol.[6] Divorce and probate court documents give ample evidence that Sundheim met several of these criteria. He was probated to City Hospital at least three times for "dipsomania." Dipsomania is a historical term referring to a sudden and irresistible need to drink alcohol. Sundheim's drinking continued despite the development of peripheral neuritis (pain, loss of sensation) in his legs and feet. Most notably, he continued to drink despite the destruction of his marriage and neglect of his children.

Sundheim was again probated (given court-ordered psychiatric hospital admission) in February 1938, which falls between discovery of victims nos. 9 and 10. A friend of the doctor completed the official complaint, which provides a fascinating bit of data: "Patient Physician at Massillon State Hospital. In Probate Court for 3rd time as alcoholic. Yesterday became hallucinated with ideas of fear. Talked about Federal men after him. Police called and taken to jail." On February 28, 1938, two psychiatrists, West and Stone, examined Sundheim and documented "that at times he has indicated symptoms suggestive of delusions, which however were transient. Also that he had been hallucinated at times when drinking, usually." Hallucinations and delusions are psychotic symptoms, which represent a loss of touch with reality. Although they can be due to a mental illness, alcohol- or drug-related problems (intoxication, as well as withdrawal) can also result in psychotic symptoms. Considering that Sundheim may, in fact, have been tailed by FBI agents, his drunken ramblings take on a whole new light. In April 1938, when he was again probated, the psychiatrist noted the absence of psychosis.

There is evidence to suggest that Sundheim may have experienced some of the long-term consequences of chronic alcohol consumption. Over time, alcoholics can develop certain vitamin deficiencies that have substantial effects on the nervous system. Peripheral neuropathies (damage to the nerves outside of the spinal cord) result in numbness, weakness, and burning pain of the hands and feet. When Sundheim was evaluated by doctors for his January 1934 inquest of lunacy, he was quoted as saying, "My wife sent me in. I'd lie around and moan all night with these hands. The legs and feet are better but they still burn like a hot pad on them." It is possible Sundheim had even more devastating neurological problems as a result of his alcohol use. Damage from thiamine deficiency can cause confusion, dizziness, gait abnormalities, and abnormal eye movements. This grouping of symptoms is called Wernicke's encephalopathy. Untreated, Wernicke's can develop into Korsakoff's syndrome, which is a chronic condition affecting memory. Unlike Wernicke's, Korsakoff's can improve with thiamine treatment, but it does not completely resolve with thiamine treatment. An individual with Korsakoff's syndrome has impairments of recent memory and the ability to form new memories (anterograde amnesia). Niacin deficiency can result in alcoholic pellagra encephalopathy. Individuals with this condition can have confusion, clouding of consciousness, and other neurological symptoms.[7] Records indicate that Sundheim continued to drink until at least the mid-1950s and possibly until the end of his life, in 1964. Thirty years of heavy drinking certainly makes central nervous system (brain) damage a possibility.

Another possible diagnosis supported by the records is barbiturate dependence. It is unclear whether Sundheim was abusing barbiturates during the time frame of the torso killings. However, he clearly was later in life, as evidenced by correspondence between the director of Dayton's Veterans Administration Center and the secretary of the Ohio State Medical Board. In one letter, the director of the VA Center quotes from the chief of the

Domiciliary Medical Service: Gaylord Sundheim "has been here in the Domiciliary on and off since 1946 . . . because the veteran still has his Ohio Medical license, he freely writes prescriptions for barbiturates. He allegedly prescribes for his aged sister who will only take the medicine he sends her. Instead, the veteran takes the drugs himself and becomes an impossible management problem. The veteran's name is also carried by all the pharmaceutical houses and he receives countless samples of drugs which he is able to become intoxicated on by overdosages." The director of the Dayton VA Center also wrote: "Although he has been under care at a mental hospital as a psychotic and is still rated as incompetent by the Veterans Administration, we have a continuing problem with him in that he writes prescriptions for barbiturates and tranquilizers in fictitious names for his own use."

With regard to other diagnostic possibilities, some of the most interesting data comes from Sundheim's own late-in-life writings. I have a few words of caution before I delve into his written communications. By the 1950s, he had been drinking and perhaps also abusing prescription medications for many years, and likely suffering many detrimental effects from doing so. The mental status revealed by his writings from the 1950s and 1960s is not likely to be truly representative of his mental status during the time of the torso killings. It would be inaccurate to conclude that whatever neurologic and psychiatric issues color his correspondence in the 1950s were necessarily also active in the 1930s. In addition, intoxication can result in mood and psychotic symptoms (hallucinations, delusions, disordered thinking). The *DSM-IV* describes substance-induced mood disorder and substance-induced psychotic disorder. Since Sundheim was impaired by chemicals for most or all of his adult life, it is hard to know if he had any mood or psychotic disorders unrelated to drug and alcohol use. To make matters even more complicated, chemical dependence problems frequently coexist with primary mood (major depression, bipolar disorder) and psychotic (schizophrenia) disorders. It is entirely possible that Sundheim had a mood or psychotic disorder and used alcohol as a way to self medicate, although this is impossible to prove now.

We can't ever really know what is in another person's mind. However, a person's writings can give us little glimpses of his or her thought processes. On September 12, 1953, Gaylord Sundheim wrote a letter to FBI director J. Edgar Hoover. It's nearly impossible make any sense out of it even after a third or fourth reading. Was he drunk or high when he wrote it? Is it an example of psychotic thinking, where the connections between the concepts make sense only to the author? Sundheim's February 14, 1954, letter to Eliot Ness and his June 29, 1956, letter to a Cleveland Probate Court judge are similarly nonsensical. They contain examples of neologisms, made up words (for example, "Nessisms"). There are also several examples of clang associations, words grouped together based on how they sound rather than their meanings or to create a logical statement.

He writes to the Cleveland Probate Court: "Evidently you are protected there by, [illegible] protectives from the seeming ever encroaching Federal Octopus or pusses promoting vicious ends by Haunt - Taunt or daunt methods." My favorite of his clang associations—"truancy in lunacy"—comes from this letter. I detect the slightest bit of paranoia in the writings but, frankly, they are so difficult to comprehend that I may be projecting my own desire to find hidden meaning in them. Whether due to the effects of drugs and alcohol or a primary psychotic disorder (or both), the letters show Sundheim had seriously impaired thinking. His letters from the late 1950s and early 1960s regarding his medical credentials are (mostly) goal oriented and not suggestive of psychosis or severe cognitive impairment.

Given my diagnostic impressions, let's quickly review the diagnoses from professionals who actually personally evaluated Gaylord Sundheim:

1934	dipsomania, alcoholism
1938	alcoholic
1953	psychosis (schizoid manic) manic depression, also considered "Incompetent," which at that time meant he lacked the capacity to care for self and property.
1956	schizoid personality
1963	alcohol intoxication, addiction to barbiturates, acute brain syndrome due to alcoholism, and chronic brain syndrome

Considering advances in science and how our diagnostic criteria have changed over the years, I agree with the doctors from 1963; I think their diagnoses are the best substantiated by the data.

I can't tell you whether or not Gaylord Sundheim was the torso killer. I can, however, examine his known history to cautiously determine whether he was at risk for violence to others. Risk assessment is a routine part of a psychiatrist's work. The goal of a risk assessment is to determine if the individual is low, moderate, or high risk of violence to self (suicide) or others. For a risk assessment to have any value, it has to be thorough. The more extensive the data collection, the more useful the final product will be. Sources of information for a violence risk assessment include a clinical interview with the individual in question; interviews with any of the individuals who witnessed threats or actual violence and with the person's family members, roommates, partner or spouse, and close friends; reviews of any threatening communications, including recorded phone messages, letters, e-mails, and Internet postings, and of the individual's medical and psychiatric records. The clinical interview is often very lengthy and can cover everything from the individual's taste in video games to his pornography preferences. In the case of Gaylord Sundheim, my sources of information are very few. Therefore, I can only make the most tentative of conclusions regarding risk.

Once a person is identified as being at low, moderate, or high risk for violence, the risk can be further classified. Is he or she at an elevated risk for high-magnitude violence, such as shooting or stabbing? Is the risk elevated for lower magnitude acts, such as hitting or spitting? Is there a specific target for the violence? (It is possible for the person to be at high risk for violence against a specific individual [i.e., a boss or a family member] but low risk as far as the general public is concerned.) Is the risk acute or chronic? Is the violence imminent or contingent on a particular event? To use a well-known example, a man who abuses his wife may be at a chronic elevated risk of violence, but that risk increases acutely at the point in time the wife decides to leave the marriage.

No risk assessment is complete without a risk-reduction plan. If the identified risk is low, the plan may be to simply monitor the individual. If the risk is moderate or high, more extensive steps need to be taken. The first task in constructing a plan is to differentiate between modifiable and unmodifiable factors. A history of past violence is the biggest risk factor for future violence, and obviously unmodifiable. Male gender, lower IQ, and age (late teens to early twenties) are other examples of violence risk factors that cannot be changed through treatment. Modifiable risk factors include drug or alcohol use, certain psychiatric symptoms, access to weapons, un-employment, and residential instability. It is important to note that not all psychiatric symptoms elevate violence risk.

Using the time frame of the torso murders (1934–38), let's now examine Gaylord Sundheim's unmodifiable risk factors. The court documents from his divorce petition allege he had a history of being physically abusive to his children and demonstrating "extreme cruelty" toward his wife. His male gender elevates his risk of violence. His divorce in 1936, ending his marital relationship and separating him from his children, is an important con-sideration in the equation. Finally, we know that Sundheim was a veteran, which means he received weapon and combat training.

Sundheim also had some modifiable violence risk factors. The most promi-nent of these was his alcohol use. In his December 1933 Cuyahoga County Probate Court inquest of lunacy, court documents indicate heavy drinking. His 1936 divorce papers discuss "habitual drunkenness" and almost continual intoxication. In February 1938, he was involuntarily admitted to hospital through Probate Court. In a statement to the court, a friend of Sundheim's said that he "became hallucinated with ideas of fear" and "talked about Federal men after him." Doctors examined Sundheim and said he "has indicated symptoms suggestive of delusions, which however were transient. Also that he had been hallucinated at times when drinking, usually." Did Sundheim's drinking make him paranoid, or was he actually referring to Ness and his men? Paranoia, whether delusionally based or due to a real world circumstance, can increase violence risk. When an individual feels endangered, he may use violent means to protect himself. Of course, if Sundheim was paranoid about federal agents, his violence risk would increase with respect to law enforcement, though not necessarily globally. Delusional paranoia is now treatable with antipsychotic medication. In 1938, however, there were no antipsychotic medications. Thorazine did not come along until 1950, and prior to that insulin shock and frontal lobotomies were the most advanced treatment.

Keeping in mind the very limited historical data and my inability to interview Sundheim or review any collateral sources of information, I conclude that Sundheim's risk for physical violence of a low magnitude was mild to moderate during periods of intoxication. This conclusion is based primarily on court documents from the time of his divorce, which alleged that he was habitually intoxicated and had been physically abusive to his family. I have no confirmable evidence to suggest he was violent when sober or that he engaged in high-magnitude violence (choking, stabbing, shooting) at any time in his life. There is nothing to suggest he was assaultive toward non-family members. Even later in Sundheim's life, correspondence from the Dayton VA does not mention violent episodes. With regards to his concern that federal agents were following him (delusional or factual), none of the documentation states that he felt in danger or was contemplating taking action against his pursuers. I chose my words carefully here because I want to make sure that my conclusions are not unsupported assertions. Now, if it could be definitively proved that Gaylord Sundheim committed murder by decapitation, it would alter my risk assessment a great deal. The more information available about the context and motivation for those decapitations, the more complete my risk evaluation would be.

I am at the end of my analysis and no nearer to proving Francis E. Sweeney, M.D., is Gaylord Sundheim is the Mad Butcher of Kingsbury Run. However, I hope I've provided some enlightenment into the factors affecting Sundheim's mental state and risk for violence during the years of the torso killings (1934–38). Most important, I hope to have given you a realistic appreciation for what forensic psychiatry is and is not. Although a part of me still longs to be Clarice Starling on the hunt for serial killers, I find rewards in the less life-threatening challenges of conducting thorough, carefully reasoned, and well-supported forensic evaluations.

NOTES

1. James Jessen Badal, *In the Wake of the Butcher: Cleveland's Torso Murders* (Kent, Ohio: Kent University Press, 2001).

2. American Academy of Psychiatry and the Law, "About the Organization: What Is Forensic Psychiatry?" *AAPL Web site*, http://www.aapl.org/org.htm

3. LAWriter, "2901.01 General Provisions Definitions," *Ohio Laws and Rules*, section 2901.01(A)(14), http://codes.ohio.gov/orc/2901.01.

4. American Psychiatric Association, *The Diagnostic and Statistical Manual of Mental Disorders*, 4th ed. (Arlington, Va.: American Psychiatric Publishing, 2000), 685.

5. Ibid., 706.

6. Ibid., 197.

7. M. Serdaru et al., "The Clinical Spectrum of Alcoholic Pellagra: A Retrospective Analysis of Twenty-two Cases Studied Pathologically," *Brain* 111.4 (1988): 829-42.

Chronology and Summary of Historical Documents Regarding Francis Sweeney, M.D.

Cathleen A. Cerny, M.D.

The following is my summary, arranged chronologically, of all the existing historical documents related to the life and death of Francis Sweeney, M.D. James Badal collected the documents and he was kind enough to share them with me. I've tried to indicate where each document came from or who authored it. I have also provided some direct quotes from this material. I have indicated that portions of the documents that were difficult to read are illegible. I used ellipses to indicate material left out of the summary because it was repetitive or unimportant. I used bold font to distinguish events not included in the historical documents, as in the dates of each torso victim discovery, for example. Unless otherwise indicated, all events take place in Cleveland, Ohio. When constructing their opinions, forensic psychiatrists use document summaries, which help organize the evidence and ensure that conclusions are well supported.

May 5, 1894   Frank Edward Sweeney born in Cleveland, Ohio. Mother: Delia O'Mara Father: Martin Sweeney.

1909   Father Martin Sweeney was committed to Sunny Acres Tuberculosis hospital.

June 12, 1923   Martin J. Sweeney dies at age 62. Cause of death: apoplexy.

Contributing factors: Psychosis with cerebral arteriosclerosis. Source: State of Ohio Department of Health, Division of Vital Statistics, Certificate of Death.

July 19, 1927   Frank E. Sweeney and Mary J. Sokol, age twenty-seven, were married by Rev. D. J. Sweeney.

October 31, 1928   Diploma for doctor of medicine issued to Francis E. Sweeney from St. Louis University.

November 28, 1928   Application by Francis E. Sweeney to the State of Ohio Medical Board for Examination for Certificate to Practice Medicine. The application indicates that Sweeney intends to live in Cleveland. Certificate is to be sent to St. Alexis Hospital in Cleveland. Physical description of applicant: white with a "ruddy" complexion, "auburn-grey" hair, "blue-gray" eyes, height 5', 10", weight 200 lbs.

December 1, 1933   Cuyahoga County Civil Appearance Docket No. 250, Statement of Proceedings, Inquest of Lunacy, in the Matter of Frank Sweeney. Judge Brewer, Dr. K. S. West and Dr. C. W. Stone: Complaint by Mary J. Sweeney filed and warrant to arrest issued.

December 2, 1933   Cuyahoga County Civil Appearance Docket No. 250, Statement of Proceedings, Inquest of Lunacy, in the Matter of Frank Sweeney. A complaint was filed by a citizen of the County alleging that one Frank Sweeney is insane. The case was heard by Judge Nelson J. Brewer. Drs. K. S. West and C. W. Stone testified. The Court committed Frank Sweeney to the Detention Hospital of the City of Cleveland.

December 7, 1933   Cuyahoga County Probate Court Inquest of Lunacy: Doctors Stone and West examined Frank Sweeney. They observed: "This patient was brought to probate court [illegible] had been drinking heavily, had become violent against [illegible] forgetful. Recommended for brief observation at D.H. [detention home]." "[illegible but presumably Francis Sweeney] said I have been drinking off and on for three [illegible] drinking when I was 19. I was in bed one time in [illegible] have been taking care of my work up to the last five days."

January 3, 1934   Frank J. Sweeney was discharged to wife.

January 4, 1934   City Hospital Detention Report for the Honorable Nelson

J. Brewer. The first line of the report is illegible. "Frank J. Sweeney with the diagnosis of Dipsomania; peripheral neuritis (mild) [illegible] to the observation wards of Cleveland City Hospital on 12/3/33 [illegible] observation in the hospital the Staff came to the conclusion that this patient was [illegible] recommended for discharge. [Illegible] released to his wife on Jan. 3, 1934. The Wassermann reaction was negative." Signature illegible. **The Wassermann test is a test for Syphilis.**

January 12, 1934   Civil Appearance Docket No. 250, Statement of Proceedings, Inquest of Lunacy, in the Matter of Frank Sweeney, Judge Brewer, Dr. K. S. West and Dr. C. W. Stone: Complaint by Mary Sweeney filed.

January 12, 1934   State of Ohio, Cuyahoga County Probate Court: "Mary Sweeney . . . believes Frank Sweeney MD to be insane and in need of hospital care." Remarks: "Discharged D.H. [detention home] Jan. 3, 1934. 'Dipsomania' can't adjust still drinking to excess wife [illegible] further hospital care."
   Probate Court order to [illegible] Sulzmann [?] commanding him to arrest Frank Sweeney, MD for an examination as to his sanity.

January 23, 1934   Sweeney examined by Drs. Stone and West. "This patient was admitted to the Probate [illegible] Jan. [illegible], 1934 for alcoholism. He had previous admission on December 2nd, 1933, for the same cause and was sent to the City Hospital from which he was discharged on January 3, 1934. Since his first admission the patient has developed symptoms of a peripheral neuritis. On January 3rd his wife requested the patient's release." The patient said: "My wife sent me in. I'd lie around and moan all night with these hands. The legs and feet are better but they still burn like a hot pad on them. I have not been drinking much, just enough to help me sleep. My wife doesn't know this is going to be a six or eight months affair."

January 23, 1934   Complaint dismissed, patient discharged.

September 5, 1934   Frank LaGassie finds victim no. 0, The Lady of the Lake, near Euclid Beach Park.

September 11, 1934   Petition of Divorce and Support and Relief stamped 413785 was filed in the State of Ohio, In the Court of Common Pleas, Mary Josephine Sweeney vs. Dr. Frank Edward Sweeney: Plaintiff and the defendant were married in the city of Cleveland on the 2nd day of July 1927. There are two children of said marriage, James Anthony Sweeney age 3 years and

Francis Edward Sweeney age 5 years. "She says the defendant has been guilty of EXTREME CRUELTY in that he has upon many occasions absented himself from his home without the plaintiff knowing his whereabouts causing her great mental suffering. She further states that he has upon many occasions humiliated her before her friends and has been abusive to her and their children both physically and mentally. She further avers that the defendant has been guilty of gross neglect of duty in that he has failed to provide the necessities of life even though he has been well able to do so. Wherefore the plaintiff prays for divorce, custody of the minor children and restoration of her maiden name."

Undated Petition   Stamped 445238 State of Ohio In the Court of Common Pleas

Mary J. Sweeney vs. Francis Edward Sweeney: "Plaintiff says that the defendant, Francis Edward Sweeney, has been guilty of Gross Neglect of Duty and Extreme Cruelty toward this plaintiff, and of Habitual Drunkeness extending over a period of more than three years...The defendant became intoxicated almost continuously beginning about two years after his marriage to this plaintiff, and remained in that condition practically all of the time until his separation from this plaintiff, which occurred in September, 1934. Plaintiff states that the defendant is a physician and his practice has been entirely ruined by said habitual drunkenness and that he was compelled to take treatment at City Hospital for acute alcoholism, but that said condition was never cured but continued until the date of her separation from the defendant. . . . Plaintiff states that the defendant embarrassed and humiliated this plaintiff continuously during such period before third persons and in the later part of said period before their children. Plaintiff further states that the defendant has completely failed and neglected to support this plaintiff or their children since their separation and for several years previous thereto . . . defendant completely failed and neglected to perform any part of his marital duties toward this plaintiff or any part of his duties to their children for several years preceding the filing of this petition, but has compelled this plaintiff to support their children by her own labor . . . defendant is the holder of an adjusted compensation certificate issued by the United States Government for services in the military forces of the United States . . . there will be due and payable to the plaintiff on said certificate the sum of approximately $775 in the month of July or thereabouts in the year 1936. Plaintiff prays that during the pendency of this action said defendant, Francis Edward Sweeney be restrained from visiting, interfering with or molesting her, that she be allowed a reasonable sum for attorney's fees in the prosecution of this action, that said defendant be restrained from collecting said money soon to become due on his adjusted compensation certificate, that defendant be restrained from spending or disposing of any part of said money until final hearing of this cause, and that upon final hearing the plaintiff be divorced from the said defendant, that she be restored to her maiden name of Mary J. Sokol, that she be allowed $500 as alimony for support of their children, and she prays that she be given the custody of the two children." Signed by Carl G. [illegible] Attorney for Plaintiff.

Undated ANSWER   Numbered 445238, State of Ohio In the Court of Common Pleas. Mary J. Sweeney vs. Francis Edward Sweeney. "Further by way of answer, Defendant denies each and every allegation contained in plaintiff's Petition except those herein expressly admitted to be true...defendant prays that plaintiff's Petition be dismissed." Francis Sweeney was represented by Roman F. Gruber.

September 23, 1935   James Wagner and Peter Costura find victims no. 1 (Edward Andrassy) and no. 2 at the bottom of Jackass Hill in Kingsbury Run.

January 26, 1936   Victim no. 3 (Flo Polillo) is found behind Hart's Manufacturing on East 20th Street.

February 7, 1936   Additional remains of victim no. 3 (Flo Polillo) are found behind vacant house on Orange Avenue.

May 19, 1936   Petition to the Court of Common Pleas (No 445238), State of Ohio Cuyahoga County, Mary J. Sweeney Plaintiff vs. Francis Edward Sweeney Defendant: Plaintiff alleges that the defendant, Francis Edward Sweeney, has been guilty of Gross Neglect of Duty and Extreme Cruelty toward this plaintiff, and of Habitual Drunkeness extending over a period of more than three years. "The defendant became intoxicated almost continually beginning about two years after his marriage [illegible] and remained in that condition practically all of the time until his separation from this plaintiff [illegible] in September 1934. Defendant is a physician and his practice was entirely ruined by said habitual drunkenness and that he was compelled to take treatment at City Hospital for acute alcoholism but that said condition was never cured but continued until the date of her separation from the defendant. The defendant embarrassed and humiliated the plaintiff continuously during such period. . . . Defendant has completely failed and neglected to support this plaintiff or their children since their separation and for several years previous. Defendant has completely failed and neglected to perform any part of his marital duties toward her or any part of his duties to their children for several years preceding the filing of this petition but has compelled the plaintiff to support their children by her own labor. She has conducted herself as an affectionate, faithful and dutiful wife. . . . Plaintiff asks that Francis Sweeney be restrained from visiting, interfering with or molesting her during the pendency of this action. Mary Sweeney asked for a reasonable sum for attorney's fees and that Francis Sweeney be restrained from collecting his VA money until the final hearing. She requested restoration to her maiden name of Mary J. Sokol and $500 in alimony. Finally, she requested custody of the two children."

Undated JOURNAL ENTRY   Numbered 445238, State of Ohio In the Court of Common Pleas. Mary J. Sweeney vs. Francis Edward Sweeney. "The Court found the allegations of this Petition to be true and that the defendant has been guilty of Gross Neglect of Duty toward this plaintiff." Divorce granted. Sweeney ordered to pay $5.00 per [illegible] per child to the plaintiff for their support.

June 5, 1936   Alum Cheeley and Gomez Ivory find victim no. 4's head (tattooed man) in Kingsbury Run.

July 22, 1936   Mary Barkley finds victim no. 5 near Big Creek.

September 10, 1936   Jerry Harris finds victim no. 6 near the stagnant pool.

September 15, 1936   Cuyahoga County coroner Arthur J. Pearce held "The Torso Clinic" at the Central Police Station to review the torso killer evidence and generate new hypotheses. The clinic was attended by Eliot Ness, Cleveland State Hospital superintendent Dr. Guy Williams, Common Pleas Court psychiatrist Dr. Royal Grossman, Anatomists Dr. T. Wingate Todd and W. M. Krogman of Western Reserve University, Police Chief George Matowitz, County Prosecutor Frank Cullitan, Sergeant James Hogan, and Police Surgeon George O'Malley.

February 23, 1937   Robert Smith finds the upper half of a woman's torso near the Lake Erie shore—victim no. 7.

June 6, 1937   Russell Lauer finds a skull under the Lorain-Carnegie (now the Hope Memorial) Bridge—victim no. 8.

July 6, 1937   Private Edgar Steinbrecher finds victim no. 9 floating in the water near the West Third Street Bridge.

February 11, 1938   Leonard F. Prendergast, DDS, swears a complaint for the Probate Court indicating he believed Frank Sweeney, MD, "to be mentally ill and [in] need of specialized observation or treatment or both." The complaint also indicates that Sweeney is neither suicidal, homicidal, nor dangerous to the community. "Patient Physician at Massillon State Hospital. In Probate Court for 3rd time as alcoholic. Yesterday became hallucinated with ideas of fear. Talked about Federal men after him. Police called and taken to jail."

February 28, 1938   Probate Court Inquest of Lunacy. Frank Sweeney, M.D., was examined by Drs. West and Stone in jail. Observations: "At time of admission to Probate ward patient was rather toxic [and] was frank in his admission of excessive drinking. Sister states that he and his wife are divorced. That at times he has indicated symptoms suggestive of delusions, which however were transient. Also that he had been hallucinated at times when drinking, usually. On probate ward his behavior has been orderly, recently moderately dejected and less talkative than on admission. His condition generally is good. He is discharged on his own request stating that he would resume work either at Massillon or Columbus State Hospital. Prognosis guarded." Patient said: "I have been assistant physician at Massillon State Hospital, past year, left there three weeks ago; have not been in touch with hospital since. I came here from Marine Hospital. I have been drinking. I don't want to lose my job."

February 28, 1938   Complaint dismissed, Sweeney discharged.

April 8, 1938   Steve Morosky finds part of a human leg on the East bank of the Cuyahoga River—victim no. 10.

April 12, 1938   [Sister] swears a complaint for the Probate Court indicating she believes Frank Sweeney, M.D., "to be mentally ill and [in] need of specialized observation or treatment or both." Sweeney was not suicidal, homicidal, or dangerous to the community. Remarks: "Discharged Probate Ward 2/28/1938. Again drinking to excess and in dejected state. Sister asks further period of observation." Agnes B. and Martin Sweeney ("bro") are listed as friends or relatives.

April 25, 1938   Probate Court Inquest of Lunacy, Frank Sweeney examined by Drs. West and Tierney in jail. Observations: "This patient was previously on probate ward in January 1934 [illegible] from February 10th to 28th, 1938. He is readmitted 11th inst. Having been drinking excessively since shortly after last discharge, living with a cousin. [At no time] has he shown hallucinations or delusions, his behavior has been orderly, he appears remorseful and discouraged at times. He is anxious to [rehabilitate] himself, thinks he has an opportunity for employment at Xenia, O. Nothing indicating a psychosis, he is again discharged in good condition in care of Mr. Walsh."

April 25, 1938   Complaint dismissed, patient discharged.

May 1938   James Badal has found evidence that Eliot Ness conducted a secret suspect interrogation at the Cleveland Hotel. Also present were court clinic psychiatrist Dr. Royal Grossman and David L. Cowles, who was head of the Scientific Investigation Bureau. The secret suspect's name was Gaylord Sundheim.

August 16, 1938   James Dawson, James McShack, and Edward Smith find human remains at the East 9th Street dump—victim no. 11. Todd Bartholomew finds more remains among the garbage—victim no. 12.

August 17–18, 1938   Shanty Town Raids.

August 25, 1938–July 30, 1940   Sweeney resides at Sandusky Soldiers' and Sailors' Home.

October 13, 1939   Railroad workers find the headless corpse of a young man in New Castle, Pennsylvania.

May 3, 1940   Railroad inspectors find three headless bodies in boxcars in McKees Rocks, Pennsylvania.

February 5, 1941–January 6, 1942   Sweeney resides at Sandusky Soldiers' and Sailors' Home.

1940–1941   Sweeney confined as a mental patient in the Veterans Administration Hospital in Ohio.

December 30, 194[6]–June 12, 1951   Sweeney resides at Sandusky Soldiers' and Sailors' Home.

July 22, 1950 Body of Robert Robertson found on property of Cleveland's Norris Brothers Company.

September 12, 1953 (FBI File 62-100240) Letter to J. Edgar Hoover at the Federal Bureau of Investigation, Washington, D.C. The return address is Vetr. Admin. Ctr. Co # 16.

Dayton, Ohio [typed at the top of handwritten letter]

Dear Sir, Since years ago, 1942-194 [illegible] I wrote you concerning [illegible] their developing connection within and upon the Federal Circuit which I then called "Nessisms." Whether or not this is a break in the Espirit de Corp or a break in the Espirit of My Person, I think would call [illegible] any obligation upon the F.B.I. to [illegible]. May I call your attention to this fact that the condition continues to prevail and that a basic principle of our individual freedoms is not at Stake, but, being Prostituted. Knowing that he was an upriser, upstarted in the Social Reforms section—Federal Security Agency. (Possibly abolished now since he can no longer twirl the baton upon the all American Turf.) Poisoning seems to have become a science which only those in the know and How come he accurately [illegible] of and seemingly I am one of *such*.

It would not take a toxicologist very long to Prove the assertion which I will make upon Proper Ground and within the, proper medium.

Whether or not [illegible] *first appeal in a question because enumerating/eminating from a place like this Vets* Admin Hosp Fort Custer Mich. Would necessarily get a "Crack Pop" [illegible] upon immediate appraisal. This *Boy* has been trying to poke/take/kick the Ball over. With apparent Phonies for years most of his Material has Psychotic Derivation – and He is quite allergic to Psychotic Formulations/Fermentations, [illegible]. All of which has been deduced by a personal interest in knowing *why*? Such a condition can prevail in Federal Institutions since *1942* and not gain any formulation for clearance—Your men pass this way from time to time and I do not see any 3 dimensional eyeware to block their natural virus/visual apparatus—or are we just upon the General highway of Social Deterioration and that come day go day philosophy of the Feeble Minded is gaining presidence over quantitative and qualitative thought the normal way of American life in decadence in *Totality*. I hope that your St [illegible] secretary does not get an Epicurious Bulge [illegible] this is translated into the small lines of "Live liberty & his pursuit of happiness. An *Apostle* from the

local field office or the Central Washington would be greatly appreciated & perhaps We can 'sing song' together [illegible] to "Sweet Adol
[illegible]"—with tow of the Big Stru[illegible] in [illegible Cleveland]
a few years back. We sort [illegible] each [illegible]—Perhaps you've
heard of same. In the mean time I hope you find sufficient significance
to at least give Me a "look See". Because eventually I am coming in
with Just Who is [illegible] U.S. *America* Why *does* a M[illegible] have
to tolerate His Weak*ness*—This is [illegible] the order of a Complaint.
You give me the Man or *Men* and I will surface [illegible] for the Good
of Everyone. I especially hereabouts.

Thank you Frank E. Sweeney M.D. [emphasis Sweeney's]

September 21–29, 1953   Letter from SAC, Cincinnati to Director, FBI re: Dr.
Frank E. Sweeney:

Attached are two copies of a communication from captioned individual
dated 9/12/1953. He is not readily identifiable in Bufiles [presumably
Bureau files], and his communication has not been acknowledged.

Bufiles contain voluminous correspondence received from one
[blacked out] of [blacked out] dating back to 1947. Letters from this
individual [illegible] most incoherent and nonsensical, and he has been
[illegible] as a chronic correspondent of the Bureau. There is the possibility
that correspondent may be identical with the individual, although the
rambling letters described above do not contain the title of "Doctor."

Your office is instructed to establish the identity and background of
the writer of attached letter, furnishing the Bureau a summary of data
available to you through [illegible] discreet inquiry, together with your
recommendation as to how future correspondence from him should
be handled. [S illegible] under caption above to reach the Bureau no
later than 10/5/1953.

October 2, 1953   Office Memorandum—United States Government
To Director, FBI From SAC, Cincinnati (62-2133). The subject of the letter is
Dr. Frank E. Sweeney, Company Number 16, Veterans Administration Center,
Dayton, OH, Research (Crime records): "Mr. Coubron Hull, Domiciliary Officer, Veterans Administration Center, 4300 West Third Street, Dayton Ohio
furnished the following information concerning Frank E. Sweeney, V.A. no.
c-274435, who entered here on July 6, 1951, as a Domiciliary patient. Frank
E. Sweeney was born May 5, 1894 . . . and was a member of the U.S. Army
from October 2, 1917 to August 6, 1919 as a Private in the Medical Corps.

His Army Serial number is not available. He claims to be a doctor having graduated from St. Louis Medical College, St. Louis, Missouri, in 1928, and a doctor who practiced from 1930 to 1934 in Cleveland, Ohio, and after this in a hospital in Glenwood, Iowa, and for the CCC in Ohio. He has also been confined as a mental patient in the Veterans Administration Hospital from 1940-1941. Sweeney gave his last residence in 1951 as [section blacked out in the document] and his nearest relative as a sister, [blacked out]. Brown hospital, VA Center, Dayton, Ohio have records which reflect Sweeney has heart trouble. He has also been found incompetent by reasons of having a mental disease described as 'Psychosis (schizoid manic) manic depression.' Mr. Hull stated further that Sweeney is constantly in trouble at the VA center with the courts there, and has been charged 10 times out of 20 appearances in court with being drunk. Mr. Hull feels that letters received from Sweeney by the FBI should not be answered. It is the recommendation of the Cincinnati Office that correspondence received from Sweeney in the future should not be answered or given any consideration due to his mental condition."

October 7, 1953 Attachment: "NOTE: No record could be located in Bu-files of the correspondent Sweeney mentioned in instant communication which he supposedly sent us in 1942-1946. It is believed advisable to handle as above since there is a possibility that the writer may be a doctor, rather than a patient in this V.A. Center. A notation is carried in Crime Records Section indicating that no acknowledgments are to be sent to the [blacked out] described from [blacked out]."

February 14, 1954 From the Western Reserve Historical Society collection, a letter addressed to Mr. Eliot Ness care of Miss [Proharage] at the Union Commerce Bldg. in Cleveland and signed by "Frank E. Sweeney, MD Ohio 7148." The return address is Vets. Admin. Center, O #16, Dayton Ohio: "Dear Sir, Enclosed a few items for your, Personal Perusal, as to Hermancy Reverence, 'Per Se,' should all or any have no significant application – Would that you present to Special Agent M.S. Cord for a Personal extraction here from and if again in the Negative, tis no doubt as of some, Perverted information having Dominant Dwelling, *a loft* in my, 'Wind sheets' I trust that we shall meet again amongst more favorable, "Federal issues" __ My apologies *Frank E. Sweeney MD Ohio 7148*
PS. 'Phony', criminalization—Is tough, at *any monetary Bargaining*? As well as Phony Psychotization?"

June 29, 1956 Letter from Frank E. Sweeney, M.D. to Walter T. Kinder, Judge Probate Court, New Court House, Cleveland, Ohio:

"Dear Sir, your resume of my truancy in lunacy over the years 1933-1938 inclusive received in good order.

It was in effect the desired detail, a previous request, of about a year ago, while at Dayton V.A. centers, applied the same negative value—only not in detail.

My apparent, frequent, requests for this information fears from—psychotic [illegible]. Safety Director of Cleveland Politically tastes of recantay(J)—lent a vicarious Bander([illegible]) of his own Psychogenisis in my behalf the present County Coroner tossed [illegible] of his own Qualities Quantities in my behalf. He should have learned – from his experiences at the cadavared mouth tells the truth by silence.

Of a recent experience there in Cleveland I was [illegible] by the mental turbulentcy @ Kings level the coutiers – dependents - carrying out Saddistic commands which could have ended on a liability to their own better ends.

So it goes in the Insane world of these times – One should think twice before assuming Sanity?

You have afforded me with the security of Cuyahoga County Court records. Evidently you are protected there by, unclear protectives from the seeming ever encroaching Federal Octopus or pusses promoting vicious ends by Haunt - Taunt or daunt methods
(Methods) I hope these items will inform you why I have to Keep appraised of my Mental level of the 1933-38 era."

September 12, 1958   Frank E. Sweeney, MD, swears an affidavit for John E. Claggett (Notary Public) in Montgomery County Ohio stating that he is the person referred to in the lost certificate to practice "Medicine and Surgery." Apparently, Sweeney had lost his original copy and was attempting to get a new medical certificate from the Ohio State Medical Board.

November 5, 1958   Letter from Frank Sweeney to H. M. Platter, MD, secretary of the Ohio State Medical Board: In the letter, Frank Sweeney indicates that he has enclosed the affidavit for the duplicate medical certificate. The return address is Section 16D x 2-49, VA Center, Dayton, Ohio.

November 29, 1958   Letter from Frank Sweeney to H. M. Platter, MD, secretary of the Ohio State Medical Board: In the letter, Frank Sweeney indicates that he has "complied with your *requirements—mailed the affidavit fully accomplished on or about Nov – 5 – 1928." Dr. Sweeney goes on to say that he may have sent the affidavit to Broad Street "not knowing whether or not you had increased office facility." This letter was sent to the Wyandotte

Building in Columbus, Ohio. The return address was from the VA Center in Dayton, Ohio.

December 3, 1958   Letter from "Secretary" [possibly H. M. Platter, MD; the letter is not on letterhead and has no return address] to Frank E. Sweeney: The letter states that an affidavit was received and would be presented to the State Medical Board on December 17, 1958, for authorization of a duplicate certificate.

December 17, 1958   Duplicate. Certificate issued Frank Edward Sweeney who was born in Cleveland, Ohio, May 5, 1894. Certificate number 7148 dated Jan. 8, 1929.

July 24, 1961   Letter from Robert F. Freeman, Executive Secretary of the Montgomery County Medical Society in Dayton Ohio to H. M. Platter, MD, Medical Board of Ohio. The letter states: "I have an inquiry from the local Veterans Administration Center concerning Frank E. Sweeney, MD, who is a patient there. . . . Can you advise if you have him listed as a physician licensed in Ohio?"

July 25, 1961   Letter from "Secretary" to Mr. Robert F. Freeman [no signature on the letter and no return address]: "Our records show Frank Edward Sweeney to be a graduate of the St. Louis University, St. Louis Missouri on June 5, 1928. He took our examination in December 1928 and received Certificate #7148 dated January 8, 1929." This letter also indicates that Frank Sweeney "made affidavit on September 12, 1958" due to loss of his certificate to practice Medicine and Surgery in the state of Ohio. "We issued a duplicate certificate" to address Sec. #16 D x 2, V.A. Center Dayton, Ohio. The 1956 directory shows him at the Soldiers' and Sailors' Home, near Sandusky, Ohio.

January 11, 1962   Letter from Ray Q. Bumgarner, Center Director of the Veterans Administration Center at 4100 W. Third Street in Dayton, Ohio, to H. M. Platter, Secretary of the Ohio State Medical Board:

> We have a veteran under care in our Domiciliary by the name of Frank E. Sweeney who is a licensed M.D. Although he has been under care at a mental hospital as a psychotic and is still rated as incompetent by the Veterans Administration, we have a continuing problem with him in that he writes prescriptions for barbiturates and tranquilizers in fictitious names for his own use. We believe it would be very helpful in caring for

this veteran if it would be possible to get his license suspended while at this Center and this fact made known to the local pharmacists.

January 18, 1962   Letter from "Secretary" [unsigned, no return address] to Mr. Ray Q. Bumgarner, Center Director, Veterans Administration in Dayton, Ohio: "I will call the attention of the State Medical Board to the case of Dr. Frank E. Sweeney and seek a way to proceed to suspend the license. This is difficult without preferring charges but we will help you when I find a way."

February 8, 1962   Letter from Ray Q. Bumgarner Center Director of the Veterans Administration Center at 4100 W. Third Street in Dayton, Ohio to H. M. Platter, Secretary of the Ohio State Medical Board: "We have received a copy of a letter which Dr. Rupert Salisbury wrote to Mr. Roger Cain in Dayton, Ohio. In it he requests Mr. Cain to pass on the information concerning Dr. Frank E. Sweeney to the retail pharmacists in the Dayton area."

May 17, 1962   Letter from Frank Sweeney to Secretary of the Ohio State Medical Board: "Will you afford me a statement of the summations of my credentials with the State Board of Medicine, State of Ohio." He requests this "pursuant to the [illegible] of the Medical Practice Act State of Ohio. The force and effects of the certification *7148* issued to Frank E. Sweeney, MD." After the signature, the letter states, "[M.B.]. If any fees are in exaction will you afford me information for '*Such*'!?"

May 21, 1962   Letter from "Secretary" [unsigned, no return address] to Frank E. Sweeney, MD: "Complying with your request, our records show you to be a graduate of St. Louis University, St. Louis, Mo. On June 5, 1928. you were licensed in Ohio on January 8, 1929 after examination, Certificate #7148."

October 23, 1962   Letter from Frank E. Sweeney, MD (Ohio 7148) to Registrar – Office of the Dean, St. Louis University Medical School: "Can you appoint me with the Procedure required in order to obtain (a) duplicates of the original Degrees, BS (Medicine 1926) – M.D. – 1928 obtained by me following the proscribed (qes) requirements for said degrees – *Originals lost* in the Hurly Burly of R.R. Transportation."

December 11, 1962   Mary A. M. [sister], age 74, buried at Calvary Cemetery in Cleveland, Ohio.

March 9, 1963   Letter from Frank E. Sweeney, MD, Ohio "*7148*" (1929) to Registrar of the Medical School at St. Louis University: "Can you furnish me a statement re credations of your school—Re Frank E. Sweeney, MD 1924-1928."

September 26, 1963   Letter from "Secretary" [no signature, no return address] to Center Director Veterans Administration Center in Dayton, Ohio: "We are in receipt of a request from Frank E. Sweeney, MD, an inmate of your institution, who is a graduate of the St. Louis University, St. Louis, Mo. in 1928 regarding his license. From correspondence in this office, it appears that Dr. Sweenbury [one name apparently typed over another] of the Pharmacy Board requested the pharmacists in your area not to honor his prescriptions. I am calling this case to the attention of the State Medical Board when it meets next week (October 1, 1963). Perhaps it will be necessary for us to suspend his certificate. Perhaps it will be necessary to formally take action to suspend his certificate in Ohio. I had thought our former efforts were satisfactory."

October 1, 1996   James Badal provided me with a handwritten summary of a[n] [Ohio State Medical] Board Meeting. This comes from page 1434 of Minute Book #5: "Frank E. Sweeney, MD, a domiciliary member at the Veterans Administration Center, Dayton, Ohio who writes prescriptions freely for barbiturates since his license is still in force, is to be cited before the Board in January (next meeting), on motion of Dr. Watson seconded by Dr. Brumbaugh."

October 3, 1963   Letter from Ray Q. Bumgarner, Center Director of the Veterans Administration Center at 4100 W. Third Street in Dayton, Ohio, to H. M. Platter, Secretary of the Ohio State Medical Board: This letter thanks Dr. Platter for his letter concerning Frank Sweeney and also for talking with Dr. B. J. Chazin, Chief Domiciliary Medical Service. The letter also contained a statement from Dr. Chazin: "Frank Sweeney has been here in the Domiciliary on and off since 1946. In 1956 he was hospitalized. He was in Chillicothe Veterans Administration Hospital and returned from there with the diagnoses of schizoid personality, heart disease and cardiac enlargement. Since then he had numerous admissions to Brown Hospital, mostly with the diagnosis of alcohol intoxication (he is being treated for it now on our Psychiatric Service). He is also a known drug addict with addition to barbiturates. His most recent diagnoses are: acute brain syndrome due to alcoholism and chronic brain syndrome. He is considered incompetent by the Veteran's administration." Mr. Bumgarner goes on to say that the director of domiciliary services reports, "because the veteran still has his Ohio Medical license, he freely writes prescriptions for barbiturates. He allegedly prescribes for his aged sister who will only take the medicine he sends her. Instead, the veteran takes the drugs himself and becomes an impossible management problem. The veteran's name is also carried by all the pharmaceutical houses and he receives countless samples of drugs which he is able to become intoxicated on by overdosages." Mr. Bumgarner requests that the veteran's certificate in Ohio be suspended.

October 4, 1963 Letter from "Secretary" [no signature, no return address] to Ray Q. Bumgarner Center Director Veterans Administration Center in Dayton, Ohio: "I called this matter to the attention of the Board this week and shall proceed to file charges for a hearing to be conducted sometime in the month of January. . . . P.S. Do I understand that this man has been adjudged mentally ill?"

October 10, 1963 Letter from Ray Q. Bumgarner, Center Director of the Veterans Administration Center at 4100 W. Third Street in Dayton, Ohio, to H. M. Platter, Secretary of the Ohio State Medical Board: "Dr. Sweeney was transferred here from the Veterans Administration Hospital in Chillicothe, Ohio, August 30, 1956. He was considered an institutional award case and as such, all monetary benefits to which he is entitled from the Veterans Administration have been paid to me as trustee of his Personal Funds Account. He has received numerous neuropsychiatric examinations since 1956 by our staff psychiatrists and consultants from Ohio State University all of which resulted in determinations that Dr. Sweeney was considered mentally incompetent. The last such examination was accomplished in 1961. There is also information in our records that he was committed to the Toledo State Hospital by the Probate Court, Erie County, Ohio and I have no knowledge of this commitment having been lifted."

October 14, 1963 Letter from "Secretary" [no signature, no return address] to Probate Court, Erie County, Sandusky, Ohio: "We are in receipt of information that one Frank E. Sweeney, MD was committed to the Toledo State Hospital in 1956 by the Probate Court, Erie County, Ohio. The Department wishes to inquire whether this commitment was ever resolved and Dr. Sweeney declared sane?"

October 16, 1963 Letter from Robert C. Winkel, Chief Deputy of the Erie County Probate Court to H. M. Platter, MD, Secretary of the State Medical Board of Ohio: "Dr. Sweeney was committed to Toledo State Hospital on October 27, 1955, and was discharged as "Improved" on June 14, 1956, the date on which he was transferred to Chillicothe Veterans Administration Hospital for further treatment. On August 5, 1957, I wrote to Doctor Sweeney at Dayton Veterans Administration Center, explaining the procedure necessary for restoration to competency, but he took no further action. He is, therefore, still legally incompetent."

January 7, 1964 Letter from "Secretary" [unsigned, no return address] to Frank E. Sweeney, MD: "It has been called to the attention of the State Medical Board that you are an inmate of the Veterans Administration Center. . . ." The letter goes on to summarize the information from Robert C. Winkel's October 16, 1963, letter. "The Department is further advised that you are still an institutional case and that you have received numerous neuropsychiatric examinations . . . all of which determinations were to the effect that you are considered mentally incompetent at the present time. This matter is docketed for consideration by the State Medical Board at its next meeting to be held on Tuesday, January 28, 1964 at 10:45 a.m. and you are requested to be present at that time. The Board is of the opinion that your license should be suspended during the time you are incapacitated. Your appearance is requested to determine whether or not your mental condition warrants a suspension."

Undated Letter from "Secretary" [no signature, no return address] to Ray Q. Bumgarner Center Director Veterans Administration Center in Dayton, Ohio: "I am enclosing a copy of the notice I am sending to Dr. Frank E. Sweeney, a ward case, concerning whom the Board desires to investigate his mental capacity. Will you please designate someone with the records of your institution to be present at the hearing to be held at the office of the State Medical Board, Wyandotte Building, 21 W. Broad Street, Columbus, Ohio, on Tuesday, January 28, 1964, at 10:45 a.m."

January 13, 1964 Letter from Frank Sweeney to H. M. Platter, MD, secretary of the Ohio State Medical Board: "Your letter re me and the meeting with the Board, read by me on the ?10th?. I will be present myself at the time specified . . . and conclude for everyone concerned, that [illegible] still about – myself. All of the above, of course, will be with the clemency of the weather, [illegible] of trains or buses and the condition of my physical being (be assured that I will not [illegible] anything)."

January 16, 1964 Letter from "Secretary" [no signature, no return address] to Ray Q. Bumgarner Center Director Veterans Administration Center in Dayton,

Ohio: This letter indicates that the 1/28/1964 board meeting about Frank E. Sweeney, MD, has been postponed. "It will be made a matter of further consideration at the April meeting."

July 9, 1964   Corrigan Funeral Homes No. 64296. Dr. Francis E. Sweeney, resident of the V.A. Center in Dayton, OH. Died on 7/9/1964 at 4 pm at the age of 70. Buried at Calvary Cemetery on July 13, 1964, at the cost of 65.00. "Sweeney, Francis E., DR. (Frank) Father of James and the late Francis E. Family will receive friends at Corrigan's Funeral Home on Lorain Ave. at West 148th St. (SAT 7-10 p.m. & SUN 3-5 & 7-10 p.m.) Funeral Mass Monday, July 13th St. Ignatius Church at 10 a.m.

July 13, 1964   Francis E. Sweeney, age 70, buried at Calvary Cemetery in Cleveland, Ohio.

July 23, 1964   Francis Sweeney's death certificate indicates that at time of death, he had been living in Dayton, Ohio, for seven years, ten months, and nine days. He was seventy years of age. He was a World War I veteran. Death was caused by cerebral edema, due to pontine hemorrhage due to cerebral arteriosclerosis and hypertensive heart disease.

† † †

There are two undated applications from Francis Sweeney to the Sandusky Soldiers' and Sailors' Home. One of them lists the following disabilities: "Major cardiac-mitral insufficiency, multiple herniated-intervertebral-spinal discs."

There is also an undated page that begins with "Local Physicians' Diagnosis." It lists mitral insufficiency and multiple herniated discs (spinal column). "Life and its stresses have contributed to the total toll, superimposed upon these conditions. No VD (venereal disease), No exanthemata, no TB (tuberculosis), ambulatory." This section is signed by Frank E. Sweeney, M.D. Residence given as 2957 East 65th St. Cleveland, OH. The middle of the page has a section titled Admission Board. The final section of the form is titled Ohio Soldiers and Sailors Home Surgeon's Report. Diagnosis: Physical and Mental "[illegible] Disability; obesity; N.O.A.; [illegible] valvular heart disease, mitral insufficiency; oh. Arthritis." It is signed by a physician and John W. Parks, Commandant.

BIBLIOGRAPHY

MANUSCRIPT AND ARCHIVAL SOURCES

American Civil Liberties Union. Files on Frank Dolezal's arrest, including various correspondence and newspaper clippings. Volumes 2116 and 2136.

Cleveland Police Historical Society Museum
Cowles, David L. Taped interview conducted by Lieutenant Tom Brown and Florence Schwein. September 6, 1983. Typescript of interview.
Limber, James M. A small collection of photographs related to Kingsbury Run.

Coroner's Office, Cuyahoga County
Gerber, Dr. Samuel R. Coroner's Verdict and Testimony on the Body of Frank Dolezal. August 24, 1939. Case no. 49869.
"Transcript of Proceedings Commencing at 10:30 A.M., Saturday, August 26, 1939, before Hon. Samuel R. Gerber, County Coroner, in Relation to Death of Frank Dolezal at County Jail, August 24, 1939." Includes depositions taken by Cleveland Police Department's Bureau of Criminal Investigation from individuals in the sheriff's office and others directly involved with Frank Dolezal's death.

Cuyahoga County Court of Common Pleas. Records.
Dolezal, Charles. Suits against Sheriff Martin L. O'Donnell and others. Case nos. 496329 and 496330.
Sweeney, Mary Josephine, née Sokol. Petitions for separation and divorce from Dr. Francis Edward Sweeney. Case nos. 413785 and 445238.
Cuyahoga County Probate Court. Records. Actions against Dr. Francis Edward Sweeney. Civil Appearance Docket no. 250. Case no. 213871.

Federal Bureau of Investigation. Records.
Sweeney, Dr. Francis Edward. File nos. 62–100340–1, September 21, 1953, and 62–100340–2, October 13, 1953.
Sweeney, Martin L. File no. 100–32378–1, July 11, 1944.

Ohio Soldiers' and Sailors' Home, Sandusky Ohio. Applications for Admission and other documents relevant to Dr. Francis Edward Sweeney's residency at the facility.

Personal Papers
Fransen, John (Cleveland Police Force, retired). Dossier on Dr. Francis Edward Sweeney. 1991–1992. Cleveland Police Department.
Lyons, Lawrence J. (Pat). Private papers held by his daughter, Carol Fitzgerald, including investigation notes, unpublished manuscripts on Kingsbury Run murders and his role as investigator, and various pieces of official and personal correspondence.
Merylo, Peter. Private papers held by his daughter Marjorie Merylo Dentz, including his unpublished memoirs, an unpublished manuscript cowritten with Frank Otwell, daily police reports, police reports from other officers, pieces of official and personal correspondence, tip letters, newspaper and magazine articles, various clippings, and photographs.

NEWSPAPERS AND OTHER PUBLISHED MATERIAL

Cleveland News. July–August 1939.
Cleveland Plain Dealer. July–August 1939.
Cleveland Press. July–August 1939.
McGunagle, Fred. "Postcard from the Mad Butcher." *Cleveland Edition* (March 9, 1989): 1+.

INDEX